LEARNING
THE HARD WAY

THE BOY WHO TREKKED ACROSS WORLDS

William Mayom Maker

A Note from the Publisher

The publisher wishes to acknowledge and thank Dr Douglas H. Johnson for his invaluable help and support for Africa World Books and its mission of preserving and promoting African cultural and literary traditions and history. Dr Johnson and fellow historians have been instrumental in ensuring that African people remain connected to their past and their identity. Africa World Books is proud to carry on this mission.

Africa
World Books
Pty Ltd

Contents

Dedication

To all my friends and comrades, dead or alive, this book is dedicated to you.

To the South Sudanese martyrs: this book is an honor of your sacrifices—your will to die for freedom and independence.

To the South Sudanese veterans: this book is a celebration of your spirit—your will to overcome unspeakable horrors to liberate the country—your will to live.

Author's Note

You are about to read an incredible story of the ultimate survivors of Africa's longest and bloodiest civil war. The people, places, and dates used in this book are real. You will find it hard to imagine that anyone, especially a small boy, could bear so many hardships in his entire life. This book, *Learning the Hard Way,* is intended to provide much-needed insights into the aspect of the civil war in Sudan and an understanding of what life was like for its fighters, especially the young fighters known as the *Jeish el Ahmer* or Red Army.

The author was born in an isolated village in South Sudan—a world without schools, televisions, or hospitals—but a world governed by strong cultural values. He grew up herding cattle. Caught up in the Second Sudanese Civil War, the eleven-year-old naked cattle-herder underwent multiples transformations. First, he became a guerrilla fighter, where constant brushes with near-death experiences turned him into a boy monster. Then, he became a refugee in the desolate wilderness of East Africa. And finally, he resettled in the West as a new immigrant in extreme culture shock. Conditioned and re-conditioned by the worst conditions imaginable, the author had to do what he had to do to survive.

As you follow the author through these various experiences, you will find some disturbing and horrifying stories. Other stories are full of humor and laughter. Some scenes may appear childish and rudimentary. And yet, others are uplifting and inspiring. The book captures these sentiments because the author has not attempted to soften his voice or alter the stories. Instead, the stories are told the way they really happened, and the original voice is maintained throughout the book.

Narrated using a combination of dialogue, narrative, and some inner thought, the book provides many different views. Some readers will find it a riveting and emotional tale to follow the author through these various scenarios. Others will visualize the scenes of the stories through the author's eyes. Meanwhile, those who have lived in similar conditions, such as conscription, isolation, desolation, and culture shock, will visualize the book through their eyes, identifying with some experiences. All in all, people of various cultural persuasions will find something to relate to in this book.

One of the main reasons I wrote this book is to convey hope to young people. Because I made it despite this adversity, young people have no reason to give up in life. The absence of parents should not be an excuse for not achieving your potentials. Living in poverty or having no opportunities does not mean you can stop trying. Suppose this book can teach people anything; it is that young persons, in the most horrible and hopeless condition imaginable, can rely on their tenacity, courage, and resilience to navigate through. If I can make it, any young person can make it, too.

Introduction

I climbed up the mountain's top and sat on the rock with the AK–47 automatic rifle on my lap. I was a thirteen-year-old guerrilla fighter, and I had been one since I was eleven years old. Overwhelmed by the guerrillas' life, I snuck out of our camp, climbed up the mountain's highest point, and sat on the rock facing West. Thousands of miles in the direction I faced was my mother's land, which I had not seen since I joined the movement several years ago. I felt nostalgic for home. And I missed my mother dearly.

My mother's land, Sudan, was sacred. It occupied the heart of the ancient continent of Africa, traversed by a network of ancient paths and rivers that had conveyed culture and traditions for generations. Divided by the world's longest river, the Nile, and its tributaries, this ancient land was vibrant with life and all things. Peace, harmony, and prosperity governed this ancient land.

However, when the war between the Sudanese government and Sudan People's Liberation Army (the SPLA) started, it obliterated everything. Strange horrors and terrors filled the land. Tanks and Antonovs rumbled, and bombs fell. Soldiers marched, and bullets whizzed. Displacement, disease, and death became prevalent in our society. Subsequently, the once vibrant land looked wretched and completely deserted, with ruins like an ancient graveyard.

The Jieng (Dinka) socio-cultural system crumbled as war forced people to abandon cultural pursuits and focus on security and survival.

Subsequently, my eleven-year-old being became keener, and I joined the rebels—the SPLA.

Now I was thousands of miles away from my homeland, my dreams, and my mother. The SPLA had confined me in the middle of mountains, along with thousands of strangers, whom I now called my brothers and comrades—the *Jeish el Ahmer* (Red Army) fighters—who were fighting for what is now known as the Republic of South Sudan. Despite being among thousands of comrades, I felt lonely and depressed.

The typical guerrilla life, including the constant brush with near-death experiences, had overwhelmed me. I was sick and tired of living in the wilderness like a wild animal, exposed to all the elements: the rain, cold, heat, scorpions, snakes, jiggers, mosquitoes, and lice. Instead of these, I longed for the familiar sight and sounds of the neighborhood I had left behind. Instead of the meanest commanders bellowing commands, I yearned for the laughter of my siblings and the smiling faces of my parents. And whenever I was overwhelmed by emotions, I snuck out of the camp to find a quiet place to cry alone. I did not want my comrades to know I was a weak soldier who cried for his mother. So, my secret crying location was on top of a mountain located just behind our barracks. It was known as Zalzal Two Mountain—named after the fourth division of the SPLA (Zalzal), who were trained there. But I secretly called it Mountain of Misery (*Kur ê Dɔɔŋ*) because it was the secret place I went to cry and feel miserable when the child in me kicked in or when I was depressed.

While sitting there on the mountaintop, I looked out over the wood, our houses, and river and took in all the beauty at my feet. Then I cried for hours; the tears cleansed my soul, relieving me from the grief and releasing me from the pressure of everything I had hidden away and all the amassed pain. I did not only sit on the top of that mountain to rid myself of frustration and grief but also communicated with my mother. Sitting there on top of the mountain and staring toward our home made me feel connected to my mother. In other words, I was communicating with my mother psychologically.

Now, the sun was setting with its most spectacular colors and sinking behind the mountain. My emotions were sinking, too, and tears streamed down my face. I got to where I did not even realize the tears were flowing. After I stopped crying, I had one more ritual to perform before returning to the barracks. I unlocked my gun and shot several bullets westward—the bullets echoed throughout the mountain ranges. My favorite moment to shoot was when it was dark so that I could see the bright, streaking tracers from my Kalashnikov traveling westward. I always felt better when my gun talked to me by rocking me back and forth as I squeezed the trigger again and again. The spicy discharge from the weapon filled my eyes and lungs; I had smelled it many times before, so it did not bother me anymore as my lungs had adapted to it. Shooting the gun was therapeutic, in a sense. The gun made me feel more secure and mature for my age. But it had not relieved me of my loneliness and homesickness.

Looking back, I do not know why I shot bullets towards our home. Perhaps the loneliness and homesickness, as well as the hardships, had unlocked my telepathic ability to communicate with my mother paranormally. That was why I stared and shot bullets toward my mother's land. In other words, the transfer of information through feelings, emotions, thoughts, and intentions was combined with staring and shooting.

Besides sitting on top of the mountain staring and shooting bullets westward, I also told the setting sun to take my message to my mother, to say that I loved and missed her so much. When I saw a flock of birds flying westward, I told them the same message.

Guerrilla life had transformed me into a boy monster who talked to the sun, the birds, and the Kalashnikov. Living in the wilderness for years, surrounded by near-death experiences, had reconnected me with my innate ability to have two-way conversations with the environment and learn from the wisdom Mother Nature offered to survive. Such narratives may sound concocted to anyone who had never lived in the bush as a guerrilla fighter. But, despite my tender age, it was amazing how my survival instinct had automatically switched to its maximum, and all the senses (sight, touch, hearing, smell, and taste) became razor sharp. For example, when I observed a flock of birds suddenly dive from the sky in a disarrayed manner, changing their course, I had to take cover, for the bombs were coming. When a herd of gazelles rushed by without even noticing me, I had to run after the gazelles or be ready to fight (fight or flight), for the enemy was coming. These split decisions made a difference between life and death.

I had now been sitting on the rock for about an hour, and I had stopped crying; I felt physically and mentally relaxed. I lay on the rock on my back with the gun strapped on my chest, my legs dangling as I gently hit the rock with my feet to calm myself down. The clear blue sky stretched above me. The sun had set, but it was still not dark. I had to wait until it was dark before I snuck back into the camp so that no one could tell I had been crying.

While lying on the rock waiting for the darkness to come, a fat rodent hopped out of the burrow under a big rock. The *faarbuz* rodents were on the top of our menu. We ate rodents and other animals because we were hungry and because we were taught that guerrilla fighters ate everything to survive. The more disgusting things one ate, the better soldier peers and commanders considered you. Luckily for this rodent, I was not in a hunting mood that day. This kitten, full of curiosity, came and stood a few feet away, just looking at me with its black eyes while squeaking. This kitten had never seen a bigheaded human kid on two legs, carrying a big fire-cracking weapon.

Soon, the frantic mother-rodent emerged from the burrow, looking for her child. While monitoring me, the mother-rodent grabbed her baby by the tail and dragged him back inside the hole. It was as if the mother-rodent was telling her kitten, "You better come back inside here. Stay away from that crazy human child with a big gun who cries for his invisible mother. He is dangerous. Don't you know human kids hunt and eat us?" Again, the kitten slipped away from his mother and hopped out from the burrow. But the mother caught him. They did this repeatedly.

As I watched this episode unfold, I wanted to tell the kitten to listen to his mother. Mothers know best. My mother specifically told me not to join the rebels. But I did not listen to her. I wished I had listened to my mother. None of these would have happened to me.

When I was only eleven years old, I left my mother because our country was caught up in a situation where it was a crime to be peaceful and prosperous. At that time, the SPLA rebels came to our village, Biling Daldiar, to eat our food and sleep in our houses. And when they left, they forced young women and men, including me, as porters to carry their ammunition and food supplies. After that, the government troops accused us, the innocent villagers, of supporting the SPLA and shot and bombed us indiscriminately. Moreover, innocent villagers who went to towns to buy and sell goods were viewed as rebel spies by the government soldiers. In addition, the rebels considered villagers who returned from cities to their respective villages as traitors collaborating with the government soldiers. With the government troops controlling urban areas and the SPLA controlling rural areas, there was no safe place for us, the innocent citizens.

Growing up in a society where children were groomed to be warriors at a young age, I knew I had to protect my mother from the insecurities caused by the men with guns. I was my mother's youngest, and in our society, the lastborn children had to care for their aging parents. Unlike in the West, where older people go to retirement homes, an Agaar aging parent moved in with their lastborn child. Since my father had passed away, my mother's responsibility was on my shoulders. I took the obligation seriously, and it affected every decision I made. Remember, I was born in a society where every individual was intricately linked to others. Every decision one made was for the betterment of the family, clan, and tribe. Therefore, every decision I made was for the welfare of my mother and the society at large.

Initially, I went to school, hoping to study hard and get an excellent job to support my mother. But the Civil War erupted, and schools were closed when I was in the third grade. Subsequently, my mother and I returned to the traditional village to rear cattle and cultivate crops—the way our ancestors had done it for generations. But again, our farms became rebels' food. What remained was destroyed by the government troops with their tanks and gunships.

Therefore, the only option left for me was to get a gun to protect my mother and the entire community. Because we sympathized with the SPLA rebels fighting against the Islamic regime in Khartoum, I had to join the SPLA. I was a pious young man who wanted to please my beloved mother and the whole community with devotion and sacrifice. The SPLA rebels were trained and equipped in Bilpam, Ethiopia—thousands of miles from our village. I was determined to walk the distance, unaware of the hazardous conditions I was getting into—the typical stupidity of a preteen who could not analyze things thoroughly before acting.

My decision to join the rebellion solidified when I heard random SPLA soldiers saying they were "fighting for justice, liberty, and freedom." Even though I had a vague idea of what justice and liberty were, I certainly knew what freedom was. The rebels received everything they wanted for free. For example, the rebels ate food they did not cultivate, slaughtered cattle they did not rear, and even married women without paying a single bride price. And this was what freedom looked like to an eleven-year-old boy.

Additionally, the AK-47 automatic rifle or Kalashnikov—Dinkanized as the *Kalany*—was the coolest rifle of all. "If I had the *Kalany* rifle," I thought, "I would be the most powerful eleven-year-old boy in the whole world, and all the girls would practically throw themselves at my feet. Then I would marry a good girl who would take care of my aging mother and me. With the gun, I would protect my mother, my future wife, and my children." Thus, having a firearm became my goal, as the benefits attached to gun ownership were too great to be ignored by an eleven-year-old boy groomed to be a warrior.

In 1987, I left, against my mother's will, and joined recruits trekking to Ethiopia, where the rebels were trained and equipped with help from the Ethiopian president, Comrade Mengistu. The heinous trek took us seventy-five days on foot from Sudan to Ethiopia. After that, I spent the next 180 days in a guerrilla warfare training center, learning how to march, salute or shoot, execute reconnaissance, ambushes, and raids. I learned all the guerrilla tactics with hard work and determination, and I was confident I would protect my mother and defend our entire village when I returned home.

However, after we had completed our guerrilla warfare training, it did not take long before I realized that the dream of returning home to protect my mother remained just a dream, not a reality. We were now soldiers of the movement, and we had to obey orders from our commanders. The strongest among us were selected and sent back to Sudan to fight. The youngest and the weakest remained in the camp to mature physically and mentally before being sent to war. I was among those who remained in the camp. While waiting, the movement opened indoctrination schools where we were brainwashed to be good fighters, loyal to the movement with its leadership. About 7000 young fighters, ages between eight and twenty, isolated in the middle of the mountain ranges, away from the outside world. We had no telephones, radios, or televisions; social media did not exist. Armed and brainwashed to the core, there was nothing else we could do other than shoot guns and sing the revolutionary song, "*Shalla abui, adiu talga* (we have no mercy. Even if it is my father, I'll shoot him)."

The movement's leadership now trained us to be the main fighters who would liberate the country. "What country?" I thought. The so-called country was created by a group of crazy men who sat somewhere in Europe and drew lines on paper. And then the European nations fought and made treaties with one another, each vying for the right to the carved up parts of Africa, disregarding the continent's inhabitants. It was the beginning of the arrival of strangers with their toxic cultural amenities such as guns, religions, rules, and regulations in our land. Now we had to fight endless wars, trying to liberate a piece of land the Europeans had demarcated? In the meeting, the chairman of the SPLA, Dr. Garang, said, "Our objective is to liberate

Sudan, starting from Nimule on the Ugandan border to Halfa on the Egyptian border." What for? We, the Agaar, had never owned the land that reached that far. I had only come to get a gun and return to free our village from insecurities caused by other men brandishing firearms. This idea of liberating a country was too abstract for me.

Nevertheless, I was now a soldier, fighting for incomprehensible things like liberation, freedom, equality, justice, etc. The term "comrade" had divorced me from the original name my mother had given me. Platoon and squad members were my siblings, battalion-mates were cousins, and commanders were the parents. The Red Army was my clan, and the SPLA movement was my tribe. In addition to this abstract background, my story as a fighter was noticeably short. I was trained to shoot and be shot at, kill, or get killed and end the story. It was that simple.

It was now dark. I got up and walked like a zombie back to the barracks, knowing this was the experience of no return. But I had no one to blame but myself. I had joined in the rebellion. Now I had learned my lesson the hard way. It was time for me to find courage, for I had to survive.

PART ONE

Sudan

"We had a reason to love our land and its bounty. The Dinkaland was full of unspoiled natural beauty. We had endless savannahs, inspiring jungles, and breathtaking swamps inhabited by animals, birds, reptiles, and amphibians. There was nothing fake or unnatural in the Dinkaland, and my brothers, sisters, and I took comfort in all of this... That was the definition of having plenty."

Visiting Rumbek Town

The rooster crowed, and I sprung up half-asleep and dashed to the door. But I banged my head against the wall. The impact jerked me awake. I rubbed my eyes with my knuckles, trying to see, but to no avail. It was pitch black inside the room. The door's outline, which signaled the arrival of dawn, was not even visible. I was going on a trip with my uncle early in the morning, and I did not know what time it was.

I was probably six or seven years old. I was born in Biling Daldiar, an isolated village without schools, hospitals, or any form of modernization, so a date of birth or even calendars did not exist. This was early 1980, and we still lived in the same way that all humanity had lived on earth since the beginning of time, in a natural world without radios, televisions, or clocks. During the day, we measured the time using the sun's position or the length of shadows. Between dusk and midnight, we used stars to measure the time. And between midnight and dawn, we used cockcrows to measure the time. Cockerels crowed three times between midnight and dawn: the first cockcrow was between 1:00 and 2:00 a.m., the second crow was between 2:00 and 4:00 a.m., and the third crow was between 5:00 and 6:00 a.m. Our departure time was the second crow. But I did not know whether what I had heard was the first, the second, or the third cockcrow.

"Go back to bed, Mayom," my mother said. "This is just the first crow. It is not dawn yet. Wait for the second crow."

I went back to bed, but I could not fall asleep again. I was anxious because I was going on a trip with Uncle Mathou. I had visited many villages, cattle camps, and fishing grounds before, but this trip would be the most adventurous of all. I was visiting a place I had never seen before: a town. I was visiting Rumbek Town for the first time in my life.

Rumbek, currently the capital city of Lakes State of South Sudan, was located just less than twenty miles away from our village, Biling Daldiar. Back then, I did not even know our village was part of a country called Sudan. Yet, despite this apparent proximity, Rumbek sounded too far away and out of reach.

Every year, Uncle Mathou and other village elders traveled to Rumbek to sell cattle and buy clothes, beads, salt, sugar, and other goods. This year he invited me to go along with him. And I was ecstatic because I had heard many fascinating things about Rumbek. What intrigued me the most about Rumbek was "*thurumbil* (automobile)—molted iron that ran faster than a grown elephant or buffalo." I had never seen a *thurumbil* before. I had only seen a bicycle, though no one owned a bike in our village. So, I was ecstatic to see all the marvelous things in the modern world.

I tossed and turned once more on the ayiek mat, made from papyrus stems. A lingering haze of sleep sat somewhere at the back of my mind but was too far away to reach, as I was floating in the pool of my thoughts about the trip to Rumbek and all the magical things of the modern world I would explore. Outside, I heard frogs croaking, owls hooting, and cricket chirping. But I was eager to hear one bird's sound, which told us what time it was: the rooster. The dawn had refused to come. Time always stands still when you are anxious.

Finally, I heard the cock-a-doodle-doo! The door's outline, which signaled the dawn's arrival, was visible, and there was a beam penetrating through the peephole. From the other room, I heard the jingling of spears as Uncle Mathou was exiting. I opened the door and went out to meet Uncle Mathou in the courtyard.

Soon my mother appeared, and the bangles on her feet jingled as she joined us in the courtyard. She came to see us off and to warn me to be careful in the town.

"Rumbek is not a good place," my mother said. "You must not leave your uncle's side at any time. And stay away from the *thurumbil*; they will crush you."

We left. Uncle Mathou balanced a thoroughly polished bundle of spears on his left shoulder, with the tips facing back. An ebony club was tucked under his left arm. Six scars running from ear to ear across his forehead demonstrated he was a warrior. He had obtained the scarification marks thirty years ago when he transitioned from boyhood to manhood, enduring the knife without sighing or blinking with fear when the scarification marks were cut bone deep into his skin, with no anesthetic. Likewise, his six lower teeth had been removed about forty years ago when he transitioned from childhood to boyhood. These rites of passage marked him as a permanent member of the Agaar people.

I had not gone through the above passages yet because I was still too young. But I had two spears and a fighting stick. Emulating Uncle, I balanced the spears on my left shoulder with the club securely tucked under my armpit. Off we went.

I looked to the east and saw a dark-gray barrier, still quite far away, stretching to the entire breadth of the horizon, with the sun's rays adding a yellow barrier to the dark gray. It was predawn. Walking on the path flanked by green spring grass, I closed my eyes and took a deep breath, inhaling the fresh, clean, and pure scent into my lungs.

Suddenly, I heard the *lual-atot* (spring weaverbirds) singing their fascinating melody. The birds were on the trees, and I saw some of them twisting nests and others collecting weaving materials and the morning worms. The air was filled with the fragrant smell of the plants. Spring, my favorite season of the year, was finally here. Finally, it was dawn, the beginning of a new day. And I was going to town to see marvelous things, such as the *thurumbil*. What a feeling!

We walked on as the trail wound its way around several zigzags, weaving through trees, grass, and anthills. After that, the forest vanished, giving way to a plain that must have been at least ten miles wide. Finally, we came to a bend that led to a landscape of gigantic mahogany trees lined up in two rows, one on each side of what seemed like a track. At first, I thought it was an elephant track. But the track was too clean, too long, and straight to be an elephant-made one.

"That is a *thurumbil* road," Uncle Mathou said.

Soon, we merged onto the road. It was straight and long, running from east to west. It took seconds for the eye to travel its length across the savannah until it melted into the blue-gray horizon in the far distance. I had seen nothing like this before. I could not wait to see a *thurumbil* running on this road.

Suddenly, a rumbling sound came from the direction we were heading to. I looked ahead and saw the big molten iron beast coming. The *thurumbil*!

"*Thurumbil* is coming," Uncle said, "Let us move out of the way quickly."

The beast was approaching fast and furious amidst the spiraling dust, trumpeting like a wounded elephant that had gone rogue. Before I knew it, the beast was upon us. Vroom! It passed, leaving us in the dust mixed with disgusting smoke. I pinched my nose to block the stench as I watched the beast disappearing in the opposite direction.

"Let's go," Uncle said. "You will see many *thurumbiil* (plural) in Rumbek."

The sun had just emerged on the horizon, and our shadows were long and pointed westward. The morning sun was still cool, but soon it would be blazing. Our idea was the rising sun would be on our backs when walking to Rumbek, and the setting sun would be on our backs when returning to our village. That was the efficient way of traveling without getting toasted by the sweltering African sun. It was wisdom acquired through observing nature.

The sun was halfway in the morning sky when we reached the outskirts of Rumbek. The first strange thing I noticed was how houses were built close to one another. It was house after house after house, with no space. The only things separating the houses were fences and roads. Back in the village, homesteads were built far apart, making sure each family had several acres of land for growing crops and rearing animals. But why would city-dwellers leave the vast land and cram themselves in a tiny space? It made no sense. City-dwellers seemed not so bright after all.

One of our distant relatives lived on the outskirts of Rumbek. We had to pass there to greet them, drink water, and rest before proceeding to Rumbek's city center. But the main reason we were visiting the relative's house was to leave our weapons there. Uncle Mathou said spears and fighting sticks were not allowed in Rumbek for "safety reasons." I did not understand the logic behind this. We kept weapons for security reasons, like protecting ourselves against wild animals. So why were the weapons not allowed in the city? "City-dwellers do not know the importance of weapons, too," I thought. "They are dumb."

We came to a homestead with three houses: two big houses with red bricks and tin roofs and a small house with a grass-thatched roof. A young woman introduced herself as Ajok and welcomed us with water to drink. She placed a bench under a tree in the compound, where we sat. Ajok sat on a bambar stool as she chatted with my uncle, inquiring about people's wellbeing back in the village.

Ajok was at home alone. No children. I had not seen a single child in the neighborhood. This was strange. In our village, you found children playing everywhere. And whenever I visited another place, I always met several friends and befriended them. But I had no friends to play with here in town.

When I asked Ajok where her children were, she pointed to the three large rectangular buildings about two houses down. "They are in that school," she said.

I was surprised to learn that some of our relatives had bought into the idea that if their children were given modern education, they would be well off. Back then, the school had always been a foreign concept to the Dinka. The only thing that mattered was cattle keeping. Traditional parents did not envision a situation where their children would be taken away from them to undergo a complete cultural transformation. When the government compelled traditional parents to send some of their children to school, the parents selected children with destructive behaviors, perceived to have no prospect in life, and sent them to school. So, it was common for parents to threaten their children, "Behave well, or I will send you to a place where bad children are taken: school." As far as they were concerned, the school was another way of enslaving their children and forcing them to learn about different cultures.

In towns and cities, an adult once said, they put children in school for up to twenty years. Can you imagine quarantining children indoors for up to twenty years?" No wonder some children drop out of school and become beggars, thieves, prostitutes, or substance abusers. This toxic environment turns them that way. Even those who remain in school to complete their education eventually become corrupted leaders who shamelessly consume public resources.

The Agaar, like any other Dinka group, did not send their children to modern schools. Instead, the natural world was a giant, open-ended learning laboratory, where children experienced the sights, scents, sounds, and textures of the outdoors. Mother Nature was the teacher and the classroom, providing countless discoveries, creativity, and problem-solving opportunities. Therefore, children spent amber time with friends climbing trees, diving in rivers, exploring the grassland and its immense inhabitants, learning animal food chains and behavior, and discovering activities for fostering development. Unlike prison-like modern classrooms where angry teachers walked with canes, telling children to be quiet, children in the village were free to explore, move about, and make noise—all delightful forms of self-expression. As a child, my games and daily activities included running, jumping, hopping, skipping, climbing, rolling, shouting, and relaxing; the activities that reduced children's tension, anxiety, and restlessness. This playing outdoors in nature benefited children intellectually, socially, emotionally, and physically. I was surprised to learn that Aunt Ajok had sent all her children to school. Perhaps Ajok had naughty children who had no future.

While Uncle Mathou was chatting with Ajok, I walked around to explore things. Of course, I was free to walk around and learn, unlike those poor children quarantined in indoor classrooms. I must go and see them. I walked toward the three significant buildings with stone walls and iron roofs, where Ajok said her children were studying. One window was wide open, so I went and peeked inside. The classroom looked precisely like the way the elder had described it: prison. About thirty children, sitting on benches, five sitting on one bench—there was no talking, laughing, playing, or any other self-expression essential for fun and development. A man, the children, called *Ustaz* (an Arabic word for teacher), was there with a cane, imposing the rules. I felt bad for the slave-like condition the children were in.

I went to another class to see if the children were just as depressed. They were. But in this class, many of the children looked like me, with black and cropped hair, and some had long curly hair with red skin, which looked like a ripened palm fruit. They were the *Laraab* (Arabs). The children wore ridiculous green pants and white shirts. They looked ugly in those clothes.

I wore absolutely nothing, the way I came into this world from my mother's womb. In our village, children and young people did not wear clothes; only married men and women and older people wore clothes. Uncle Mathou wore a long robe called the *jalabia*. I was naked, but my body was anointed with butter oil from head to toe. If I came from a cattle camp, I would coat my body with fine cow dung ashes. Ashes were more prestigious than oil because the Dinka were (and still are) devoted cattle-keepers. Yes, I was the only naked boy in Rumbek, but I was unconcerned. Neither was my uncle.

I stood there at the window, watching these depressed children in the class. Soon, a man wearing a long white robe with his head wrapped up in a white scarf walked in. The children stood up, and the man said something. Then the children uniformly yelled back before sitting down. He had a cane and a box full of what looked like pieces of chicken bones. The man talked briefly before turning his back to the children and faced black plywood attached to the wall. He then took a white thing and scratched the plywood with it, making different shapes. Next, each of the children took out writing twigs and white leaves (pencils and papers) to copy what the man was writing. Then the man pointed to the written conditions one by one, calling the name of each shape, as the children repeated after him: "A B C D . . ."

What nonsense to teach to the children. Human beings are not a uniform entity to be taught this nonsensical ABCD. An effective learning environment must accommodate individual differences. In Dinka land, adults did not deliberately train children to answer their questions and provide the help they sought. Instead, adults treated children protectively but did not attempt to control their learning. They assumed young people would learn what they needed to know through their self-directed play and exploration, and therefore they allowed children ample free time for those activities. That was why Uncle Mathou let me wander around to play and learn things naturally, instead of letting me sit around listening to their boring adult conversation, like these poor children forced to recite this nonsensical ABCD.

A boy sitting next to the window noticed me. He seemed surprised. He nudged the boy beside him and muttered something. They both looked at me and giggled. Now all the boys sitting at the window noticed my presence. They continued giggling.

I did not know what was so funny about me. Perhaps it was my nakedness? But there was nothing wrong with being naked. I should be the one laughing at these children because they looked ridiculous in those clothes. Back in our village, the only reason a young person wore clothes was when they had some disability, especially in their private parts. For example, when your manly thing was too tiny, or it had grown out of shape, or the skin was absent from it, as the Agaar were not circumcised, then you had a perfect reason to wear clothes. And when you wore clothes, people automatically knew something was wrong with your genitalia, whether you were a girl or boy, and people mocked you. Only grownups wore clothes. But young people still growing should not wear clothes or anything that would restrict some body parts from growing naturally. So, the private parts of these schoolboys wearing shorts would grow crooked like a tree trampled by an elephant. That was why I should be the one laughing at them, not the other way around.

10

Now the entire class was looking at me and not paying attention to the man. Then the man saw me. It was my first time meeting an Arab, and he looked scary. He was short and crooked in build. His teeth were yellow-stained and bent inward, making him looked like a dog scratching its backside when talking. He barked in that peculiar language while pointing at me with the stick before exiting and approaching me. Back in our village, children were the responsibility of the entire community, as expressed by the phrase, "Children belong to all." So, when an elder approached me, it meant he wanted to know my name, parents, clan, or general wellbeing. But the look on the man's face told me he was not coming to enquire about my wellbeing. His right hand held the stick; he looked fierce, like a hungry lion focusing on its prey. Without warning, he tried to seize me. I ducked aside just in time as he leaped, avoiding the arms reaching for me. He swung wild. In the nick of time, I ducked out of the way and took a couple of steps backward, and the cane whistled past my ear. I had never seen a grownup whip a kid for no apparent reason. This was a madman. I left the school feeling bad for those poor children under this madman's responsibility.

I returned and found Uncle Mathou and Aunt Ajok still talking. When he saw me, Uncle Mathou said we should leave to reach the market before noon. On the way, we came to a field where a game was happening. I had heard this game was called *kura*. We stopped to watch for a while. There were two teams, one wearing yellow jerseys and the other in green. A man in black with a whistle was in the center. There were two oversized door frames, one on each end of the field, and a man was standing there obviously to prevent the *kura* from entering the wooden frames. On each side of the field, there were about ten people. The mood was intense. I figured this was a crucial game for the town-dwellers.

Soon, the man blew the whistle. They started kicking the *kura* and running around. Finally, the *kura* reached the end of the frame on the east side. A man kicked it. The frame-keeper caught the *kura*, preventing it from passing. The frame-keeper then kicked the round *kura* to the other end. A man there was alone with the opposing frame-keep-er. He tried to kick the *kura* to the house, but the whistle blew. He left the *kura* in frustration. The game was fascinating to watch. But the annoying whistle-man kept disrupting the harmony of the game.

We continued to Rumbek city center. What caught my eye im-mediately was the number of people in the city. It was packed. The crowd had a life of its own; their vibrant clothes shone in the sun, and they moved like enchanting shoals of fish. No, they moved more like confused, migrating wildebeests. So many people were walking up and down, seemingly not settling down. Also, cars, bicycles, and motorbikes were everywhere, all in different shapes, sizes, and colors. There were loads of clothes, hides, salt, beads, and other strange items displayed everywhere. Trucks were loading or unloading. The hustle and bustle were chaotic and spoke of life I would not want to be a part of.

But the smells! The city's smells were alien to me, and their cha-otic fragrance set me on edge. There was no tinge of earthy loam to the air, no scent of spring growth, or heady warning when rain was due. Instead, the fumes from belching vehicles, coupled with strange food from nearby vendors, created an awful smell. The *thurumbil* I had wanted to see so much turned out to be noisy beasts that produced unpleasant smoke.

Nausea clawed at my throat, literally, and I had to force down the bile. My stomach kept contracting violently and trying to move ev-erything up and out. Luckily, I had nothing in my stomach because I had eaten nothing that morning. Nevertheless, I sneezed, had watery eyes and an itchy throat. That disgusting smell was not good for life. I wondered how people lived here.

Then the noise. The town's noise was unprecedented. You see, people say, "a bad arrangement of sound is noise." That was precisely what was happening: bad arrangement sounds—the honking, the dis-organized drumming, singing, and ululating from a nearby pub. It was the noisiest place I had ever encountered. I hated it.

In contrast, our village was vibrant, not noisy. All you heard was the sweet melody of nature, birds chirping, cows mooing, mother singing lullaby songs, or a young man singing, and all sounded pleasant. But this town noise was unpleasant. But what happened at cattle camps was simply pleasant. From a distance, you could see and smell smoke, indicating the position of the camp. When you got closer, all you heard was the singing of a young man parading his beast, punctuated with the bellow of the beast or the jingle of the bell on the neck of the ox or bull; the laughter from a byre; and the singing and dancing of children, which all summed up the general wellbeing of the society.

After buying our groceries, salt, sugar, and a brand-new dress for Uncle Mathou's recently married wife, we sheltered under a mango tree. We had to wait for the sun to cool and go down to walk with the sun on our backs, returning to our village. Elders from other villages were also sheltering under the same mango. They were playing a *wet* game to pass the time. *Wet* is a game where players take turns distributing the counters around the board, and each player tries to capture the opponent's counters—a common board game in Africa.

While Uncle Mathou joined the game, I had the opportunity to explore more. The noise was still deafening. One singer was the loudest in the entire city. He sang the same song repeatedly: "*Allah-U-Akbar!*" he chanted. The voice came from a big circular house with the moon crest on top. The singer's voice was loud and firm. Many people were entering the building where the singer was located, so I wondered if he was the best singer in town.

Even though he sang in a peculiar language, there was nothing unusual about singing. Singing defined Agaar life. Every young man had a personal ox, bull, or both. The bull's horns were sharpened, so the beast defended itself against other bulls, lions, or hyenas. On the other hand, the ox's horns were carved when they were growing, so the horns grew asymmetrically. Then, horns were decorated with tassels made from buffalo tails. The young owner then composed songs which he sang when parading his beast. The songs attributed to the bull were known as tuar songs, full of aggression, violence, and bulls sexual potency. The songs attributed to the oxen are known as kêp songs; these songs were slow in pace and gentle in tone, designed for beauty and attraction. Whether angry or happy, the young man would sing tuar or kêp songs, accordingly, depending on his mood.

But I was unsure if this city fellow was singing a tuar or kêp song. I went to see. I approached the entrance of the building and noticed many people were entering the house. Shoes were left at the door. I peeped inside to see what was happening. There were many people inside, hundreds of them, wearing white robes and white headscarves. There were no women or children. I knew where their children were: locked up somewhere in those prisons, called classrooms. The men were sitting on spread-out mats, facing the same direction. They stood up uniformly, mumbled something, sat down, smelled the floor, and stood up again. The crowd did this repeatedly while the singer continued singing, "*Allah-U-Akbar!*"

It looked like they were praying to their divinity, not singing tuar or kêp songs. It was not that exuberant to watch. As I was about to leave, a shadow appeared behind me. Looking back, a man wearing a long robe had lifted a leather whip, ready to hit me. I try to dodge it, but it was too late. The whip found its mark on my naked butt with the tip of the whip wrapping around, missing my manly thing by a few inches. My eyes flashed with red, green, and yellow colors as this excruciating pain shot up to my brain. He had swung so hard that the whip cracked on my butt, creating a welch. He tried to hit me again, but I ran away, back to my uncle.

I never left my uncle's side again. Now I knew why my mother had told me, "Town is not a good place." Rumbek was full of mad-men who beat people for no apparent reason. My seven-year-old mind could not understand why these *Laraab* were mean and violent. No wonder weapons were not allowed in the town. Unfortunately, the exciting trip turned out to be the most terrible experience I had ever encountered.

When the sun was down and cool, we walked back to our village, reaching home at dusk.

Family and Lineage Continuity

I did not know the exact date of birth because there were no calendars, watches, or hospitals for record-keeping. But, like any other Dinka, there were stories and occurrences which point to the time I was born. For example, my mother said my older brother, Manyang, was born a couple of years after the great war between southerners and northerners had ended. The war ended in 1972, so it was assumed my brother was born in 1974. My mother also said I was born two years after my elder brother. Therefore, it was assumed I was born in 1976. My day and month of birth were just a matter of guessing. My mother said I was born in the middle of the dry season, where all the big birds had migrated to the Toc Swamp. The dry season is usually between December and April. So, I was likely born in the first week of February. Therefore, my date of birth is February 1, 1976. That was how real things could get in the Agaarland.

Like the date of birth, the relationship ties among family members tended to be overly complicated, so foreigners found it unfathomable. Levirate and ghost marriages make this relationship even more complicated. Men were (and still are) expected to bring children to their lineage. If a young man dies before he could have children, it is believed that his spirit or soul will be unhappy. An unhappy soul stays here on earth as a ghost (*thuöm or atïëp*). If this happens, the unhappy ghost causes sickness and other misfortune for his lineage. To appease the *thuöm*, the living relatives must negotiate and pay the bride price for a bride for their *thuöm*. If a man dies, leaving a wife behind, the deceased's brother betroths the widow. In both cases, the ghost will have children with the wife, who will, of course, belong to their father's lineage. Since a ghost cannot father children, what normally happens is that the new bride forms a permanent marital agreement with one of the living men of her ghost husband's lineage, most likely one of his brothers. The brother will be the biological father of her children, but her ghost husband will be the cultural father.

When a living brother or relative inherits his deceased brother's wife, this is known as *lohot* (**lɔƳɔ̈t**), literally meaning "entering of the house" of the deceased. And when a living brother marries a wife for his deceased brother, this is known as koc nhom (**kɔ̈ɔ̈c ë̈ nhom**), literally meaning "standing of the head" of the deceased. The purpose of these arrangements is to ensure the legacy of lineage posthumously; therefore, any resulting children in these marriages are considered children of the thuöm. That way, the deceased person's name does not vanish utterly on the face of this earth without a child carrying his name forward.

I was born posthumously in a levirate arrangement. I referred to Mathou Majok, who took me to Rumbek Town, as my uncle. But he was more than that. Mathou was my biological father. Malei, the older brother of Mathou, married my mother, and he died before I was born. Subsequently, Mathou, the younger brother to Malei, betrothed my mother, and I was born in that union. Even though Mathou was my biological father, I would not, under any circumstances, consider him as my father; he was my uncle, and I was his nephew. So, I was named after my deceased uncle; therefore, I became Mayom Malei Majok at birth.

After this levirate arrangement, Uncle Mathou conducted two ghost marriages. Uncle Mathou had a brother, Makomot, who had died unmarried. So, Mathou ghost-married another wife, named Aliu Keer, for Makomot. Mathou also had a sister named Cholhok, who died unmarried. Yes, ghost marriage is not for men alone. Women who die without children must have children posthumously to carry their names forward. So, Mathou married Akec Wacwel as his deceased sister's wife.

Added to this arrangement was polygamy. After one levirate marriage and two ghost marriages, Mathou finally married his two wives: Adut Agany and Acigam Agok, making five wives, including my mother.

Now things got even more complicated. Mathou's youngest brother, named Maker, had also died unmarried. So, another ghost marriage was required. But Mathou, the only living brother, was utterly overwhelmed with five wives and their children to take care of. Additionally, Mathou could not afford another bride because he had no cows. This was troubling because the ghost (Maker) could be unhappy because he had no wife and children to carry his name forward. This unhappiness could bring sickness and even death into the family.

Mathou did the unthinkable to solve this problem, something that had never been done before in the Agaar system. He decided to take the lastborn child of Malei and named him after the deceased—Maker. Guess who that child was? Me. I was taken from Malei and given to the ghost as his child. I was five years old when this happened, and I became known as Mayom Maker Majok.

Surname does not exist among the Jieng people. The tally of names from father to grandfather to great grandfather defines one's identity. That is why it is crucial for any born child, including those who die as infants, to have their children to carry their names and lineage to the next generation.

Each of the five wives had their separate homesteads, and Uncle Mathou took turns visiting each homestead accordingly. The five wives relied on each other for support that was emotional and logistical. They cared for each other's children. The children, including me, took turns visiting each home, and each mother was expected to treat us equally. The good thing about having many mothers was we did not go hungry because there was always food available in the homesteads. I never run out of people to love and people to love me. I grew up with siblings and nieces and nephews my age. The generations grew up together, with both the mothers and the older siblings looking out for them.

Uncle Mathou exercised much of his control over the five wives with their children through leading wives—Acigam, Aliu, and Akur (my mother). Leading wives meant those who were married first were responsible for the younger wives. These senior wives wielded considerable authority and demanded respect from junior wives.

Rivalry and jealousy occurred from time to time, but Uncle Mathou had stringent measures to suppress them. Based on the severity of the situation, the punishments included reprimanding, beating, or abstaining from the wife's food and bed. The abstention from the wife's food or bed was the severest punishment against the woman. If not settled urgently, it could lead to divorce.

Solving any dispute was a delicate matter. If the woman knew she was right and her husband was wrong, she would go to her husband's relatives to make her case. The relatives would come and judge the settlement and reconcile the couple. If the woman knew she was wrong, she usually went to her relatives. In this situation, the relatives would come and apologize to the husband or even offer him a cow or two, based on the severity of the wrong committed, as a token of appeasement. Culturally, a man who married a bride with many cows was most likely to be appeased by their in-laws when he felt his wife was not fulfilling his wifely duties. The reconciliation usually ended in a ritual, where a goat or sheep was slaughtered to conclude the abstention or bring the woman back into her husband's home if she had left during the fight.

Polygamy, levirate, and ghost marriages were prevalent in the Jieng society because the mortality rates were extremely high. There was no single family who had not lost a child or children during or after the delivery. For example, we were seven children from our mother, but four had died, leaving Mabor, Manyang, and I. Our sister, Yar, had died in 1996.

Looking back, we grew up poor. But we did not notice it. Happy children do not always know how poor they are. Even though we were born in this complicated levirate arrangement, we still had our mother, uncles, and aunts that loved and took care of us. We cultivated our land, reared our animals, fished our rivers and lakes, and hunted all we wanted. That was the definition of having plenty.

We had never owned shoes or nice clothes to wear. We did not have a modern house. But it never occurred to us we needed these things. We were content with what we had, and we missed nothing.

How could you miss something that did not even exist?

We had a reason to love our land and its bounty. The Agaarland was full of unspoiled natural beauty. We had endless savannahs, inspiring jungles, and breathtaking swamps inhabited by animals, birds, reptiles, and amphibians. There was nothing fake or unnatural in the Agaarland, and my brothers, half-brothers, sisters, and I took comfort in all of this.

Biling Daldiar was a beautiful village. However, it was an ancient village with different names. The first settlers who founded the village named it Madieng Thon, named after a bull, sacrificed there during the arrival. But eventually, the place changed to Biling Daldiar, named after an ancient *biling* tree still standing there today. Located two houses away from our homestead, the *biling* tree was a holy ground where the Maayuäl divinity lived. Sacrificial pegs were planted under the tree to mark the site's holiness, and anyone who passed offered something to the divinity and sought blessing. This was before the arrival of Christianity.

On the village's western side was an ancient palm tree named Akan Ayak, which stood majestically overlooking the entire village. It was believed the palm had stood there for hundreds of years. So, our village was also called Akan Ayak. North of the village was an extensive stretch of salty open ground, named Loyic, where animals and birds gathered to eat these minerals. So, the place was also called Loyic. Finally, to the east was an incredibly famous dancing ground, called Nyilumic, dotted with trees encircling the field that broke the monotony of the savannah. For decades, the surrounding villages had danced in Nyilumic, making it the biggest dancing ground in that area. For this reason, the place was also known as Nyilumic.

Further down was a low-lying area where numerous pools were found. Located in the center was one pool, the biggest of all, known as *Maan-Puot* (Mother of All Pools). Being surrounded by so many water locations, the sounds of frogs, crickets lulled people at night and woke them up early in the morning.

Between December and April, the pools and the tall elephant grass dried up, and the land looked extremely thirsty, except for scattered open canopy trees, which flourished all year around. Young men moved to the Toc Swamp, the world's largest swamp along the Naam River, a tributary of the Nile. There in the swamp, the young men would have plenty of fish to eat, and their cows would have plenty of grass and water. At the end of March, it would rain, and the swamp would flood. The young men returned to their villages to grow crops, such as sorghum, millet, maize, groundnut (peanut), sesame, and so much more.

The same cycle (planting, cattle-keeping, and fishing) took place at my maternal relatives' village, Kakook. I enjoyed staying with both my paternal and maternal relatives. My paternal relatives are Palou (people relating to the bamboo), and my maternal relatives are Pacuer (people relating to the lion). However, these two sets of relatives treated me differently. There is a saying that goes, "If a paternal relative wakes you up at night, he has killed someone, and he wants you to be ready for a fight. But if a maternal relative wakes you up, he is giving you food." I found the times I spent among my maternal relatives to be the happiest part of my life. Living with my maternal relatives, I was the center of attention. They called me *wën Akur* (the son of Akur), and I was never whipped or yelled at. That is why people say, "Your maternal aunt smells like your mother, and your maternal uncle is your master alone." The Dinka believe maternal relatives possess spiritual powers to bless or curse their daughter's children.

I remember days when I stayed with Uncle Turich, my mother's elder brother, a *raan kec,* "the bitter person" endowed with special curative powers. I enjoyed sitting with Uncle Turich, just conversing, and listening to his wisdom.

I took part in children's activities, such as taking cattle for grazing and watering. We also hunted, fished, gathered wild fruits, or dug groundnuts, cassava, or yams. Then, of course, there would be fighting as boys challenged each other individually or as a group, sometimes clan versus clan. The fighting involved wrestling, open-handed boxing, or clubbing. Some boys wore sharply barbed bracelets called *nyuiny*, used for fighting. Serious injuries occurred in these fights, and sometimes adults had to intervene. Sometimes, the case went to court, but it was dismissed as boys' things in most cases.

Pachong Primary School

I always thought that school was a place where naughty children who had no future were sent to. But in a very twisted turn of events, my brothers (Manyang, Makis) and I were taken to school. Uncle Mathou made the decision. I was shocked by the fact we were taken to school. So was the entire clan.

The idea came to Uncle Mathou when he attended a conference in Rumbek shortly after we had visited together. It was initiated by politicians who wanted to hear from traditional elders. At that time, Rumbek was the capital city of Lakes Province, governed by Dhol Achuil. Jaafar Mohamed al Nimeiri was the president of Sudan. Other prominent politicians included Aru Bol, one of the most powerful politicians in the region, elected to the parliament of Sudan in 1968. Dhol Achuil, Aru Bol, and other educated southerners formed the conference's bridge between traditional rural Sudan and urban Sudan.

It was the first time Uncle Mathou met influential leaders and politicians, and he was intrigued. Uncle Mathou noticed that all people, including the Arabs, stood up in respect whenever MP Aru Bol and Governor Dhol Achuil passed. And this was very new and strange to Uncle Mathou because, in Agaar culture, you would never stand up for anyone, not even traditional chiefs and spear masters. To do so was a sign of weakness or submissiveness—a trait the Agaar loathed.

Uncle Mathou had enough courage to ask MP Arou Bol and Governor Dhol Achuil how they got their status. "Through the education," the politicians replied. "You have to send your children to school to be educated and powerful, too."

Uncle came home that evening puzzled by what he saw: "Aru Bol and Dhol Achuil are so educated that when they passed, the entire

21

Agaar, as well the Arabs, stood up," Uncle Mathou said, as he kept shaking his head in disbelief. "I have seen nothing like that before. There is power in education!"

With that, Uncle Mathou made the unthinkable decision to send me and my two elder brothers, Manyang and Makis, to school. The move upset the entire clan because the school had always been viewed as a place where children learned about foreign cultures. Some family members even accused Uncle Mathou of mistreating us because we were not his biological children. But none of that dissuaded Uncle Mathou.

"There is a future in modern education," he argued. "Educated children will become tueny, powerful authorities who see faraway things. Aru Bol and Dhol Achuil are immensely powerful that even the Arabs bow down for them in respect just because they are educated. Modern education is powerful."

Being a man of strong will and determination, Uncle Mathou appeared to have taken this as a challenge, and he could not be dissuaded. "Educated children will see faraway things from other worlds," he concluded.

With that, we were taken to school. We moved from Biling Daldiar to Pachong, where a primary school was located. But because I was small, my brothers Manyang and Makis were taken to school while I waited for a couple of years.

I would never forget the day I was sent to school for the first time. My mother took me on the morning of April 2, 1980. I was in a state of shock or awe about the school. As a little boy, I had always been a good cattle-herder and crop cultivator. I had never lost a single cow to wild animals because I always took good care of my herds. I was a good cultivator, too, because I always helped parents and siblings cultivate crops such as sorghum, millet, groundnut, sesame, and other crops. I was a typical Agaar boy. I did not understand why I was sent to school, but I had no choice, mainly because my mother supported the idea that school was good. I was nervous. I felt like a baby gazelle being introduced to an unknown world for the first time. But like any other offspring, I trusted my mother and followed her, no matter how nervous I was, because my survival depended on her.

We went into the office, a rectangular building with a grass-thatched roof and unburned brick wall, where we found a tall man with a short beard who introduced himself as Ezekiel Roor Makuer, the school headmaster. Upon seeing us, he got up, and the chair creaked from his weight to welcome us.

"*Ci bäk!*" Ezekiel greeted me with a big smile, extending his hand to shake my mother's hand. "Greetings!"

"*Acïn kë rac!*" my mother replied. "Nothing bad; all is well!"

The headmaster wore black trousers with sandals. Sunlight gleamed from the golden top of his pen that was hooked on his shirt's pocket. After shaking my mother's hand, Ezekiel turned his attention to me: "And who is this young man here?" he said.

"This is Mayom," my mother said, "my lastborn son. I'm bringing him to school to learn."

"Good," said the headmaster. "I hope you are as smart as your brother, Manyang. He is starting grade three this year."

I was extremely nervous, and I do not remember if I said anything.

"Now," Ezekiel continued. "Do you know how to count?"

I was not sure what he meant by that.

"Yes, he does count from one to a hundred," Mother replied.

"You have to be quiet now, Mother," he said. "Let me talk with my pupil."

Before I knew it, the headmaster put my knowledge to the test in Dinka. First, he asked me to count from one to thirty, which I did. He found me fit. And I hoped he would not put me in *dhël noot* (grade zero), which was equivalent to kindergarten. But I still had an advanced knowledge test. The headmaster opened a drawer, took out a book, opened a page to display pictures of several animals, and asked me to name them one by one.

"This is a lion," I said. "This is a giraffe. This is a tiger. This is a hyena. This is a . . ." I had never seen this animal before. It looked like a zebra, but it was brown instead of black and white stripes. My heart started thumping. I was going to fail the test. I looked at my mother, hoping she would help me with this one, but she did not. The headmaster had told her to be quiet. I was on my own.

"This is a . . ." I stammered. "This is a . . . This is a brown zebra!"

Both Mother and the headmaster roared in laughter. "Very good," the headmaster said in his laugh. "You are a brilliant boy. But this is a horse," he corrected. "And this (he pointed at ridiculously looking animal with two humps I had never seen before) is a camel. They live only in the Arab countries."

The headmaster opened another drawer, pulled out a binder, and wrote my name down. I was placed in *dhël noot* (grade zero).

I could not attend the class on the same day because I was naked. The headmaster told my mother to fit me in a white cotton shirt and green shorts before attending class the following day. Mother could not afford to buy me a new uniform, so she fitted me with Manyang's old uniform he had outgrown.

The following morning, I was on my way to school with my elder brother, Manyang. Manyang was starting grade three, and I started my grade zero or *dhël noot*. Not only was I nervous, but I was also uncomfortable. Extremely uncomfortable! To begin with, I had to wear clothes for the first time. Having run around all but butt naked for the first eight years of my life, wearing clothes was an awkward experience for me. The shirt felt weird on my back; the seams under my armpits tickled me. Shorts were rubbing against my thighs, and my buttocks and manly assets felt restricted; I could not wait to get home to take them off and let my skin breathe. Finally, we came to the school compound and found the headmaster standing there. All the children were in classrooms. We were late.

"You are a little late, Manyang and Mayom," he said. "Run to your classroom quickly, Manyang. I will show Mayom his class."

The headmaster took me to another class, located next to the office, where he introduced me to another teacher named Yai Makuei. Pupils called him *Ustaz* (teacher, in Arabic) Yai. *Ustaz* Yai, a medium-built man, welcomed and showed me a seat between two boys.

To the left was a tall and skinny boy named Mapuor Makuach. To the right was a very talkative boy with a lisp named Marial Machuei. Marial Machuei (currently in Ontario, Canada) was Corporal Macuei Thondok's son, who commanded the police squad in Pachong.

There were about thirty-five children in the classroom, all seated on benches made from palm tree planks. After I settled down, *Ustaz Yai* started a song which all the children, except me, sang: "A B C D…" in Arabic. They sounded exactly like the Arabic children I saw in Rumbek last year.

At first, I did not understand why there were so many teachers. Soon, the bell rang. The class teacher left our class, and another teacher came in. All the students in our class again stood up. Other students looked at me curiously. "People stand up when a teacher walks in," Marial said. I should have known that because I had watched the pupils stand in Rumbek when their teacher walked in.

"*Sabah el kheer!*" the teacher called. "Good morning!"

"*Sabah el Nuur!*" the pupils said, except me. "Good morning to you!"

The teacher wrote some words on the blackboard. And the singing began again: "1 2 3 4 5 …" in Arabic.

Then the bell rang. Another class began. A new teacher asked us to read pictures from a book in that class. He called everyone's name one by one, and you had to get up and answer the question. Some of the children faithfully read it one after another. I was glad the teacher did not pick on me that day; apparently, he knew I did not know how to read yet.

After three consecutive classes, there was a recess of half an hour. After that, children ran to the playgrounds to play games. Both boys and girls had separate games. I did not know what to do; I did not have friends, nor did I know how to play any games.

Marial and Mapuor approached and asked my name and where I was from. It turned out that Mapuor was my next-door neighbor and Marial lived two houses away. We instantly became best friends. They knew a lot about town stuff, and I knew cattle camp stuff. The boys seemed impressed when I rattled off the names of cattle camps that

I knew. Holding their attention made me feel special, like somebody in school.

Marial and I were nine years old, and Mapuor was eleven years old. Marial spoke with a lisp, and the boys made fun of him a lot. Mapuor Makuach, on the other hand, was tall and skinny. He was nicknamed Matang-tang because he ran with his elbow stuck out like a plane taking off.

My nickname was even more derogatory. Other kids enjoyed making others miserable by giving them nasty nicknames. I was the victim. They nicknamed me *Dhiom-riec*. You see, when my teeth were growing, the two front teeth grew first before the rest of the teeth, so children thought my two protruding upper teeth looked like a rodent's teeth. Out of that came *Dhiom-riec*, meaning "the big, fat mother-in-law of the rat." I was not too fond of the name. I had fought many times, trying to get rid of it, to no avail. The more I fought, the more famous the nickname became. Eventually, I gave up, especially when big boys started calling me *Dhiom-riec*. The name stuck.

I rushed to the playground, and my classmates, Marial and Mapuor, and I became instant friends. Marial and Mapuor, who had been to school before me, knew how to play football and taught me. When I saw the size of the ball, I was scared. I could not believe that you had to kick such a big hard, round thing the size of a grown pumpkin. Then the rules! You were not allowed to touch the ball with your hand. Why? I had no clue. You could only kick it with your legs. It was tough for me to keep my hands away from the ball. I could not get a successful kick for ten minutes or so as the ball kept eluding me. Knowing I kept catching the ball, my friends avoided passing it to me. Then the ball came my way; I let loose of my foot and kicked it as hard as possible. Big mistake! My toes hurt so badly I had to sit down in the middle of the field. The other boys laughed. Mapuor and Marial came to me and helped me stand and warned me not to use my toes directly to kick the ball but the side of my big toe or the back of my foot.

I left the football and went to the other side of the field to watch the girls sitting down on the ground, counting spherical tones collected from the well's shore. The stones were placed inside a hole where the three girls were sitting around. One girl threw a stone in the air and scooped the other stone out of the hold before grabbing the stone with the same hand. Then she threw the stone up again, shoved the stones back inside the hole, leaving one outside. "One," she counted. She repeated the same steps as she counted "two," "three," and "four." When she missed, it was the other girl's turn.

Soon the bell rang, and we ran into our classroom for our last class of the day. The next classes included science and hygiene, where we were shown pictures of people washing their faces, brushing their teeth, combing their hair, and cutting their nails. We were told to do the same activities every day before coming to school.

After school, I ran home and took off all my clothes, and walked around nude. I did not want others to think I had some deformities in my private parts by always wearing clothes. Most importantly, wearing it all the time would make my manly thing unnatural. For example, a tree that grows in the shade unnaturally grows because it lacks sunlight. This practice also kept my uniform from wearing out quickly, saving money for my mother, who could not afford to buy uniforms twice a year.

The primary school lasted six years and was often divided into two levels: the lower level included grades one, two, and three; the upper class had grades four, five, and six. After completing grade six, you went to secondary school in Rumbek. Those who did not do well were sent to Akot Secondary School.

The secondary school lasted six years and was divided into junior secondary school (grades seven, eight, and nine) and senior secondary school (grades ten, eleven, and twelve). Most of the students ended their education in grade six, and only a few made it to secondary school and completed it. Colleges and university graduates were unheard of. I had never seen or heard of any student from Pachong who had advanced to college or university. Even though Rumbek was the Lakes States' capital city, there was no single college or university.

Students went to Juba or Khartoum, but only a few wealthy people could afford higher education.

The official language was Arabic, so was the lecturing language. The subjects were all taught in Arabic in primary schools, such as mathematics, science, geography, history, and civics. English was taught in secondary school and just optional. In grade seven, you learned the English alphabet or ABCD. The Arabs discouraged English because if you failed Arabic, you would not be admitted to any university or college even if you had scored one hundred percent in English.

At the beginning of 1983, I was in grade three, and Arabic had finally started to make sense. I knew how to read and write in Arabic. We also sang Arabic songs. In addition, I learned simple arithmetic and multiplication tables.

In grade three, I was also introduced to the Dinka language. I began learning Dinka alphabets in grade three. I found it hard to write from left to right after learning to write Arabic from right to left. But Dinka was not in the school curriculum. It was taught on weekends and after classes.

Ustaz Yai taught us the Dinka alphabet after school. And on Sunday, we would attend church services conducted by Abuna (priest) Maker Nyinde. At that time, Christianity went hand in hand with education. And so, the reason Dinka was taught was so new converts could read the Scriptures. The mass population, however, did not practice Christianity; only students practiced it. For this reason, Christianity was known as "pupils' God."

In the first year that I went to school, we ate lunch at school. But in the second and third years, the lunch program was discontinued. When asked, the headmaster said Khartoum had cut off the budget. Teachers were not even paid, so parents were asked to pay extra school fees to support the teachers. Some teachers went to teach in Rumbek, and others stopped teaching and became farmers to provide for their families. Books, desks, classrooms were worn out, but no replacements were provided because the government had cut all budgets.

I was now beginning to understand politics, and I sensed something was wrong in the country. Elders talked about how the Arabs were oppressing us, the southerners. I had had a bad experience with the Arabs in Rumbek, so I was not expecting something good from them, especially since they ruled the country. Rumors had it that the war was about to break out between the south and north. The conflict was brewing.

Jumping into the Bush

I remember hearing about the First Civil War (1955-1972) from our teachers and village elders in Pachong. Because of its magnitude and devastation, this period was known as the earth's ruin (riäk ë piny). Southerners trekked to the bushes of the neighboring country, Congo, where they trained and were equipped before returning to Sudan to fight the central government. Thus, the act of joining the rebellion was known as "jumping into the bush."

In 1955, one year after Sudan received its independence from the British, Southerners rebelled, forming *Anya-nya* One. In 1972, the Addis Ababa Agreement was signed between the rebels and the government of Sudan, ending the First Civil War. One of the main reasons the Southerners rebelled was the rejection of Arab culture and religion. Therefore, Southerners were exempted from the Islamic laws, according to the Addis Ababa Agreement.

In 1983, when I was in grade three in Pachong Primary School, the Islamic regime of Khartoum resumed business as usual by imposing Sharia Islamic law in the country—a direct violation of the Addis Ababa Agreement. When asked, President Nimeri of Sudan said, "The Addis Ababa Agreement is neither Koran nor Bible," meaning it must be abolished. Subsequently, Southerners rebelled against Sudan's government, forming a military unit called Sudan People's Liberation Army (SPLA), with its political wing, Sudan People's Liberation Movement (SPLM). The SPLA/SPLM fighters jumped into the bush and trekked to Ethiopia, where they were trained and equipped. This meant the Second Civil War had erupted, the biggest, longest, and the bloodiest of all the wars the Sudanese people experienced. But the war had not reached our area yet.

In Pachong, the First Civil War memories were still fresh in elders' minds when the Second Civil War erupted. Elders who grew up during the first war swore, "I hope I am dead by the time the war reaches us." I was born four years after the war ended, but my mother often talked about how we had lost everything during the war. She said our land became a vandalized yard instead of organized farmland. War had wreaked havoc on it. There was no mooing, chirping, or bleating of prosperity. Instead, the once vibrant land looked wretched and completely deserted, with ruins like an ancient graveyard.

In 1984, a new phrase flew around the school. It was the phrase I had heard in the stories told during the First Civil War. It was all pupils, and even teachers talked about. The phrase was "jumping into the bush." News had it that the rebel fighters who had trekked to Ethiopia had returned, armed with AK47 automatic rifles, and they were hiding in the bushes, ready to attack Rumbek. Because the mass population in rural areas sympathized with the rebels, young men, mostly students, escaped from the government-controlled areas and jumped into the bush in large numbers. The government responded by cracking down on those suspected of joining the rebels and arrested them. So, the phrase jumping into the bush was only whispered among friends and relatives because people feared arrest.

There was one platoon of police in Pachong, commanded by Corporal Machuei Thondok. But because the rebels were reported to be closing in, an army battalion was brought to defend the little town and deter people from jumping into the bush to join the rebels. But many students were still jumping into the bush, anyway.

Some students swore they had seen rebels armed with the most powerful automatic rifles—the *Kalany*, a Dinkanized acronym for Kalashnikov or AK47. My friend and classmate, Marial Machuei, was the expert when it came to guns because his father, Corporal Machuei Thondok, commanded the police platoon in Pachong. Marial was obsessed with guns. Because he spoke with a lisp, he called *Kalany* "*Kayang*," and GM-three was "*GM-Thiyii*." Because Marial was the police commander's son, he was well informed. He often told us about the rebels and where they were. He also told us the SPLA had an army called the *Jesh Amer* (Red Army) fighters, who, according to him, were boys of our ages.

Mapuor came to me one day with the news. "Mayom," he said, "This is between you and me. I am jumping into the bush. Several boys are going to Bilpam, and I'm going with them."

Before I could even open my mouth to answer him, Marial Machuei appeared out of nowhere. "You will not believe this, guys," he said. "I heard that students from Rumbek Secondary School are jumping into the bush tonight."

"Perfect," Mapuor said. "I can't miss this opportunity. I'm jumping into the bush."

"Me too," Marial said.

"Me too," I said, not wanting to be left by my friends.

That was that. We were going to Bilpam to join the rebels. When? Tonight! That was how stupid we were. I mean, this was a decision between life and death, and we made it in less than five minutes. We had no food supplies, no water containers, and no money. We had nothing other than the cotton school uniforms we were wearing.

We met at 2:00 p.m. to discuss our escape strategy. There was a big problem, though. Pachong was guarded by a heavily armed police force, commanded by Machuei Thondok, Marial's father. And Marial swore that when his father caught us going to Bilpam to join the rebels, he would shoot us himself. Marial was sure of that.

We planned to stay in school late, and when it was dark, we would start our journey. We had to sneak out one by one to avoid being detected by police or our parents. Our gathering place was Pan-Awach, a small village located forty-five minutes' walk away. You would think we were joking, but we were not. And remember, this was 1985, and I was nine years old; Marial was my agemate, and Mapuor was eleven years old.

Time flew by, and the darkness came on. It had to be dark to pass under cover of darkness and loud enough to hide any sounds I might make. As the animals and birds overtook the forest, I knew I would not be heard. It was black everywhere. There was no moonlight that night, and I had to run with hands rigid in front of me. My heart pounded as I ran as fast as I could.

It must have been 9:00 p.m. when we met in Pan-Awach. I found Mapuor and Marial standing on a clearance beside the road. Two other bigger boys (I forgot their names) arrived after us.

We had to wait for people from Rumbek to go with them to Bilpam. Then, as chance would have it, we spotted a deserted homestead set off the road. The homestead consisted of three houses that belonged to a man call Yak Aduol. It was summer, and the family had gone to the fishing camp, where they would spend the entire summer.

We took refuge in a house adjacent to the main road, and I hardly slept on the worn-out mat because it was cold by South Sudanese standards. Summer days in the Agaarland were hot, but the nights were cool. I put my hands between my legs to keep them warm. At home, I had a small blanket to cover with, but not here in this little hut. I was getting the first taste of what it felt like to be an *Anya-nya* (rebel).

At around midnight, Mapuor woke us up, whispering in the corner. "Get up, get up, guys. They are here!"

Listening, we heard a commotion on the road. We knew these were people trekking to Bilpam to join the rebels. So, we rushed out to join them. They were mostly students from Rumbek Senior Secondary School. Three soldiers armed with G3 rifles had deserted the government and joined the rebels.

A soldier wearing a green uniform shone a flashlight on our faces to identify us. He realized we were just a bunch of kids. "Where do you think you are going?" the soldier asked.

"*Biipam*," Marial, our lisped spokesperson, said, meaning "Bilpam."

"Biipam?" the man mimicked, chuckling. "You are just kids. What kind of gun do you think you can carry?"

"*Kayany*," Marial replied, meaning "*Kalany*."

"*Kayany*," the man mimicked. "You can't even pronounce *Kalany* properly. So how the hell are you going to handle the gun?"

Mapuor opened his mouth, trying to convince the soldiers to let us join them. But the soldier slapped him in the mouth. "Go back to your mothers, now!" the man yelled.

We ran back inside the house like chickens. The flashlight moved slowly over our heads and then spread further. The soldiers continued throwing shards of light around in the compound, making sure we were inside the house. Then the compound went dark again.

As we were contemplating what to do next, we heard another group. Again, we rushed to join them. But they chased us away also, saying we were too young to trek to Bilpam. Every group rejected us.

Now we were in big trouble. We could not return home because we could be arrested by the police, not to mention our parents' beating. Moreover, Marial was sure his father would shoot us himself.

Mapuor suggested we should walk on our own behind the people. After two days, we would join them, and they would not turn us away. We agreed. Off we went, after the crowd in the darkness. We followed the main road, heading east. We were determined to go to Bilpam to get our guns.

At dawn, we reached Bhar Naam Bridge. This was where our nightmare began. Sometimes, government troops were stationed there guarding the bridge against being destroyed by the rebels. We knew the people we had followed had either exited left or right to avoid being detected on the bridge. We exited right and walked for about one hour before reaching a crossing point. The river was full, and I did not know how to swim. Neither did Marial Machuei. Mapuor and the other two boys knew how to swim, so they jumped into the river and swam across before we knew it. The stunt, Marial, and I just stood there hopelessly as we watched our friends' backs vanishing on the other side of the river. Our dreams of going to Bilpam to get our guns had ended abruptly.

Hungry and exhausted, we returned to Pachong to face the wrath of our parents, teachers, and, of course, the police. This time, though, I told

Marial to keep his mouth shut when we reach Pachong and let me do all the talking. I knew his lisped tongue would do more harm than good. We planned to say the rebels abducted us, and we managed to escape.

Pachong was in turmoil when we arrived. The mysterious disappearance of five children had turned the little town upside down. Search teams were sent to look for us in the nearby bushes, thinking we might have gone to play in the bushes and lions had attacked us. The report of the missing pupils had even reached Rumbek. We arrived before noon and found our parents, teachers, and police in the meeting, discussing our whereabouts.

My mother ran and grabbed me hard until my ribs hurt. Finally, she hauled me on her hip and walked away, taking me home. But the police wanted to ask questions first. The crowd had gathered around Marial and me like children who had died and woken up.

"What happened? Where have you been?" the policemen, teachers, and the crowd bombarded us with questions.

"The *Anya-nya* rebels abducted us yesterday," I said. "Marial and I escaped, but Mapuor and the other boys didn't get the chance."

"Where were you when they abducted you," the police said.

"We were playing soccer there," I said, pointing to the soccer field located behind the school. "When it was dark, we just sat down and talked. Then, before we knew it, three rebels emerged from nowhere and took us. They wanted to take us to Bilpam."

I did not think they would believe our sad story, but they did. We were praised as clever boys who had escaped our abduction. The report reached Rumbek that rebels had abducted pupils. Tanks and jeeps swamped Pachong as troops patrolled the area.

The school was closed indefinitely because no parents wanted to send their children to school for fear of abduction. So many people, including Marial's family, moved to Rumbek. Others moved to the countryside in the swamp, where they would be safe.

The same year, government troops came from Rumbek and attacked Pachong and killed people, including Chief Maker Kanac *Ustaz* Achuoth. The entire town, including the school, was burned to ashes. Subsequently, my mother and I moved back to our traditional village, Biling Daldiar.

Mapuor Makuach: After Mapuor crossed the Bhar Naam River in 1985, he made it to Bilpam, Ethiopia, and he was trained with the Kazuk, the Third Division of the SPLA. In 1987, I successfully made it to Bilpam, and I was trained with the Zalzal, the 4th division. In 1992, I finally met Mapuor at Khor-Bulldozer near the Sudan-Ethiopia border, where he was deployed, and I was on my way to Kapoeta from Ethiopia. When the SPLA built the road from Dimma, Ethiopian to Buma, Sudan, one of the excavation machines broke down. So Mapuor's platoon was deployed there to guard and protect the machinery. Hence, the place was named Khor Bulldozer, meaning the bulldozer's stream. It was a great reunion. We laughed as we remembered that escape episode. Mapuor told me that the other two boys who went with him had died of thirst and exhaustion in the Tingli Desert.

Mapuor and I agreed to return home to see our families together. While Mapuor was waiting for written permission from his commander, I proceeded to Kapoeta to wait for him. Two days later, Mapuor was tragically killed in action.

Marial Machuei: After that incident in Pachong, Marial and his family moved from Rumbek to Khartoum and finally to Egypt. From Egypt, he migrated to Canada in 2000. He is currently in Ottawa, Canada.

Halima, the City Girl

After the school was closed, I went back to my roots in cattle-keeping. Even though I was acquainted with town life after several years studying in Pachong, I readjusted smoothly to the life of cattle camp.

Some urban dwellers who were forced out by war found it harder to adjust to rural life. One of them was a girl named Halima, whom I met at Aramweer Cattle Camp in 1986. Halima did not belong to the cattle camp; she was a city girl. Born and raised in Khartoum, Halima visited relatives in Rumbek, and while she was there, the SPLA captured Rumbek. So, Halima fled to a remote village, where one of her uncles lived. The uncle took Halima straight to the cattle camp. The life there petrified the city girl.

Halima, who spoke half-baked Dinka flavored with Arabic vocab-ulary, did not know how to milk cows, pound grain, or clean dung. She called the cow dung *urara bagar,* an Arabic word meaning cow feces. People found it despicable to term anything coming from the noble cow with such a graphic term.

Cow dung had numerous functions. The dung was collected, pro-cessed, dried, and burned as fuel. The ashes from the dung are im-portant elements with many practical uses. People who live in a cattle camp, young and old, coated themselves with ashes from head to toe. The ash is used to protect their skin from heat and insect bites. But the main reason people wear ashes was to show they were *awuot* or cattle camp dwellers, as it was honorable. For decoration purposes, water was added to ashes, and the paste was applied to the body in desired patterns and left to dry, forming living art on the body. Additionally, in the swamp where there were no twigs to use as toothbrushes, you grabbed a handful of ashes and used your index finger to clean your teeth and gums with it, and then rinsed your mouth with water. Your teeth and gums would be clean and germ-free. Furthermore, ashes were also used for spiritual purposes. Not any ashes, but cow dung ashes called *arop.* Ashes were carefully processed and mixed with a special clay, forming a red or white powdery mixture stored in sacred gourds (*gut*) specifically used for this purpose. It was stored to be used by spiritual leaders for blessing, healing, and other spiritual purposes. In fact, there was a free divinity called *arop*, meaning ash.

Boys and girls processed the dung. But Halima, the petrified city girl, did not want to touch that thing with her polished fingernails. Her uncle punished her all the time, trying to make her do chores like any other girl, but the Khartoumer could not cope. To the Dinka, cattle keeping must come naturally. But to be this incompetent was unfathomable. No one sympathized with Halima.

Other girls also bullied Halima because of her inability to con-form. Back then, girls wore few clothes, and they were not afraid to be nude when necessary. Unmarried girls had nothing to hide. But Halima, who was used to city privacy, could not part with her clothes for any reason. Even when swimming, Halima always wore her underwear. The girls and the boys were dumbfounded why Halima was so secretive with her body.

"Something must be wrong with Halima's private parts," a girl mocked, "and that's why she is so discreet with her clothes."

The boys, who wanted to sneak a peek but to no avail, were just as bad. "Maybe her womanly thing is not even there. I hear they cut them off in Khartoum!" one boy joked, referring to the female circumcision that Arabs practiced.

Halima was called other nasty names, such as "*athuma*," "*adhaba*," or "*thaluk*"—derogatory terms used against "city-dwellers who lack decent manners and competencies." Halima was visibly depressed.

When I met Halima, she noticed I had all my teeth, unlike all other boys who had removed their six lower teeth, marking them permanent Dinka members. She smelled some city in me, and she was right. I was once a pupil at Pachong Primary School until the civil war intensified. I had returned to my roots, but I did not remove my lower teeth or received scarification marks because I planned to join the SPLA movement.

Halima befriended me instantly. She was a gorgeous girl, by the way. The fact that she was older and more educated than me, as she was twelve- or thirteen years old and I was ten years old, did not matter to either of us. I did not even speak Arabic that well, but I understood most of what she said, which was soothing for both of us. Besides, she had no other friends. Not only did the boys and girls comment on her private parts, but other people, including her uncle, call her a city-dweller who lacked decent manners and competencies. Even young fellows (*aparapuööl*) did not want to court an athuma. Lucky me. I had the Khartoum beauty all to myself because I was the only one who did not judge her.

I taught Halima how to milk. Her uncle had given her a lactating cow for her consumption and told her to milk her cow or starve to death. I asked her what her cow's color was, and she described it in Arabic as "a black and white-headed cow." That is *kuei*, I gathered.

Kuei is a name given to a cow with this coloring. *Kuei* also means fish eagle because it has black and white coloring.

Their byre was not far away from ours, so I promised to go there every day, after I finished milking my cows, to teach her how to milk. I just wanted to be closer to this Khartoum beauty. Do you know what I mean? But Alima perhaps did not realize my perverted thinking. As far as she was concerned, she had found a good friend to learn from, someone who had not judged her.

Knowing how to milk was crucial. You could not go to the next phase in life without mastering milking. In fact, a warrior is called an *apälräk* or *apäräpuöl*, meaning "one who has stopped milking." You had to master milking before transitioning from boyhood to manhood. You could not call yourself an *apäräpuöl* when you had not mastered cattle-keeping skills. Similarly, you can not call yourself a graduate when you have not attended classes and work hard to pass all your courses.

You see, milking a cow is not as easy as it looks. It is a delicate task that every boy and girl must master. There are three containers needed for the job, all made from gourds. *Theu* is used for milking, *amuj* or *ajieb* is used for storing the milk, and *göm* is used to churn the milking into butter.

To milk a cow, you must be on the right side of the cow. You can never, ever milk on the left side of the cow. And please do not ask me why. It is just a rule to be adhered to, just like driving on the right side of the road. I mean, you can drive on the wrong side of the road if you want to, but that makes you an idiot. So, you must milk on the right side of the cow. No exceptions.

Similarly, when tethering cows to their pegs, you make sure that the rope's adjustment loop faces the right, not the left. All ropes are woven in similar patterns, right? You can never invert the rope when weaving or tethering. Never!

After the cattle had returned from the pasture and milked my cows, I went to help Halima. As we walked among the cows, Halima always jumped when a cow swung its horns. I told her to relax and that the cows get nervous when people jump. I showed her how to calm a cow down by caressing and speaking in a soft clicking language called *cin*. Then, I also grabbed a handful of ashes to clean the cow with it. The cow was very cooperative, but I was just showing off. Like a young man driving a car with a beautiful girl sitting beside him, the young man makes all these unnecessary maneuvers to impress the girl. That is what I was doing. I wanted to impress the Khartoum beauty. I mean, who wouldn't?

After calming down the cow, I released her calf to suckle first so that the cow could release the milk. Then I tethered the calf to milk the cow. I squatted on the cow's right side and held the container between my bent knees. First, I grabbed the cow's bushy tail and cleaned the teats with it. I advised Halima not to use a cloth to clean the teats because the cow would identify it as fabric and withhold her milk. Then I wrapped my thumb and two fingers around the teat base and squeezed; the milk squirted out of it into the container. I synchronized with both hands, from teat to teat, as milk rapidly squirted into the container.

The Khartoum beauty just stood there, watching in amusement as I showcased my skills. I handed her the milk and told her I would come tomorrow morning to help her again. I returned to my byre, hoping the Khartoum beauty was impressed by my skills. Indeed, she was. After one week, Halima asked me to escape with her to Khartoum, where we would resume our studies. "And then when we finish our studies," she said, "we will get married." *El-ham-dhul-li-laih,* I said to myself in Arabic. "Thank God!" I did not speak Arabic that well, but hey, when a beautiful woman falls for you like that, you think you know the language, especially if it is the language the girl speaks.

But as tempting as it was to escape with Halima, I did not want to go to Khartoum, where the Arabs were. I told her Arabs were our enemies. My first encounter with the two Arabic teachers in Rumbek had made me hate all of them. So, I turned down the offer and told Halima I wanted to join the SPLA, and I was waiting for the right moment to escape and trek to Bilpam, Ethiopia. "If you like it," I said, "you can go with me to Ethiopia." Surprisingly, Halima said she wanted to go to Ethiopia with me. The Khartoum beauty had surrendered; *Walaih lazim!* (for sure!).

But before we could find people heading to Ethiopia to join them, Halima and her uncle moved their herds to another camp called Wunju, leaving me in Aramweer. They suddenly left when I was out in the pasture, and we did not even say goodbye to each other. I was devastated. I heard Halima had escaped from Wunju. By then, the Khartoum government had recaptured Rumbek, and I believed she returned there and went on to Khartoum, where her parents were. Since then, I have never heard from Halima again.

The Trek

In 1986, the war between the government and the SPLA movement had peaked, with us, the unarmed civilian population, being the principal victims. Besides heavily armed Arab tribes, the well-equipped Sudanese troops ravaged the countryside, repeatedly attacking villages across Southern Sudan. Antonovs bombed indiscriminately in rural areas. Civilians were slaughtered in large numbers; cattle were looted or killed, houses were burned to ashes, fields, and crops were torched or destroyed.

While the government and its militias were killing civilians directly, the SPLA rebels were killing them indirectly. The rebels consumed crops and cattle the government troops had not destroyed. The SPLA fighters solely depended on civilian food. The SPLA had multiplied in number by now, and having many soldiers meant many mouths to feed. They went from village to village, house to house, cattle camp to cattle camp, fishing ground to fishing ground, demanding food and porters to carry their ammunition and food supplies. The civilians suffered more than the men in uniform. Dinka Rek sang the following song in the Bhar el Ghazal region summed up the civilians' predicament:

Cë piny riäk kacïn kë ber Yo kony?
Muɔnyjäŋ da, këdït acë Yo jäl yök.
Acë tek nhom në diäk:
Bë naŋ jieny ë Marälïn,
Ku nɔŋ jiec ë Junub,
Ku nɔŋ jieny Arab-malual,
OO! Muɔnyjäŋ da, këdït acë Y o jäl yök!

Has our country fallen apart that there is nothing to help us?
Dinka, we are in big trouble.
It is divided into three:
There is an army of Marahaliin (Islamic army)
And the army of the South (the SPLA army)
And the army of the red Arabs (the government army)
Oo, Dinka, we are in big trouble!

I was eleven years old when the ruin or spoil of the land was at its peak, and I still believed I could protect my mother and our belongings if I had a gun. Also, I was confident I would make it to Bilpam. I had learned a lot from the rebels. I knew Bilpam, where the rebels were trained and equipped, was in Ethiopia. Obviously, the heinous trek to Bilpam was not for the timid; it was the most agonizing trek, which tested your endurance and pushed your boundaries. If you were looking for a relaxing walk in the woods or savannahs for a few days, this was not the hike for you. It was a combination of rugged, long, and dangerous terrain. Dangers such as wildlife, falling rocks, roaring rivers, and a lack of trail markers defined the trek to Bilpam. On top of that, you had to leap over landmines, dodge bullets and bombs, and run away from wild animals and poisonous snakes. All these dangers made the trek exciting for a young warrior who wanted to test his manhood.

I needed to save money for my journey to Bilpam. I also wanted to buy some clothes. So, in 1986, I grew tobacco at a deserted cattle camp called Adiid, located several kilometers away from Biling

Daldiar. After spending the entire summer planting, watering, weeding, and harvesting the tobacco, I sold the product and generated enough money to buy items for the trip. My tobacco sales earned me thirty Sudanese pounds, the largest amount I had ever had.

I bought a pair of shorts, called totin, and a robe called *cop-wong*—famous clothes worn by young fellows in Rumbek at the time. Totin shorts were tied yet comfortable, specifically designed to keep manly assets in place as the young man walked, ran, or danced. On the other hand, *cob-wong* was a thigh-length robe that was so beautiful and so pricey that a young fellow would "chase the cow" *(cob-wong)* to the market to sell it and buy the cloth. That was how the name came about, and the pair cost ten pounds. I gave ten pounds to my mother and kept the remaining ten pounds for my trip.

Now correctly dressed and with the money in my pocket, I took a small tin of peanut butter from my mother, and off I went, heading to Bilpam, Ethiopia. It was 1987. I joined Second Lieutenant Manyang Magom with his twin brother, Aheu and Madit, in Baar Aguoch. The three brothers had deserted from the government and were also heading to Bilpam. Hundreds of other recruits joined us as we set out as the red African sun descended into a horizon clad with pines. There were hundreds of recruits on the first leg of this long and agonizing journey. I wanted to go to Bilpam and get my gun, the AK47, and return to protect my mother and the entire village from both the Arabs and rebels. I would be the most powerful young man in the town with the gun, and all the girls would practically throw themselves on my feet. Then I would marry a good wife to take care of my aging mother and me. The enthusiasm and positive thinking kept me going.

We walked from Rumbek through the lands of Ciec, Atuot, Aliab, and finally Bor. We avoided main roads and towns by walking in the forest to avoid being detected by Sudan government soldiers who patrolled the area. In the first few days, walking day and night, every one of my muscles was swollen. The weather was either colder or hotter than I had anticipated. When the rain came, it came in wild, concentrated bursts, flurrying all around us. We spent our days, weeks, and finally, months trekking from village to village, bush to bush, and mountain to mountain.

We reached the marshland of Jonglei, where we followed the Nile River and its tributaries, dominated by papyrus. The paths were virtually nonexistent as we walked on what felt like a waterbed; the reeds held our weight, but there was always the sensation that they might break at any moment, plunging me into the stagnant marsh beneath.

My first near-death experience began when we crossed a river, one of the Nile's tributaries. The shallow crossing point was in an open area. There were human bones and skulls scattered all over the place, and we knew this was a killing zone where government troops laid in ambush. Nevertheless, we had to cross quickly.

It was around 7 p.m. and getting darker. The river did not seem deep. I still did not know how to swim. There were no rivers in Pachong where I was studying, so I had not learned. When I went to a cattle camp, it was summer, and the Naam River shrunk during the dry season. I was waiting for the rainy season to overflow the river so that I could learn to swim. But I left before the rainy season arrived. I was now facing the consequence of this.

Everyone slipped in the cold water to cross. Without even thinking, I slipped in as well. I waded slowly to let my body adapt, and the sensation of cold was diminished. As I waded, I sank a little until my head was below the water. Suddenly, I do not know how I was drowning. I could not breathe because the water had entered my nose and mouth quickly, and subsequently, my lungs. I was aware I had to stay above water to be able to breathe again. And I was flailing my hands to keep above water, hoping I could bring my face above the surface, but I was not successful at it. Other people were only a few feet away, but each was busy in their world, trying to cross quickly before the government soldiers arrived. I drank water twice and could not shout, and my mind was blank. Then, out of nowhere, a man from Jurbel grabbed my hand and pulled me to safety. My mind recorded all those things, but I could not react. Maybe I was in total shock and could not respond or shout. When we were on the other side, the Jurbel threw me on the ground like a wet sack and moved on. I was coughing and vomiting loudly in an area where absolute silence was needed. A few minutes later, after water cleared out of my lung and was replaced with nice clean air, I got up and ran to join the trekkers.

Throughout the journey, I had tried to avoid Lieutenant Manyang Magom because he had first said I was too young to go with him to Bilpam. So, I avoided him, thinking he would send me back home, like the first group who rejected us when we first attempted to trek to Bilpam. But now that we were far from the Agaarland, I joined them because I knew he could not send me back home alone. He said nothing when he saw me. And after walking for weeks, he was impressed by my strength. He even trusted me enough to give me his mosquito net to carry. Manyang led the way throughout the journey, followed by his brothers, bodyguards, and another young fellow, Mading. I followed Mading.

Mading became my instant friend. He was extraordinarily tall and gaunt and a typical Dinka that Jacob Akol described in his book, I Will Go the Distance, as "a waste of two children in one." Because of his height, no river was deep for him. Whenever we came to a river, Mading instructed me to hold on to his backpack, then kick my legs in the water to float as he dragged me along. We crossed several rivers that way. I never left Mading side throughout the journey.

Hunger was not my primary concern. Boys were trained to cope with hunger. It was a process of being groomed into a warrior. Sometimes, the herd boy was intentionally starved. While he was away tending the animals, people would cook food and eat it all, leaving nothing for him. When he returned from the wilderness with the animals, there was nothing to eat. You would think he was being mistreated. No. He was being trained to cope with the hunger so that when he became a warrior, he would be fasting for days. When there was a war, warriors spent days fighting in the wilderness without food or water. When food was scarce, a warrior always fasted, letting the women, children, and elderly eat the little food available. When un-expected visitors came, an *apäräk* usually left their food to the visitors. Complaining about hunger was a weakness—an utterly unacceptable trait. This stamina was instilled in me at an incredibly young age. And it had helped me during the trek to Bilpam and throughout my entire life.

Even though I was hungry, I reserved my ten pounds and the tin of makuanga. I was starving to the point that I was dizzy. Whenever I stood up, I had to hold on to something first until my feet were steady before walking, or else my eyes would flicker black, red, and green lights as if I were about to faint. But I pressed on.

After walking for several weeks, days and nights, we came to a village called Manydeng. There was a little restaurant where a woman was selling porridge (*cuin-thou*). I checked my precious ten pounds in my pocket; they were still there. I did not want to spend the money before even reaching the desert. But the aroma of the food was ir-resistible. I went to the woman and asked how much a plate of food was. She said it was one pound and a half. I bought one dish, which I shared with my cousin, Mabor Turich. It was the tastiest food I had ever eaten in my life. But it was not enough. I wanted to buy another plate, but I stopped myself. Greediness was an unacceptable trait; I had to economize my money accordingly. So, I stuck the 8.50 pounds into my pockets. We left Manydeng, heading to the Ajak-Ageer Desert.

The vast, golden sun rose over the edge of the barren world, and its harsh rays beat down on me, trying to shove me down onto that bare ground. The stiff desert breeze blew salty sand into my face, making breathing even difficult. My swollen tongue felt as if it was coated in thorns, and my lips were chapped, dried, and cracked by the time I was in the middle of the Ajak-Ageer Desert.

I longed for crystal, cold water, but there was none! In my tattered backpack was a three-liter bottle full of water, wrapped up in a mos-quito net. It was all I had for this four-day journey across the desert.

We had been walking all night into the desert. Now it was midday. When I shaded my eyes and peered away across the broken waste of the desert, I saw nothing but scattered human bones and skulls. Back in our village, every dead person was buried correctly. Not in this desert. Bones and carcasses were scattered everywhere.

"This is a good sign," someone said. "These bones tell us we are heading in the right direction."

It was unbelievably hot. The air entered my lungs like lava. There was not a single bird in the sky, and even the flies had taken cover. Only a few scattered trees stood, with no leaves, their spindly branches pointing to the sky, begging rain to come.

As I walked, I wandered around, looking for something to distract me from the problem at hand. First, I counted the skulls to take my mind away from the thirst. One, two, three. Small, big, tiny, big. Then something else caught my attention. Each skull had scarification marks, distinctively telling me which tribe the victims hailed from. Scars running from ear to ear indicated that the victim was Agar, Ngok, or Nuer. V-shaped scars told me the victim was from Atuot, Aliab, or Bor. And marks running from front to the back of the head meant that the victim was from Rek. I kept counting the skulls as I walked—anything to distract me from this carnage. I knew if I gave up, my skull would tell people coming behind they were heading in the right direction.

Two days passed, and it was now morning in the middle of the Ajak-Ageer Desert. We had seen no visible water source yet. The cruel sun beat down on me, without even a wisp of cloud to soften the harsh rays. With each step, I had sunk into the burning sand; the air was thick and hazy, each breath like drowning in the lava.

The desert lizards took shelter in the shadows of the anthill, where the sand was not hot enough to roast them, but there was no shade large enough for me. The lizards possessed certain characteristics and behaviors that allowed them to adapt to the desert environment. For example, these Lizards adjusted color due to temperature fluctuations, and this regulated their body temperatures and provided the means to survive. And when standing, the lizard danced by raising two feet and a time to avoid burning. Unfortunately, I could not adapt like the lizard because my color was fixed, and I only had two legs. I was at the mercy of the blazing African sun.

To be thirsty in a desert, without water, exposed to the burning sun, without shelter was the most terrible situation a human being could be placed in and one of the greatest sufferings they can sustain. My tongue and lips swelled. I heard a hollow sound in the ears as if I were losing my ears. My brain appeared to grow thick and inflamed. I knew death was nearer because I had never felt that way before. So, I took my bottle and gulped down three mouthfuls and a half of water. That was the end of my water. Mading had also finished his.

Everyone had fallen behind, even Manyang's bodyguards (Aheu and Madit). Manyang was leading, followed by Mading, and I was behind Mading, following like a thread with a needle.

We had been in the desert for three days. By now, everyone depended solely on the last drop of their mother's milk left in his heart. Death crept and lurked closer, day by day. Hour by hour. Minute by minute. Second by second. It was all around me now. The thoughts of it filled me with fear and dread. I wondered what death would be like when my time came! How would my last breath escape my body? Violently? Or peacefully? Would it hurt badly? I did not know the answers. No one knew the answers. I wished I could ask the bones lying around, "How was it?" Unfortunately, that was not possible either.

"A green tree! It could not be," I thought. "This must be a mirage." But it was not a mirage. Everyone saw a big green tamarind tree that was less than a mile in front of us through a shimmering haze. Everyone knew a green tree meant water. Morale and smiles lifted. We would not die.

But when we arrived at the location, the lonely tamarind stood on the dry land with no water. We spent several minutes running up and down like madmen, looking for water, but to no avail. Hope soon turned to dismay; there was no surface water, not a drop, and the sand was as dry as the bones.

I started to feel nothing, see nothing, or smell nothing. My survival instinct was the only thing keeping me alive. I was no longer thinking, caring human being. I was just a wild animal trying to stay alive.

I looked left and right before removing my bottle of water. Some individuals in the group went around, seizing other people's water containers by force. There were a few drops in the bottle. I had learned a new trick from other people: after completing your water, you started collecting the liquid that came out from the other end and recycling it back to the container. You would be surprised to what extent you were prepared to drink when you have had nothing for over three days.

I lifted the bottle and sipped the urine. It tasted and smelled awful. My throat was dry and swollen, and it hurt when swallowing. Despite its disgusting taste, the concoction of liquid wet my swollen tongue and throat.

I tried to find Manyang, his two brothers, and Mading, but I had difficulty doing so. My brain was sluggish, tired, and confused. I did not even know how long we had been walking in the desert. I was on my last legs—another twenty-four hours without water, and I would be dead.

The urine seemed to have helped because I got up and walked when people started to move, although several remained under the tamarind tree. Most of the people who had remained were from the Jurbel and the Rek sections. Exhausted, weak, and dehydrated, they had lain down to rest. And that was it. They would rest for eternity. Their bones would tell those behind them they were heading in the right direction.

You see, when someone dies, people often say, "Rest in peace." But I find it hard to believe that people who had died in the desert had rested in peace. Dying in the desert was not a clean death; it was a horrific, painful way to die. In the first stages of dehydration, they felt thirst set in, and their mouths went dry. As thirst intensified, saliva thickened, faces flushed, skin wrinkled, heads ached, arms and legs cramped, strength dwindled, and body temperatures soured. As dehydration became severe, the victims' tongues swelled. Their eyes grew sunken and tearless; stomach bloated, major muscles contracted severely and painfully, and blood pressure fell. Their pulse rates became feeble and rapid as consciousness faded. They died, but that was not the end. Their bodies baked in the sun for months, and their bones still litter the desert. Tell me, are they resting in peace?

We moved in a single file with drooping heads, dragging feet along the trail littered with bones. It was getting dark in this waterless world. Finally, we slumped down for the night.

I saw a group of people lying down like logs, and I joined them. Lying on my back, staring up at the stars, I started to feel uneasy. I rolled over onto my side, trying to look at Mading or Manyang. It was too dark to see the expressions on their faces. The fact that they were not even moving spoke volumes. I rolled back onto my raw, skinless, throbbing back to wait for my fate.

When the weather was cool in the middle of the night, the elders beside me sang traditional hymns. It was then I realized I was in the wrong group; they were elders from Twic who were ahead of us, but they were exhausted and thirsty to walk, so they had lain down waiting to die. The last option was to call Ajingdit, their spear master back home, to send the rain or water. Finally, the oldest encouraged everyone to call his God, Divinity, or Spearmaster.

While the Rek elders were singing and praying, our clan song dedicated to Mading-ding Divinity came to mind. My lips and tongue could not move to sing the song, but I sang in my heart:

Kë ci wën ë Wundiör maan,
Aye thimic ë nyier,
Maadiŋdiŋ aba kuompiny në duaar,
Acë möön cë mënë luät e,
Madïŋdïŋ aba kuömpiny në duaar.

Anything that the son of Wundior hates,
He sprinkles it with rain,
The giant, dark Divinity will cover me with the clouds.

The moon came, and we were on the move. The night had been long, hot, and sleepless. My skin felt like it was on fire, my head felt like it was going to burst, and my eyes felt like they were popping out of my head. I was no longer sweating, as there was no more fluid in my body to sweat. I shuffled along. The Maadingding Divinity did not hear my prayers to send water or rain. Neither did Ajingdit and the other spear masters and divinities summoned.

After walking for about one hour, the weather suddenly changed; it was more relaxed. Then I smelled water in the air. At first, I thought my nose was playing a trick on me again. I had been chasing mirages earlier in the desert, which looked like a river, all day. But this was real. Water! The flood came rushing on our feet. It was a miracle, the act of divinity.

It had rained heavily ahead of us. The rainwater from Mount Gumroh flooded the desert once or twice a year. We were lucky to have been there then. To me, this was a miracle, a divine manifestation; Maayual Divinity had sent the water. The older men from Gogrial thought Ajingdit had heard their calls and sent the water.

People lay down on their stomachs to drink the muddy water full of debris. I put a piece of mosquito net in my mouth to sieve water as I drank. My throat and stomach hurt when I swallowed, but every organ welcomed the soothing wetness of water in the body.

Flash flooding could become a threat. The desert sand did not soak up water quickly, so heavy rains could rapidly produce flood conditions without warning. It did not take much water for a desert to flood, either. The ground was usually baked hard, like concrete. If the water could not percolate into the soil, it had to go somewhere.

After crossing the desert and coming to Gumroh, a town on the other side of the desert, I was utterly exhausted and hungry. The vegetation in that area looked strange, so I could not scavenge for food. Knowing I was already halfway into the journey, I decided to spend my 8.50 Sudanese pounds. Unfortunately, I learned the Sudanese pounds no longer worked on the other side of the desert. Instead, they used Ethiopian money (birrs). Therefore, my 8.50 pounds were now useless papers and coins. I was angry with myself. I should have at least eaten that extra *cuin-thou* and bought many other things at Manydeng. What a waste! I was disappointed with wasting my hard-earned money.

Now my only hope was the tin of peanut butter, which I had not even tasted since my mother gave it to me. One piece of advice I was told by another soldier back in our village was, "Don't finish your water and food before you find another source."

In Gumroh, I met another soldier named Makuer (currently in Rumbek). Makuer was from Pachong Primary School; I have forgotten his father's name, but I remember his nickname. Like me, Makuer was the victim of those boys who nicknamed people. So Makuer was called *Makuer-ci-dhuel,* meaning Makuer with sagging testicles.

Makuer told me that my brother, Manyang, was in Pibor, a town on the outskirts of the desert. This changed everything. I decided to keep the makuanga until I met my brother to share it with him. He had gone to Bilpam a couple of years earlier, and he was now a soldier. So, I figured it would be nice to give him a little taste of our mother's finest produce, the *makuanga.*

I gathered some edible leaves, which I boiled and drank the green, slimy soup. There was no taste, no nutrition, nothing in the soup. But it temporarily eased the pain of starvation. I did not even know the name of those vegetables in Murle land. Mading had taught me how to pick soft edible leaves and boil them.

We left Gumroh, reaching Pibor four or five days later. I heard my brother had left that morning with his battalion, heading to Pachalla. No problem. We would pass through Pochalla, so I hoped to find him there. I did not touch the *makuanga.*

A couple of days later, we arrived in Pachalla at nighttime. In the morning, I started looking for my brother, but to no avail. Eventually, I met Sabah Malok, another student from Pachong, who told me that Manyang had gone to Gilo yesterday. Now I had given hope of finding my brother. From Pochalla, we headed in the opposite direction to Dimma, a newly established training center. The chance of sharing the *makuanga* with my brother had just vanished. Now I had to open my tin of *makuanga* and eat it alone.

I opened the bag, and I could not believe my eyes. My tin of *makuanga* was not there! It had been stolen last night when I was sleeping. It was devastating. A complete disaster! I had wasted my money, and now I had lost my *makuanga*! How foolish was I? The anger or hopelessness I felt at that moment was hard to describe. I had absolutely nothing to hope for. My money was useless, the *makuanga* was stolen, and I was not even meeting my brother.

But you know what? When you are in that situation, your survival mechanism always increases in levels. So, my survival mode automatically shifted to the next level. I sneaked out of Pochalla and walked for about half an hour, where I found an Anyuak village. After going from house to house offering my *chob-wong* robe for food, I found an Anyuak man who barter-traded the robe with a half-gallon of maize. After selling the robe, I walked naked, wearing only my shorts from Pachalla to Dimma, Ethiopia. But I survived on the maize until I reached my destination.

We had walked for ninety days and nights through the jungles, deserts, savannas, and mountain ranges, braving hunger, thirst, disease, wild animals, and attacks from government troops. When I finally reached Ethiopia, everything was gone: I had no buttocks left, my ribs were exposed, and my arms and thighs did not have any meat left on them. Without visible curves, I looked like a bamboo pole.

Shortly after arriving in Dimma, I was taken to the Red Army training center called the Multi-Purpose Youth Center. After that, Lieutenant Manyang Magom was sent to Bongo Training Center to take cadet courses. His twin brothers Aheu and Madit and Mading Ruc-juny were sent to Marketh Training Center with the Black Army forces. Our division was Zalzal Two.

Aheu Magom was killed in action in Kapoeta in 1987.

Madit Magom was killed in action at Bhar Naam Bridge in 1991.

Manyang Magom: Manyang is currently a general in the South Sudan army, and he is living in Lakes State.

Mading is currently in Rumbek. To this day, Mading keeps talking about the "strong-hearted boy" (me) who trekked to Ethiopia with him.

PART TWO

Ethiopia

———◇◆◆◆◆◆◆◆◆◆◆◇———

"I stopped longing for the home I had left behind and started belonging to the home I was now living in. Therefore, I discovered my new identity through the replacement of longing with belonging."

Dimma

After the gruesome journey, which took us nearly three months from my village in Southern Sudan to Ethiopia, we finally reached our destination—a place tucked away somewhat anonymously in the middle of mountains. It was a land my ancestors had never seen or heard of before. When I looked around, the horizon stretched across the entire field of view most spectacularly. The gigantic mountains soared up high, determined to challenge the heavens itself, majestically standing and dominating the horizon in every direction. The only distance I could look at without anything blocking the view was straight up. This was Dimma.

Located in the western part of Ethiopia, Dimma, established in 1986, was the third training center of the SPLA, after Bonga and Bilpam. Unlike the other training centers, Dimma specialized in training and indoctrinating young fighters, the Red Army. Even those trained in Bonga and Bilpam, and they were too young to fight, were sent to Dimma for further indoctrination until they were mature enough to fight.

When we arrived in Dimma, there were battalions of the Red Army from the three divisions of the SPLA: Koryom, Muormuor, and Kazuk. Thus, we became Zalzal, the fourth division of the SPLA. Zalzal was divided into Zalzal One and Two, and they trained in Dimma and Bonga, respectively.

Dimma was divided into five sections. The first section was a residential area called *Hela*, where women and children lived. Multi-Purpose Youth Center (MPYC), where Jeish Amer (boys and girls) were trained and indoctrinated before being sent back to Sudan to fight, was the second section of Dimma. The third section was the

Katiba Nuur Center, where old men and women were trained to become *Katiba Ajathiin*—the Elderly Battalion, whose functions included mobilizing resources for the fighters. The fourth section was the Markath Center, where the Black Armies were trained. The fifth section was Korchum, later named Pakhok, located between the Sudan-Ethiopia border. Later, Korchum became the training center for Ugandan rebels, called Aringa, who were fighting the government of Museveni of Uganda.

The three prominent leaders who commanded Dimma were Late Commander Marko Chol Machiech (1986–1988), Commander James Hoth Mai, former South Sudan Chief of Staff (1988–1989), and Dr. Atem Nathaniel Riak (1989–1992).

When we arrived in Dimma in 1987, I wore only my totin shorts, and nothing was covering my visibly exposed ribs because I had sold my *chob-wong* robe in Pochalla after my tin of peanut butter was stolen. The first person I met in Dimma was Manyang Akoldit. Manyang, from the Kazuk Division, was a student from Pachong, and he was my brother's classmate. When Manyang saw I was naked, he gave me a shirt. Even though the shirt was too big for me, I still wore it because it was the only thing I had. The second person I met was Dut Malual, from the Kazuk Division, who took me to his place to eat. It was the first time I had a decent meal since I left the Agaarland three months earlier. Such trivial gifts may seem insignificant to others. But a small gift in a desperate condition equates to a piece of diamond in value.

Shortly after our arrival, we were categorized in two: the Black Army—the ages of eighteen and above, and the Red Army—up to eighteen. As a result, twelve battalions (ten battalions of the Black Army and two of the Red Army) formed the fourth division of the SPLA: Zalzal Two. The ten battalions of the Black Army were taken to Marketh Training Center, and the two battalions of the Red Army were taken to the Multi-Purpose Youth Center.

We had less than one month to recuperate from the agonizing journey before starting our guerrilla warfare training. Then we were arranged into platoons, squads, companies, and battalions.

I was put in the first platoon, the third squad, the fourth company in the first battalion. It was my first time meeting other people from other tribes, and I became uncomfortable. Remember, there were more than sixty tribes all bundled together. My platoon members were primarily boys from Dinka Rek, aged between eight and twenty. At first, the members of each tribe stuck together because of the language barrier and cultural differences. I had no one from the Agaar, so I languished in loneliness and isolation for a while. Every night I went to bed lonely, hungry, and scared.

It was then that I realized loneliness was as painful as hunger. When you are hungry, you feel the emptiness inside your stomach, and if you do not eat, the pain will spread all over your body. The same thing applies to loneliness. When you are lonely, you feel the pain and emptiness in your heart, and it will eventually spread all over your body. The loneliness was overwhelming. The dreary routine of loneliness and isolation in the middle of the mountain was excruciating without parents, brothers, sisters, or relatives.

Luckily, I met Jima Anyar, who was about my age—I was eleven. Jima was in the second platoon. Like me, Jima was the only Jurbel, so he was lonely too. We became friends instantly, and we enjoyed each other's company—two sad individuals. I walked from Rumbek to Ethiopia with Jurbel members, and it was a Jurbel man who saved me from drowning. So, I was accustomed to them more than another Dinka group. Despite our cultural differences, Jima and I were both from the same region: Lakes State. Jima and I became inseparable. We ate and played together and slept side-by-side.

But there was one problem. I only knew Dinka, and Jima only knew Jurbel. I also learned a few Arabic words, but Jima had none. So, communication was almost impossible. Fortunately, though, Jima knew some Dinka vocabulary, which became crucial in our conversations. The only problem was that Jima awkwardly constructed sentences, making it hard for me to understand him.

First, Jima addressed me as "*raan* Mayom," which means "person Mayom," and he called himself "*raan* Jima" or "person Jima." The common and proper nouns were not supposed to be together in any language. Only Jima did that.

When it came to speaking in sentences, Jima said things up-side-down. For example, he would say: "Eat come to Mayom." I had to rearrange the sentence in my mind to figure out what Jima meant: "Mayom, come to eat." And this was in a good case scenario. In a bad-case scenario, he would throw a bunch of jumbled words to me, and I had to put them together myself to form a sentence and figure out what he meant. For example, he would say: "Tomorrow, water wood Mayom; pound cook Jima." I had to rearrange these words and added all the necessary verbs and conjunctions to form a meaningful sentence and figure out what Jima meant: "Tomorrow, Mayom [will collect] water [and] firewood [and] Jima [will] pound [and] cook [the] food." Our conversation was pathetic. But it was better than nothing. We needed each other for survival, so we cherished our friendship.

One day, Jima's platoon members cooked and ate the food, leaving him with nothing. Jima was furious and started to fight: "*Raan Jima acin nisba?*" he said. He was belligerent. No one understood what he was saying, so his sergeant called me to come and translate.

"What happened, Jima?" I asked. "*Raan Jima acin nisba,*" he said. I translated to the trainer that someone in the platoon had eaten his share (*nisba*).

My platoon leader was Piol—a very arrogant fellow. We never got along, and he always punished me for no reason. But Piol did not know a single word of Arabic. So, every morning after the parade, when orders were given in Arabic, Piol would ask me to explain to him in Dinka what was said. But because he punished me, I always told him, "I don't know what was said." But when my friends asked, I usually explained it to them. So Piol retaliated by finding every excuse to punish me whenever he could. When sent to cut the grass for roofing, for example, Piol would say my bundle of grass was either too tiny or too messy. And then he sent me right back to the wilderness.

Then the wheels turned around. Because Piol did not know Arabic, he was demoted, and I became the platoon leader instead. You know how the SPLA treated people. "The SPLA sticks an ostrich *nok* (plume) on your head, and before you knew it, they take it off your head and sticks it to your bottom." That was what happened to Piol. Now he had to obey my orders.

But do not let my boasting fool you. It did not take long before the SPLA took the nok-plume off my head and stuck it to my bottom. We were reintegrated to begin our training, so I lost my rank during the integration.

Guess who was in the same squad with me after the integration? It was Piol. Of all the people, Piol and I landed in the same squad, again! He was in the third platoon, and I was in the first platoon. I tried to avoid him as best as I could. Even though both of us were privates, Piol would not hesitate to give me a slap or two when we met in a dark corner. I could be sure of that. He was a big guy, probably eighteen years old, and I was only eleven.

But soon, Piol became a minor problem. After that, there was a significant problem: food was scarce. About ten people shared the same plate. We all stood in a big circle, and we took turns, each stepping in to cut the food with a spoon and stepping back to let others cut. Some people did not cut the food and step back to give others a chance. You had to shoulder your way in; otherwise, the food would finish without even getting a single cut.

What made things even worse for me was that two of my two new platoon-mates were each armed with a spoon nicknamed *katul-akuk*, literally meaning "kill your brother." Handmade from a sheet of tin, *katul-akuk* was the most oversized spoon that was supposed to be used as a scoop, not a spoon. With little food from the training camp, the spoon lived up to its name, "kill your brother," because the food did not last when used. When a *katul-akuk* was dug into the plate, you saw the damage with your own eyes. It was troublesome enough to share a plate with one *katul-akuk*. But two? I did not know how I would survive the grueling guerrilla warfare training of the SPLA.

Kuedi, a boy from Murle, and I were the youngest in the squad and the entire company. It was hard for us to shoulder our way in and have access to the plate. And with two *katul-akuk* spoons, food did not last on the plate. Kuedi and I suffered.

Fortunately, Mayak Malet, the squad leader, noticed our suffering and came to our rescue. Being a squad leader, Mayak ate separately. And he always had plenty of food because every cook wanted to appease the boss by giving him enough food. Sergeant Mayak ordered that Kuedi and I share with him, and he ordered our platoon leader, Tong Chol, to add our rations to his. From then on, the three of us shared the same plate. Kuedi and I became comfortable.

Additionally, Mayak also ordered that Kuedi and I should not do heavy duties, such as going to the wilderness to get building materials, pounding the grain, or even cooking because we were too young. The entire squad agreed with Mayak, except Piol, who said it was unfair to make some people do all the jobs while others eat and sleep.

"No one brought them into the bush," Piol said. "They should work like everyone else."

But despite his constant whining, Mayak's orders endured. Because the squad leader protected us, Piol tried to accuse Mayak of tribalism. But he could not find the link: Mayak was from Bor, Kuedi was from Murle, and I was from Agaar. Piol and I were from the same region, Bhar el Ghazal.

Nevertheless, Piol, who could not find any tribal link among Mayak, Kuedi, and I, ended up saying it was because we were all *ayuk* (uncircumcised), and that's why Mayak treated us favorably. He kept whining and complaining until the message reached Madut Mabior, our company leader (currently a general in the South Sudan army, Armor division). Madut reported to the battalion leader, Mathiang Mathiang, who forwarded the case to the overall commander, First Lieutenant Paul Anyuat, currently a general in South Sudan in the wildlife division. Lieutenant Paul agreed we were too young to do heavy duties, such as going to the wilderness, cutting thick poles using stones (there were no axes or machetes), and carrying them back to the camp. Subsequently, Lieutenant Paul ordered anyone below eleven years old to be selected from our two battalions and taken to the headquarters. It was then that the terms *Marek-rek, Dikdik,* or *Nyawanyiu,* were coined in Dimma to describe the youngest of the Red Army fighters.

After the orders, Kuedi and I packed our belongings immediately and moved to the headquarters. We did not do anything, not even cooking—the cooks who cooked for trainers cooked for us, so we just ate and attended the training. We stayed comfortably in the headquarters until we completed our training. Piol's actions were a blessing in disguise.

Training

The selection was made before training. Those with physical disabilities remained in refugee camps because they could not make it because of the training's intensity. Only the strongest and fittest were expected to complete the training and make good fighters. Registration was also thoroughly done: your full name, clan, tribe, location or town, and chief were recorded before attending the training. Every SPLA fighter was fully documented, though these documents were lost or damaged by the elements.

Because of the intensity of the training, deaths were expected. As recruits, we knew it was acceptable for trainees to die; it was the cost of producing the top-class fighters of the SPLA. Anyone who had attended training had seen relatives, friends, or platoon-mates die. Beating, kicking, running up and down mountains, soaking in cold water, and rolling in the mud, as well as the deprivation of food and sleep, were parts of the regular drill. Some recruits died in the trainers' hands, others fell off the mountain cliffs, and some died purely from exhaustion. Those who died during the training were known as kusara medan, meaning "training center casualties." The SPLA training was designed to separate the strong from the weak.

The trainers or drill instructors, known as *talimjiin* (singular, *talimji*), were responsible for the imposition of this training program. Our leader training was First Lieutenant Paul Anyuat (currently in Bor).

The second in command was Second Lieutenant Deng Deng, who was killed in 1990. The third in command was Comrade Geng Maker (currently in the USA).

Lieutenant Deng was the meanest trainer—a nearly seven-foot-tall guy from Gogrial. We nicknamed him *Enbuu* because he liked to yell "*enbuu!*" instead of "attention!"

To introduce himself to us on the first day of the training, Lieutenant Deng stood the two battalions at attention and ordered, "I do not want anyone to move, talk, sneeze, cough, or even breathe. I need absolute silence!"

We thought he was joking. He was not.

Soon, a young fellow named Chol Bol (currently in the USA) could not hold in his cough. Chol was Lieutenant Deng's brother-in-law. In Dinka culture, in-laws are the most respected relatives. So, we thought Lieutenant Deng would not punish his brother-law. We were wrong.

As soon as Chol coughed, Lieutenant Deng ordered, "Take him to the river, soak him up, and beat him thoroughly."

The entire battalion was scared. A guy who beat up his brother-in-law was not joking.

Another mean trainer was First Lieutenant Anyieso Ajang (who passed away in Juba in 2021, as I was writing this book). He was one of the few officers trained in Cuba.

A few of our comrades had their mothers at the residential area, located half an hour away from our center. These lucky guys sneaked out of the training center on the weekend and went to the residential area to enjoy their mothers' cooking before sneaking back without being noticed. However, while with their mothers, some made the mistake of sharing what was happening in the training center. Not a brilliant idea! You cannot share such things with mothers because they worry too much.

One day, a boy visited his mother. While eating, the inquisitive mother asked her son how the training was going on. Without even thinking, the son told her everything in detail: "We are severely punished every day," he said, "many boys have already died."

Though she could not take her son out of the training, the worried mother went wild with this rumor. She mentioned it to her neighbor, who told her neighbor, and so on. It did not take long before the word spread like wildfire. All mothers who had their children in the training center went nuts: "Our children are being punished to death in the training center. We need to write a letter to Dr. Garang, the commander in chief of the SPLA."

It did not take long before Comrade Anyieso heard the rumor. He was belligerent. Fuming, he came early in the morning and blew the whistle. He did not even want to find the culprit who gossiped to his mother. No, he had to punish all 3,000 of us. It was unfair to most of us who did not have a single relative in the camp.

"What kind of soldiers are you to share military secrets with your mothers?" Anyieso said. "I will show you what death looks like today, so you will be able to explain it to your mothers properly if you survive."

Comrade Anyieso stood us at attention and disappeared, leaving us standing in the blazing sun. Shortly afterward, he returned marching a battalion of *Jesh Amer* from Zalzal One, armed with sticks and whips, apparently to come and beat us. First, we were driven into the river and soaked in the water. Then we ran, frog-leaped, or rolled up and down the mountain several times while being mercilessly beaten. The punishment lasted for hours.

On the first day of the training, we made a dummy gun. We had to treat the wooden gun like the real gun. You carried it everywhere you went. When sleeping at night, you made sure no one stole your weapon. Sometimes, the trainers snuck into our houses and stole people's wooden guns. Those who lost their weapons were punished.

On the same day that we made our dummy guns, we learned how to pledge allegiance to the SPLA. First, you punched the air with your left fists and yelled, "SPLA *Oye!*" You chanted this phrase before you talked, sat, stood, or sang. Then, when dismissed, you stood at attention, turned right, stamped the left foot, took one step forward, stamped your right foot, and then yelled, "SPLA *Oye!*"

We had to take many classes, including military courtesy, general orders, and a chain of commands. In the first week, we were bombarded with information, directives, orders, and instructions from the trainers, officers, and senior ranking officers. For example, we were ordered to eat, sleep, and wake at specific times dictated by the trainers. At 4:00 a.m., we started jogging and exercising, which lasted for two hours. At 6:00 a.m., we returned to clean up. At 8:00 a.m., we went to the mountain top to train. At 2:00 p.m., we returned to eat lunch. At 4:00 p.m., we returned to the mountaintop for training. At 6:00 p.m., we returned home to eat dinner. At 8 p.m., we gathered on the parade ground to sing revolutionary songs and receive instruction for tomorrow. At 9:00 p.m., we went to bed.

The trainers highly emphasized teamwork and comradeship during the training. The point was to make everyone the same. Individuality was not an asset in basic training; it would not be an asset in battles. We trained, bathed, ate, slept, and even used the restroom as a team. If one person wanted to use the toilet, the entire platoon or squad would jog to the restroom while singing revolutionary songs. If one person did something wrong, the whole squad, company, or battalion would be punished. The concept was for everyone to think of themselves as part of a unit and think of the team first and foremost.

The training began with physical endurance and stamina. Guerrilla fighters had to have a series of vital physical and mental characteristics. Soldiers lived in the bushes, so they ought to endure extremities such as rain, cold, heat, thirst, hunger, and disease. While enduring, they must walk or run distances without getting tired. So, jogging and marching for miles were part of our regular activity during the training period.

After jogging for about two hours, we started physical or muscle-building exercises such as push-ups, sit-ups, and so on. Physical strength was crucial because, as guerrilla fighters, we would carry our house on our backs like tortoises. During this exercise, we also performed a drill of carrying injured or dead comrades. After these physical exercises, we would relax our muscles with easy activities such as matching, saluting, and rolling.

At 7:30 a.m., we were released to brush our teeth, washed our faces, use the latrine, and rest. We only had thirty minutes to do all of that. There was no breakfast. We ate twice a day: lunch at around two and supper at eight. The food was reduced significantly so that the recruit did not eat to their satisfaction. We were prepared to cope with hunger because, in a real battle, we could go for days without food on the front line.

Our training consisted of necessary soldiering skills for the first weeks, including matching, saluting, weapon handling, and bayonet fighting. This training would help us for battle survival. Then we learned all the guerilla technical moves and maneuvers, including camouflage and reconnaissance. The *giamat* (tactical maneuvers) were derived from animals' movements. For example, *giam dud* was crawling on the stomach like a worm; *giam tigil*—walking like a monkey; *giam sogur*—squatting and walking like an eagle; *giam gowonya*—leaping like a frog, and so on. *Giam lel* (nightly tactical maneuvers) was also emphasized because guerrilla fighters like to attack at night.

As the weeks went by, we learned more, and we were harassed slightly less. We had courses in navigation, field sanitation, camouflage, close combat maneuvers, and in-filtration. Camouflage was emphasized. We dressed up like trees to conduct reconnaissance or execute raids and ambushes.

We learned how to launch successive attacks on an enemy convoy or town using a platoon, squad, company, or the entire battalion. The attack ought to be uniform and in an established order: the first platoon was always the vanguard, followed by the second, third, and so on, still in the same order—this built routine and momentum.

Bayonet training was also emphasized, and we learned the techniques of bayonet fighting. Because I was groomed to be a warrior armed with spears, the thought of needing to use a bayonet did not leave a queasy feeling in my stomach. The instructors had a course laid out, in most cases, with life-sized figures stuffed with straw which the trainee would traverse, practicing his bayonet thrusts. There were many techniques of killing with a bayonet. The simple technique was to jab, withdraw, swing the butt of the rifle to deflect the enemy's thrust, strike the enemy in the head or neck to knock him down, jab, and withdraw. Every thrust, blow, or swing was followed by the phrase, *Hi, hi, ya!* to maximize the spirit of the bayonet.

The act of fighting with a bayonet was known as Atan-ten-atan. One of the Red Army battalions sang the following morale-boosting song, demonstrating how they killed the enemy using the bayonet, sung in Juba Arabic:

Jes komondo jayi,
Taradu Jalaba, Jalaba jere e sambala.
Budukia nimir talata, timtish arazi.
Bundukia nimir arba, timtish arazi.
Song-ki, hi ya!
Jalaba jere,
Adu fi kalfi, atan-ten-atan!
Jes Komondo jayi.
Anina jes gurilla!

Translation:
Commandos arrived and defeated the enemy (Arabs).
The enemy scattered.
Third and fourth gunners check and kill the enemy.
Use bayonet, hi, ya!
The enemy is running,
Atan-ten-atan!
The enemy is in the back
Atan-ten-atan!
Commandos have arrived.
We are guerrilla fighters!

We were also trained about what to do when the enemy captured us. You were not supposed to give the enemy any information, no matter how much they tortured you. And if you had documents with sensitive information in your pocket, you had to destroy them or even chew and swallow them so the enemy could not read them. The chewing and swallowing of documents sounded simple, but it was not in reality.

I remember one day when we set up an assault exercise in a defended position. The objective was to cross an open field, maybe 500 yards from the tree line, where we would begin our assault. From there, we would proceed to climb the hill where we would have a vantage point of shooting down at the enemy. From the hilltop, we would run through a ravine where the enemy was waiting in ambush. By then, we would be exhausted, outnumbered, and low in bullets. The enemy would capture us.

The theory of this assault called for a minimal number of fighters because the enemy had the advantage of cover and protection. However, the reality of this situation was that we did not want to lose many people, so a few people would have to be sacrificed to test the enemy's capability.

In this exercise, the unluckiest fighters selected to test the enemy's capabilities included me. I oversaw the highly classified documents during this exercise. I was teamed up with Madut Mabior, the company leader. When captured by the enemy (the trainers), I had to either destroy or swallow these two documents.

We followed a trail carrying our wooden guns as we walked up and down a mountain. Soon we emerged into a clear field near the enemy base. The enemy opened fire. We shot back. Remember, the enemy (trainers) were using live bullets, and we were using our wooden guns. The bullets were hissing above my head, and I thought I would get hit and die.

Nevertheless, we crossed the field and climbed up and down the hill. The midday sun was sweltering, and we were exhausted, but we had no time to recuperate. Somewhere ahead, the enemy had laid several ambushes, waiting for us. We had to be vigilant. Madut Mabior warned me I should run faster when we fell into an ambush to avoid being captured and beaten. Most importantly, we had to avoid swallowing the papers if possible.

As we entered a dry stream, the enemy (trainers with live ammunition) started shooting. We were caught in the ambush. We used our wooden guns to shoot back, "*ta, ta, ta, ta,*" then we took off running. "*Saabit! Saabit!*" the enemy shouted. "Stop! Stop!" But we did not stop. We made it out of the ambush.

In the next round, I was teamed up with another person. In this drill, the enemy had to capture and torture us. But we were not supposed to give away any information. We walked up and down the mountain before we fell into the ambush. We were surrounded, and we put down our weapons and raised our hands. The enemy started slapping, kicking, and gun-butting us. "Who is your commander?" "How many are you?" "Where is your location?" They bombarded us with questions as they tortured us.

I took the documents out of my pocket and stuffed them into my mouth to crumble and chew them. But before I could swallow them, Manut, the trainer, squeezed my throat, preventing me from not just swallowing but also breathing. When the instructor inspected the document, some of the words in the papers were readable; I had not destroyed the documents, meaning I had put the entire battalion at risk. We were beaten and kicked mercilessly. That was how elaborately brutal the training was.

Nevertheless, it prepared fighters for the real thing. "You are unconscious and alive, fortunately," the trainers warned us. "But in war, you would be dead when caught by the enemy."

After we had tactical maneuvers, we were trained on how to handle the weapons. We learned all the parts of the AK47 and how to disassemble and assemble the rifle. And this was my favorite part of the training. I came from my village to get the gun, and I had to clean it thoroughly to protect my mother and the entire village when I returned.

Ten of us stood at attention. In front of us were AK-47s, lying down, their long black barrels beaming against the rocky ground. My heart was thumping as I tried to remember everything I had learned about disassembling, cleaning, and re-assembling the rifle. It was one of the final steps of the training. I had to get it right, or else I could not be a competent soldier.

"Stand at ease," the trainer said. "Kneel before your gun."

I kneeled, making sure the butt of the gun was between my knees.

"Get ready," the trainer said. "One. Two, Three. Go!"

I picked up the gun with both hands, feeling the magic metal's coldness. It was heavier than I thought, but I held it firmly. To have a firm grip, I rubbed my hands on the floor to get rid of the sweat when the trainer was not watching. I removed the magazine and set it to the far right before unlocking the gun and pulling back the charging handle to eject any loaded rounds. Then I removed the cleaning rod located at the rifle's front below the barrel and placed it next to the magazine. I removed the bolt cover by pressing the button on the back of the bolt cover forward. Then I pressed the same button toward the gun's front, sliding it out of its channel, and removed the bolt spring by pulling it backward. I placed the cover and bolt spring to the far left. I pulled out the bolt and charging handle and put them in the front. Then I remove the gas tube. I cleaned all the parts and performed these steps in reverse order to re-assemble the firearm.

The training ended with us being given real guns for practice shooting or *zaref-naar*. But we did not want to waste our precious bullets, so we used dry shooting. And this was how it worked: you aimed at the target, and the trainer was ready with a chalk or pencil. When the pencil pointed in the area you aimed, you asked the instructor to mark your target area. Then, each recruit had three shots: standing, squatting, and lying down. When the three marked spots formed a pattern, such as a triangle or a circle, you passed. If they were random, you failed.

When my turn came, the instructor yelled the following instructions:

Afta mufaraden el akiir (switch your rifle to single shot)
Neshin ala rah-tak (aim as you wish)
Shit el ula (first tuck of the trigger)

Shit el Tania (second tuck)
Shit el talta (third tuck)
Akfil el nefas (hold your breath)
Azuruf (fire)!

"Over there," the trainer said, sending me to the group of winners.

"Yes, Comrade." I got up and ran off with a big smile on my face. I had passed the final test. I was a competent fighter. "Soon," I thought, "we will graduate and be given guns. Then I will return to my village to protect my mother and the entire village."

The commander in chief, Dr. Garang, first paid a surprise visit during our training. We were rehearsing raid tactics when he showed up, flanked by his bodyguards.

"What are you doing today?" Dr. Garang inquired.

"We are conducting a raid attack on the enemy," Lieutenant Paul Anyuat said.

"What is the position of the enemy?" the chairman asked. "In other words, what do you know about the enemy you are attacking?"

"There is one battalion in this location," Lt. Paul said. "Their artilleries are deployed to the east, and their headquarters are in the center. So, we are trying to launch an attack from the west."

"How did you know this?" Dr. Garang interjected. "Did the enemy tell you?"

"No," Lt. Paul said. "We sent out a reconnaissance earlier to gather all these facts on the enemy."

The chairman nodded. "Continue with the good work," he finally said. "I will return after six months to graduate this division, Zalzal Two."

And now the commander in chief was here to graduate us. The entire camp was frantic. Women, children, and disabled people started pouring in from the residential areas. The arrival of the chairman was the only time women were allowed into our barracks. We marched to the parade ground amidst the chanting and ululating of the women.

The Black Army battalions also came from the Marketh Training Center. The mood was exhilarating, and morale was high; each battalion sang their revolutionary songs.

Soon, the advance guards who heralded the chairman's arrival strode into the parade grounds and surrounded the entire place, all armed with AK-47s, RPGs, and PKMs. Several jeeps had already sealed every exit and entrance.

Then, Dr. Garang arrived flanked by around twenty bodyguards. There was clapping, chanting, thrilling, and cheering from the civilians. The Red Army and Black Army just stood at attention as the chairman entered the parade grounds.

After the civilian had quieted down, Lt. Paul stood the entire parade at attention and reported to the Camp Commander, Dr. Atem, who finally reported to Dr. Garang.

After saluting and stuffing the report papers in his pocket, Dr. Garang strode toward us, his AK-47 slung on his right shoulder, a pistol on his left hip, and a bayonet securely tied on his left thigh. Standing over six feet tall, he had a broad chest, thick neck, and a prominent jaw set off by his unkempt beard.

"SPLA *Oyee!*" Dr. Garang bellowed, punching the air with his left fist.

"SPLA *Oyee!*" the entire Dimma crowd roared back.

A lead singer of one of the Black Army from the Gradall Battalion got up to start a revolutionary song:

Adɔm baai (X2.)
Kalanykob arƐc Wau,
Aweil, Wandit, ku Juba, ku Malakal abuk ke dɔm në yom tök, RPG-9.
Rïny dan ci puou riak, ku bi ku lui ë kë piath.
Miɔc Ɏok në këdan dhiƐƐ.
Këdan cɔl Kalan abuk teŋic ë rou, rou; abë yic lɔ rou, rou!

Translation:

We will capture our country.

We will capture Aweil, Wau, Juba, and Malakal in one day with the RPG9.

Our youths are angry (with the enemy),

Give us our usual thing, the Kalashnikov to shoot, rou, rou, rou!

"I will give you our usual thing, the Kalashnikov," Dr. Garang said, capitalizing on the song. "But you must go and do our usual thing: capture towns and cities from the enemy."

Educated in the USA, Garang was a great leader and a very eloquent man. He flavored his speeches with humor, stories, and jokes.

"I greet you all in the name of our movement," Dr. Garang began. "I'm happy to be with you here today in Dimma. The purpose of my visit is to come and brief you about our movement, how far we have come, and what we have achieved so far. But, most importantly, I come today to graduate Zalzal Two Division officially."

The hue and ululation rose as our lead singer, Majok Fanan, started a morale-boosting song:

Katiba Jiec el Amer,

Jundi munazil, rajil sora

Ya munazil (X2) rajil wathon

Amer John Diktor Jai alela

Kalanykob fok

Anina bi yah-rar adaf bita thora

Min Sadik al Mahdi

Red Army Battalion

A soldier of struggle, the man of revolutionary.

He is a struggler and the man of the land.

The Red Army of Dr. Garang is coming today.

Holding Kalashnikovs up high.

We will achieve the objectives of the movement.

From Sadiq el Mahdi

"I congratulate you," Dr. Garang continued, "for completing your training. Some of you will go back to Sudan to fight. Those who are still young and weak will remain here in Dimma to mature before they are sent to battle. Schools will be opened to study while you wait. Education is also crucial."

I did not want to go to school, I thought. I did not come here to study; I came here to get a gun and return to protect my mother. It had been eight months since I left my mother, the longest time I had been away from her since I was born. I could not wait to return home again. I would be different. Now I knew how to march, salute, and shoot; I also knew how to conduct raids and ambushes and throw a grenade. I had learned it all. I was a complete soldier. Nobody would mess with my mother and me when I returned home.

"There is a reason why your center is named the Multi-Purpose Youth Center," my mind drifted back to the speech. "You must learn how to shoot and how to write. There are a lot of things that you need to know in education." Dr. Garang bent down, picked up a stone, raised it high, and let it drop to the ground. "Why does this stone fall on the ground instead of staying up there in the air?" he asked. "You will learn this in school."

The illiterate population who knew nothing about the law of gravity gasped in awe, puzzled by this wisdom. It was this wisdom that qualified Dr. Garang to be referred to as a leader who was "half-human and half-divine." Indeed, the way he solved some problems supported the theory that the chairman was full of divinity.

One day, he was traveling with his troops. One car had stuck in the mud, and soldiers gathered rocks to be placed under the tire to gain traction. One soldier was exhausted and hungry after working all day. So, he came with a big rock and threw it down forcefully, splashing mud on everyone, including the chairman.

"Fuck the people who bring us into the bush to come and suffer like this," the angry soldier said and went to sit down under a tree.

The air stood still. People wondered how the commander in chief, a man so powerful, would react to a soldier who insulted him in his face. Some thought he would arrest him. Others said he would fire-squat him right there.

But Dr. Garang did none of the above. Instead, he went to work in the place of the angry soldier. The chairman went to gather rocks, bringing them one by one. When he was tired, the chairman went and got his final rock and threw it down forcefully, splashing the mud all over the place. "Fuck the son of a mother, who followed me into the bush when he knows he was not man enough to keep up," the chairman said.

The crowd roared with laughter, including the mutineer. Subsequently, the mutineer got up, saluted, and apologized to the chairman for his bad behavior. After that, the morale was high again.

Dr. Garang spoke for six hours straight, each critical point punctuated by clapping and songs. He talked about the history of the SPLA as written in the manifesto. He also spoke about the division which was happening within the SPLA. His second in command, Commander Kherbino Kuanyin Bol, had fallen out with the chairman. It was alleged that Commander Kherbino wanted to take over the chairmanship from Dr. Garang.

"Let me tell you the story of cat and mouse," Dr. Garang said. "A rat and a cat were crossing a river on a boat. The boat was made from dry *dura* canes. And you know rats like to eat dry *dura* canes. The cat was sitting rowing the boat, and the rat was paddling from behind. When they reached the middle of the river, the rat started to chew the boat. Water started coming into the boat through the hole where the rat had eaten. The cat was unaware of this until his tail got wet. He saw the rat was busy chewing the boat when he looked back, and water was seeping inside the boat.

"'Rat, my brother,' the cat said. 'Why do you do this terrible thing? Why don't you wait until we cross the river before you can start eating the boat?'

"That is precisely what Commander Kherbino Kuanyin Bol and Commander Arok Thon Arok are doing," the chairman said. "They are eating the boat while we are still in the middle of the river. Why do they want to destroy the movement when we are still in the bush? Let them wait until we achieve our objective and return to our country, and then they do whatever they want to do.

"There is nothing left in our country," the chairman continued. "This is because the Arabs killed (and still killing) our people, raped our women, and destroyed our cattle and farms. That is why we came to the bush, to get the power: AK-47. Because if you have no power, your oppressor can lie to you or force you to do something you do not want, but you have no choice. Your oppressor, for example, can point at a tree and say it is a stone. But you would accept, even though you know that is not true because you are powerless. But if you have power, you say no, this not a stone; it is a tree."

After the chairman completed his speech, the crowd dispersed. The women, children, and disabled persons returned to their residential areas. The Black Army battalions returned to Marketh Training Center to get ready. They would be armed and equipped tonight, and they would return to Sudan to fight.

We, the Red Army, remained in the parade grounds. It was time for a selection. Those who were strong physically would be selected and equipped to join the Black Army in front lines. We all stood at attention as commanders went from platoon to platoon, pushing strong boys to one side and the weaker ones to the other.

A commander approached our squad, grabbed Tong, Piol, and Mayak, and pushed them on the right side, where instructors took charge. The rest were shoved toward the other side of the field. Then the commander came up to me. He did not even bother to look me over. Instead, he just grabbed my shoulder, turned me around, and shoved me to the rejected group. "Go there," he said and moved on to the next boy.

I shuffled over to the rejects, who were now wailing. I knew crying would solve nothing. I had to look strong; perhaps, I would be selected. I had to be tenacious.

I ran to our house and put on layers of clothes to look puppy and increase the chance of being selected. I also stuffed cardboard inside my shoes to look taller. Then I dashed back to the other platoon, waiting for the selection. But again, my baby face betrayed me. The commander came over to me, grabbed my shoulder, turned me around, and shoved me out of his way. "Go there!"

I cried terribly. My dream of returning home to protect my mother and our belongings had vanished before my eyes.

When I look back, the selection was thorough and fair. If you were not physically strong to carry heavy fighting equipment, you stayed in Dimma. I emphasize this point because I read books and articles of people who claimed they were sent to fight when they were only eight years old. The SPLA was not that brutal, which separated the SPLA from the Lord's Resistance Army. Only a handful of boys had escaped from Ethiopia to join the Black Army. Otherwise, there was no battalion of eight-year-olds trained, equipped, and sent to fight. A handful of boys managed to escape, but it was exceedingly difficult to leave Dimma without being officially discharged.

The Red Army forces were categorized into three: the *Dikdik* comprised of boys aged ten and below. Even though they were trained, they were not allowed to carry guns under any circumstances. Instead, they had soldiers who guarded them and a couple of elders who acted as their caretakers.

The next group was *Marek-rek* and was aged between ten and fifteen. Some of the *Marek-rek* members were armed to protect themselves from Kachippo and Anyuak militiamen, who were heavily armed. They attacked South Sudanese, whom they assumed to have occupied their territory. I was in the *Marek-rek* forces. But I was not just a member. I was both an adjutant and logistics officer who kept food and ammunition supplies for three battalions of the *Marek-rek*.

The third category was *Mutawasat* (Medium). These were ready-to-go fighters. When there was something urgent, such as if the SPLA needed an urgent reinforcement, the *Mutawasat* forces were dispatched because they were more mature. The *Marek-reks* and the

Dikdiks were left alone to continue their indoctrination.

Nothing was more upsetting than seeing your comrades returning to Sudan to fight while you remained in Dimma. The selected were delighted, and the rejected cried. I thought those who were sent back to Sudan to fight were the luckiest. They would be promoted to higher ranks in the front-line, unlike us who remained in Dimma. Additionally, those who went to fight would capture towns and cities and get clothes and even money in the places they captured from the Arabs. Some of them would be lucky to meet their parents, finally. Even those killed in action were lucky because they rested in peace as martyrs, unlike us who were confined in the middle of the mountain, eating *arec-gon*, a food so disgusting that even vultures rejected it. Also, the *tuk-tuk* jiggers, insects that entered your body to feed and breed, were eating us alive. For the next five years, a selection was made; those who appeared strong physically were sent to Sudan. But I was not selected.

Adapting Resiliently

In my first year in Dimma, I was always depressed. Some thoughts got stuck in my mind in most cases, and I could not get rid of them. These thoughts emerged whenever I found it challenging to adapt to my new reality and deal with the tremendous changes and challenges of living in the wilderness as a young guerrilla fighter. As a result, I frequently climbed to the top of the "Mountain of Misery" to cry. I was highly afflicted with nostalgia.

Experts believe that nostalgia or homesickness can be dangerous. It made a day, week, month, or year seem too long and yet too short. Illusions developed in your mind confused the past and present, and real and unreal events. This constant daydreaming or longing jeopardized your daily activities and schedules. And when it became your obsession, you began to waste away.

In the Bible, Lot's wife was inflicted with nostalgia. Lot and his wife lived in Sodom. Because of the evil in that city, God sent Lot and his wife away to safety. The Bible tells us that instead of focusing on the problem at hand or looking forward, Lot's wife felt nostalgic for the home she had left behind and looked back, subsequently turning into a pillar of salt, a sad moment to illustrate her grief.

However, I stopped looking back to the home I had left behind and focused on the present and future. I realized I had no power over the hardships and near-death experiences, such as hunger, disease, or the constant attacks from local tribes threatening my life, and my adapting mechanism kicked in automatically. Mother Nature dictated that unwanted change of all types and degrees required me to adapt if I wanted to succeed in my endeavors and find happiness in my life. It was not about the environment; instead, it was about me and how I reacted to the events. I needed something that came from within, a strength that could help me move forward despite the challenges and find joy in my journey. To achieve that state of mind, I had to develop emotional intelligence and resilience.

These attitude shifts proved to be my most important asset on this long journey. I finally accepted that I was destined to be a guerrilla fighter. I would have to make the best of this place because there was no way to go back home, only forward. I stopped longing for the home I had left behind and started belonging to the home I was now living in. Therefore, I discovered my new identity through the replacement of longing with belonging.

I was entirely indoctrinated by now, and I thought about liberating all of Sudan, not just my mother and our village. I had accepted the new and vague terms "Comrade" and *"Jeish el Ahmer,"* even if it meant the names were divorcing me from my traditional roots. The platoon members became the siblings I had never had; the squad and company members were my extended families; the battalion was the clan; the SPLA was the prominent tribe, and the commanders were my parents. My life could not be any better.

In 1988, our forces were reshuffled, and I became a prominent member of the Marek-rek Forces: First Battalion, Third Company, First Squad, and Second Platoon. I was just a private when I graduated from the training. But with my newly acquired positive attitude, I was beaming with what we called *nashataat* (guerrilla competencies). Additionally, I was one of the few boys who knew how to read and write. I had completed grade three in Pachong Primary School in Arabic. I also knew how to read and write in Dinka. And since Dinka letters are like English, it was easy for me to write and read English.

Because of these credentials, I became an asset at age fifteen. First, I was promoted to sergeant. Then I became both an adjutant and a logistics officer. As an adjutant, I oversaw and supervised administrative personnel. And as a logistics officer, my duties included keeping the inventory of guns, ammunition, and food rations.

These jobs may sound simple, but the benefits involved were great. First, I did not do hard labor such as going to the wilderness to collect building material (poles, grass, ropes, vines, etc.), nor did I perform *doria* (sentry duties) at night. Instead, I woke up early in the morning and went to the parade to gather all the reports. Included in my reports were how many soldiers were present, absent, on-duty, off-duty, sick, recovered, etc. Then I took the report to the Dimma general headquarters. After that, I would take a copy of the report to the commander responsible for logistics to receive supplies (ammunition and food rations) for the three task forces. After each task force received its supplies, my job was done for the day.

Second, I always had extra food and bullets because of my jobs. Having reserved shells meant I could hunt animals and practice target shooting all I wanted. There were plenty of animals to hunt in Dimma, but bullets were scarce. So, if you had extra bullets, you could hunt all you wanted. This improved my shooting capabilities, and I became one of the best shooters in Dimma, which gave me another job. I was one of the people selected to go on hunting trips during the hunting seasons.

Third, my jobs allowed me to have access to guns twenty-four hours a day. I did not want to part with my gun—it was the only thing I had in the world, the only reason I left my mother several years ago. I always felt safe in the presence of my Kalashnikov.

We locked away guns in the store, so the UN did not see them. Our food rations came from the United Nations, which would not bring food to soldiers and had accused the SPLA of practicing child soldiering. So, we had to be careful not to betray our movements. When we heard the UN was visiting Dimma, we hid our guns and all military equipment and pretended to be refugee orphanage boys. We had our informants in Addis Ababa, who informed us as soon as the UN staff landed. Since I was the logistics officer, my job was to ensure that the UN members did not discover any military equipment at our camp.

My jobs made me feel proud and important in the movement. Dimma became enjoyable simply because my contributions made me happy. After all, happiness is never about the environment; rather, it is about how you perceive the environment and adapt accordingly. People receive their happiness differently, but the result is always the same. For example, a young man from Tuareg driving a camel in western Africa is just as happy as a young American driving a Mercedes. A Canadian bride wearing diamond jewelry is just as happy as a Dinka bride wearing ivory jewelry or Jang traditional necklaces.

All the negative stuff which made me depressed in the beginning now turned into positive things that made me happy. The absence of parents meant the freedom to do what I liked without anyone bossing me around. At first, meeting people from other tribes shocked me. But eventually, it turned into a beautiful thing called diversity. My stereotypes about other people quickly evaporated, replaced with camaraderie. Loneliness disappeared because I always had countless companies. The other languages and dialects that sounded peculiar at first became familiar because I learned several languages, including Murle, Toposa, and Lotuko. The same change was happening throughout the camp. And Dimma became the face of the New Sudan we were fighting for, a society where diversity was embraced.

Some of our comrades, whom I thought were weird, turned out to be comedians full of humor that everyone needed in these conditions. One of these comrades was Achiek Akuak. Achiek means "Creator" or "Divinity" in Dinka. And anyone name Achiek means they have some physical abnormalities, which the Dinka believe to be an act of God or the Creator. In Achiek's case, he had six fingers and toes on each hand and foot. Because of this, he was nicknamed Abu-sita, meaning "sixer" in Juba Arabic.

Abu-sita was a hilarious character. He was tall and so skinny you could not see a visible curve on his body. He looked like a bamboo pole. But he had a sharp tongue. When Abu-sita insulted you, you died of shame. "You farted so loud until your battalion sprung up and loaded their weapons, thinking they were shot at," he insulted one comrade.

One day one of our comrades was suffering from diarrhea. And Abu-sita was far from being sympathetic. "Vultures had taken their complaint to the commander," he insulted the sick comrade. "They wanted to take you to court because one of the vultures stepped on your watery feces, and the vulture slipped and broke its neck. So, the vulture family wants you to produce thicker feces instead of watery ones."

One day, we were ordered to go to the wilderness to gather poles for our building. This was when we first arrived, and there were no knives, axes, or machetes. Yet the trainer wanted us to bring long poles.

"How can we cut the poles without an ax or a machete?" Abu-sita asked.

"Use your teeth or your penis," the trainer barked. "I don't care. But you must bring a pole. Understood?"

When the trainer left, Abu-sita let leash with his tongue. "Did your sister tell you that a penis is capable of cutting trees? Even your mother, who is an expert, will tell you that penises are useful, but they don't cut trees."

Because of funny comrades like Abu-sita, and I enjoyed my jobs, I began to appreciate simple things, and I found Dimma unique and exciting. We bonded together as comrades. This meant that everyone—your bosses, buddies, and those who served under you—were responsible for each other's well-being and morale. If someone seemed sad, irritable, or in danger, every soldier who saw it would step up and do everything he could to help. We became one big family after adapting resiliently.

The First Casualties

The main reason guns were kept in the store was that the boys did not accidentally shoot each other. Even though we were thoroughly trained to handle guns, our child mentality kicked in, and boys accidentally shot each other. Taking the guns away from us was not an option because local tribesmen, the Anyuak and Kachippo, were armed and dangerous. So, we needed our weapons to protect ourselves. But there were always consequences of giving automatic rifles to immature people. Remember, our adult commanders lived in residential areas with their families and only came in the morning for inspection. So, we were always on our own, boys age between eleven and eighteen, and armed with powerful weapons. What a deadly combination that was. It was no surprise that there were several deaths in the camp.

The first casualty of accidental shooting was Ring Machar (Ring Adhardit), a sixteen-year-old comrade who died in 1990 or 1991. Ring was one of my best friends. Our forces went to the wilderness camp every summertime for three months, located twenty miles away from Dimma, where we gathered building materials and played hunting games.

One morning, I went hunting with a group of comrades, including Ring, Akot Pap, and two other fellows. After walking the entire day without even seeing an animal, we returned home in the afternoon. Thirsty and hungry, Ring invited us to his hut for lunch. Ring was a sergeant (three chevrons) who commanded a squad.

When we returned home, some of us unloaded our guns, and others did not. Ring liked to keep his gun loaded and locked. We were in the Kachippo territory, and the Kachippo tribesmen were armed and dangerous. Some of their girls were recently raped, so they were now very hostile toward any Sudanese. We were always ready to fight them.

After we finished the meal at Ring's place, we started chatting. Ring lay on his bed, cuddling and caressing his gun like a baby. As teenagers, we were emotionally attached to the guns, and nothing was as soothing as touching and feeling that smooth metallic surface— which helped dissipate all the fear and doubts we had in mind. We called ourselves soldiers, not small boys.

After chatting for a while, I excused myself to go to my hut to nap. We were supposed to resume our hunting at around 4 p.m. when the sun was cool. So, I went to my hut, located a few yards away, leaving Ring, Akok, and two other boys in their hut.

About an hour into my nap, I heard a gunshot. At first, I thought the Kachippo tribesmen had attacked us. I grabbed my gun and exited my hut. When I did, I saw people bursting out through the grass wall of Ring's hut, not even wanting to exit through the door. Something terrible had happened inside the hut. As I rushed over there to investigate, Akok Pap, who had no time to find the door, burst through the grass wall covered in blood and white brain tissue from head to toe.

At first, I thought Akok was shot. He ran past me like a madman. I ran after him and saw him jump into the river to wash, so I knew he was not shot. The blood had come from someone else. But who? I had left four guys inside that hut. Who shot whom? Millions of questions ran through my mind as I headed to the scene.

When I looked inside the hut, I was shocked when I saw who the victim was. It was my friend Ring. He was lying face down on the bed, and his gun was on the floor in a pool of blood. (I cannot describe his wounds in detail because it was so gruesome.)

My mental picture snapped the images. My stomach twisted, and I felt nauseous. It was unimaginable to see one of your friends in that situation, a friend who had just eaten with you a few minutes ago. That feeling is hard to explain in words. One minute, we were laughing and joking; the next, he was lying in a pool of blood from a bullet wound in the head. It was the first time I had witnessed death since I joined the movement; the first time I saw what damage a bullet could cause to the head.

But the irony was that I could not even shed a tear. Gone were the days I used to climb up the mountain and cry just when I thought about my mother. Now my tear reservoir no longer produced tears. My body had become taut muscles and bones with no excess fluid to waste in the form of sweat or tears.

As I stood staring at my friend's lifeless body, a big greenfly came and sat on the twig next to Ring's lifeless body. The fly looked at me, looked at the dead body, and looked at me again. It was as if the fly wondered why these "lost boys" with big guns had such a short lifespan. Finally, the fly looked at me once more, and I swear, it seemed to shake its head before flying away. The fly probably had seen enough of these malnourished boys, wearing tattered clothes and carrying big guns, who died quickly, just like the flies.

I was fifteen years old at that time. So were all my other comrades. We did not even know what to do with the body. Some said we should bury him. Others said we should take him to Dimma to bury him there. Finally, some wise boys said we could not touch him until an investigation was conducted. We were alone in the wilderness, and our grownup commanders were in Dimma, so we had to trek for three hours to Dimma to fetch them.

Ring's mother, Lieutenant Adhardit (now a retired general in the South Sudan army), was one of our commanding officers. Ring's three other brothers were in Dimma, including Ager Machar, the former spokesperson of the vice president of the Republic of South Sudan, General Taban Deng Gai. To inform Adhardit her son had died, the commanders first went to Lieutenant Adhardit's place and ordered her to surrender all her guns. Lieutenant Adhardit knew something had happened. She started crying, saying, "Tell me, which one of my children had died?"

Later, the eyewitnesses to the shooting explain what had happened. They said the deceased was lying on the bed, and his gun was leaning against the bed with the muzzle pointing at his head. As he was chatting, Ring absent-mindedly played with his rifle by unlocking and locking it. As a result, his thumb slipped and pulled the trigger while the gun was switched to auto, and several bullets discharged simultaneously, all shooting him in the head.

Nevertheless, those who were inside with the deceased, including Akok Pap, were arrested. After the investigation was completed, it was determined that the deceased accidentally shot himself. As a result, Akok Pap and his crew were released. Now a USA citizen, Akok Papa has been deeply affected by that incident. However, he still does not talk about it.

The death of Arok Atem and Akoi Mabior shook the camp the most. This was intentional, not accidental, like with Ring. The incident occurred in Pakhok, the fifth section of Dimma. When President Mengistu was overthrown, Ethiopians and the UN staff in Dimma were evacuated, leaving everything behind. We went to the Ethiopian residential areas to scavenge for whatever they had left behind, both food and non-food items.

Akoi Mabior, who had five chevrons, found a tape recorder in the Ethiopian shops. Back then, tape recorders were like diamonds. We used them for music, entertainment, and the news. However, First Lieutenant Arok, senior in rank than Akoi, confiscated the electronic from Akoi.

Akoi was not happy when his precious possession was taken. Subsequently, Akoi reported the incident to high-ranking officers. But there was no time to solve the problem because we were preparing to fight. President Mengistu fled the country and was reported to be in Zimbabwe, where he is currently living. The TPLF rebels who dislodged President Mengistu were closing in, ready to attack Dimma and other SPLA camps. So, we evacuated from Ethiopia to Pakhok right at the border. Arok still had the tape recorder, which he now used for entertainment.

After evacuating from Dimma and settling in Pakhok, Akoi raised the issue again. He wanted his tape recorder back. But Lieutenant Arok did not want to give back the recorder, and the other commanders did not want to solve the problem either. Akoi was furious.

Finally, left with no option, Akoi decided to take the matter into his own hands.

Akoi, from the Koryom, the first division of the SPLA, was around twenty-five years old. He was the overall Red Army commander in Dimma, who reported directly to high-ranking commanders. We, the adjutants, took our reports to Akoi, and he took them to the camp's overall commander. Akoi was an amicable person who liked to get along with anyone. He always joked with me after I took the report to him. Akoi had a thick Twii accent, and he pronounced "N" as "L" and vice versa. For example, when reading names of the guns, such as *Kalany, Fal,* and *Luot,* he said *"Kanany," "Fan,"* and *"Nuot"* instead.

That morning when I took the report to Akoi in Pakhok, he was withdrawn and did not want to talk. So, I ended up taking the information to his deputy, Majok Majok, famously known as Kadis, now in the USA. I did not realize Akoi was about to commit suicide in a very gruesome manner.

After I took the report to HQ, I went to Commander Maper's house, where I usually hung out when there was nothing to do. One block away from Maper's home was a tent where Captain Dau, Lieutenant Arok, and other officers lived.

Thirty minutes later, I saw Akoi entering the tent. A few seconds later, we heard two gunshots inside the tent. Captain Dau and the other officers burst out through the tent and ran away. Comrade Maper sent Muothich Jalla (now in Rumbek) and me to investigate what was happening.

It transpired that Akoi had gone to the tent where Arok lived with his fellow officers and shot Arok in the head at point-blank range. The other officers tore out the tent as they ran for their lives. But Akoi did not intend to kill them. After he shot Arok, Akoi exited the tent, turned the gun to his head, and pulled the trigger.

Muothich and I were the first ones on the scene. We found Akoi lying outside the tent, face up with a bullet wound in his forehead. He was moving his bloodied head from side to side while his left hand caressed his head, and he moaned and grunted softly, his eyes closed. Arok was inside the ten, lying down sideways, his knees bent and eyes closed. There was a single gunshot in his forehead, and the bullet had not exited. He was not bleeding or moving like Akoi; he was so calm as if he were sleeping. The picture of my friend, Ring Machar, who shot himself a year ago in Dimma flashed into my mind. By now, I had seen three of my comrades with bullet wounds in their heads.

It was not long before the news of the deaths spread around the camp. Jonglei peoples (where both Arok and Akoi hailed) divided themselves into two. Sub-tribal fighting was brewing even though both were from the same area: Twii. Luckily, the conflict was averted. But the event shook the entire Pakook.

Akoi died on the spot. And Arok was airlifted to Loki, Kenya, where he also died.

Some incidents, which occurred in Dimma, were hilarious. There was one incident where a boy named Ladule shot his friend, Kuer. Although it was not fatal, it was a dramatic scene. The incident took place in 1989. That evening, I distributed guns to soldiers who were doing sentry duties; each task force member received their firearms. Then, in the morning, each soldier returned his gun to me to put away. But one gun registered to Ladule from Taskforce One was missing. So, I took it upon myself to retrieve the weapon.

As I was near the rectangular house where Ladule, Kuer, and their platoon-mates lived, I heard a gunshot, followed by a cry. I rushed to the scene to investigate and saw Kuer wallowing on the floor, holding his arm, blood oozing from the gashed elbow. Ladule's gun had gone off, shooting Kuer in the right arm, destroying the elbow joint. While Kuer was crying on the floor, Ladule was saying, "I'm sorry, I didn't mean to shoot you." The other platoon members ran away from the scene, and I did not know why. It did not take long before I realized why people ran away. Ladule, who had shot his comrade, kept pointing the loaded gun at people, with his index finger curled around the trigger, trying to demonstrate how he accidentally shot his comrade.

"*Ana amulu jede sakit,*" he said. "I just did it like this."

Both Kuer and Ladule were my best friends, so I approached them. Kuer was in much pain holding his elbow, trying to stop the bleeding. Ladule was crying too.

When Ladule saw me, he said, "Mayom, I didn't mean to shoot him. *Ana amulu jede sakit.*"

I ducked, trying to avoid the gun's muzzle, which was pointed directly at me. I ran away to take cover.

The fact that people were running away seemed to agitate Ladule more. He would not put the gun down even when order by his superior. The boy had lost his mind: he was shocked, scared, and disoriented. No one could attend Kuer until we could persuade Ladule to put the weapon down. When his superior ordered him to stand at attention, Ladule obeyed. But when ordered to put the weapon down, the boy went insane: *Yajama, ana ma gasidu,*" he said. "*Ana amulu jede sakit!*" "People, I did not mean to shoot him. I just did it like this!"

Eventually, he regained consciousness and put down the weapon without further incident. Afterward, he was not even arrested because Kuer confirmed it was just an accident. Later, Ladule confined it to me that he did not want to put the weapon down because he thought he would be fire squatted.

Ladule's explanation was hilarious, though. He had loaded the gun at night during his sentry duty. In the morning, he unlocked the gun and pulled the lever to discharge the bullet in the chamber. But because he did not remove the magazine first, the firearm discharged one bullet and reloaded another. Then Ladule removed the magazine, unaware of the bullet in the chamber. One mistake!

Another mistake was that instead of testing the gun up in the air as an experienced soldier did, Ladule tested the weapon as pointed toward Kuer. Luckily, he only shot him in the elbow. He could have killed him. But Ladule explanation was that he did everything right, but one bullet somehow hid in the chamber.

At that time, bullets were extremely valuable. They were counted daily, and if you lost one bullet, you could go to jail. But my friends, Lhat Mabor, Andria Buoth, and I wasted eight-six bullets, and we got away with the crime.

Lhat Mabor, who was sixteen years old, had five chevrons. He commanded Taskforce One of the Marek-rek, and he reported directly to a grownup commander. Andiria Buoth, who was also the same age and rank, commanded Taskforce Three. I was a sergeant, and because I was a logistics officer and adjutant, I always dealt with Lhat and Andiria when collecting reports.

As mentioned earlier, when schools were closed during the summer, our forces would move to the wilderness (about twenty miles away) from Dimma. We spent up to four months gathering building materials (poles, grass, ropes, vines, etc.) for constructing our houses and classrooms for the next semester. We also hunted, picked wild fruits, and harvested wild honey. The adult officers who commanded our forces did not go to the wilderness with us. Instead, they gave us orders and remained in the camp with their families. And this gave us, the *Jesh Amer,* the opportunity to be by ourselves without adult supervision. It was rare freedom. Remember, we were a bunch of fifteen- and eighteen-year-old boys. As teenagers, we were young and dumb! And that was not all: we were also armed with AK-47 automatic rifles. And we had no adult with us? What a deadly combination!

My job was to travel back and forth between Dimma and the summer camps, ensuring the troops had adequate food and bullet supplies. Lhat and Andiria also traveled back and forth, monitoring the work progress, and bringing reports to our commander, Athuai Machartat.

One morning, Commander Machartat ordered Lhat, Andiria, and I to go to Camp Two to inspect the troops and bring him a report. Accordingly, the three of us left early in the morning. It was not good to put Lhat Mabor and Andiria Buoth together as they argued and fought constantly. There was nothing that Lhat and Andiria would not argue about: politics, guns, tribes, school, you name it.

We grabbed our guns and left early in the morning. We followed the main road, which passed through Ethiopian residential areas. Technically, we were supposed to bypass the Ethiopian residential areas because the UN staff sometimes stayed there. If they saw us with guns, they could take photos and accuse the SPLA of recruiting children. Nevertheless, we did so anyway to show off our weapons. Every time we passed, the Ethiopians would come out of their houses to look at us, small boys holding the most powerful automatic weapons. "*Abet! Abet! Abet!*" the Ethiopian women would cry when they saw us. "Oh, my! Oh, my! Oh, my!"

The Ethiopians cried for us poorly fed, skinny boys carrying automatic rifles almost taller than them when we should be in school learning. But for some reason, we liked the attention, for it made us feel special.

After we had passed, Lhat and Andiria started their first argument. The topic was city stuff. Lhat was born and raised in Rumbek, and he was obsessed with this town. That is all he talked about. Andiria, born and raised in Bentiu, said he was way better than Lhat because he had been to Bentiu, Ayod, Nasir, and Malakal.

Because I was born in an isolated village, Biling Daldiar, where there were no schools, hospitals, roads, or any form of modernization, I knew nothing about cities. So, I could not participate in the conversation. I only visited Rumbek once with Uncle Mathou, and I did not like it because it was a noisy and smelly place inhabited by madmen who beat people for no apparent reason. The city-dwellers were insane that people were not allowed to carry weapons. The only place I knew was Pachong, where I went to school for three years. When Lhat and Andiria asked me which towns I knew, I mentioned Pachong. But Lhat dismissed the idea, saying I was embarrassing myself talking about Pachong because it was a mere village, not a town, not even close.

I changed the subject and talked about cattle—a subject I knew well. I told them I was born at a cattle camp and learned how to milk, groom, and herd the cows. Lhat Mabor and I were from Agaar Dinka, and Andiria was from the Nuer. Both the Jieng and the Nuer are proud cattle pastoralists obsessed with cows. So, I thought Lhat and Andiria would be impressed by my cattle camp capabilities.

But the city boys were not fond of the subject. When I talked about cattle camps, they started calling me *fara sakit*—meaning "typical primitive." I had no choice but to shut my mouth. I did not like to be insulted. But what could I do? Not only were Lhat and Andiria bigger than me physically, but they were also senior in rank: they both had five chevrons each, and I only had two. So, challenging them physically or militarily was a suicide on my part. I was sure of that.

Members of the *Jesh Amer* punished each other to death. Two of my friends, David Paulino Mayuir and Waiwai (I forgot his full name), almost died due to these punishments. Their superior, a young fellow named Garang Metod, tied their hands and legs behind their backs so that they sat on their exposed shins and chests. It was a punishment style called *rubut tamania*. I watched the entire episode in awe. In just seconds, David and Waiwai were thrown on the floor and tied up. The ropes became stiff and tied, and their arms and muscles craved for blood and air, and their teeth crunched on their tongues because of pain. Next, their hands and bent legs were tied on their backs, forcing them to rest on their chest and necks. The ropes dug deep into their skin, and blood oozed out from the cuts.

Some bullies, like Garang Metod, for example, abused their authorities. They punished subordinates for no apparent reason. The irony was that a subordinate could not complain to senior commanders alone; it had to go through your corporal, sergeant to the top. Even if a commander saw you being punished to death, he would not intervene unless the report was channeled through proper steps or protocols. But the sergeant who punished you for no reason would not take you to a commander to make your case. Instead, he punished you for no apparent reason and then asked you: "*mazulum?*" This means, "Was the punishment unjustified so that I can take you to the commander?" If you said "yes," he would say, I will take you when I am done with you. Then he punished you more. And he would continue punishing you until you gave up the complaint. The smart thing to do when asked, *mazulum?* was to say "no." That would save you from a lot of pain and suffering.

So, when asked, David and Waiwai kept saying, "*Ana Mazulum,*" meaning "I am unjustly punished, and you should take me to the higher authority to make my case."

But Garang Metod maximized their punishment instead. He tied their arms so tied that the rope cut their bodies, and they bled profusely. Garang Metod then took the hottest peppers and rubbed them in their bleeding wounds to maximize the pain and suffering. The young men cried in agony as they were punished all night.

After the punishment, their arms were severely damaged. Subsequently, Wawai's left hand was amputated from the shoulder. And David's left hand was crippled permanently, though it was not amputated. Garang Metod was eventually arrested for a couple of months before being sent to the front line. But his barbaric act had destroyed two people's lives permanently.

Therefore, you can see why I kept my mouth shut when dealing with senior officers like Lhat Mabor and Andiria Buoth. It was not a joke. The fact that I played my game smartly explains why I still have all my limbs today. A good soldier always knows the battle he can or cannot win.

Thankfully, Lhat and Andiria stopped making fun of me and resumed their argument. The topic of discussion was now school. Lhat said he was smarter than Andiria. Lhat was right, though. We were in the same class, grade two. Or was it grade three? During the final examination, Lhat was listed as number twenty-nine, and Andiria was number thirty-five out of about seventy-five pupils. I topped all my classes in three consecutive terms. As I was number one in that class, I could get involved in this argument because they knew I was the smartest. If they were not senior to me in age and rank, this would have been the opportunity for me to mock them back. I would have told them they had called me a primitive, yet none of them had beaten me in class. But I was not dumb enough to antagonize these big fellows in the wilderness. So, I shut the hell up.

Now the subject of the argument was bravery. Andiria said he was braver than Lhat.

"You talk too much, Lhat," Andiria said in Arabic mixed with Nuer language, "but if a *lony* comes along right now, you'll be the first one to run."

"Why should I run?" Lhat said. "I can kill *lony* with my bare hands. I don't even need a gun."

"*Lony?*" said Andiria, sounding incredibly surprised. "It will eat you!"

Lhat laughed, saying, "You are a dumb Nuer. Who told you *lony* eat people?"

What was happening in this conversation was a complete cultural misunderstanding. You see, *lony*, in Dinka, means a small animal, like a mongoose. But in Nuer, *lony* means lion.

When Andiria translated *lony* in Arabic, we knew he was talking about the lion. And this took them to another argument in which Lhat said Nuer do not know how to name animals.

"Why do you name this powerful animal *lony*? It is called *koor* or *ajuong*."

By now, we had exited the main road and followed a narrow footpath heading into the middle of mountain ranges. We were heading into Kachippo territory, who were unpredictable tribespeople and armed and dangerous, so we had to stop being teenagers and act like soldiers. We discussed our shooting strategy if we were ambushed. The idea was that Lhat and Andiria would switch their guns to automatic, and I would shoot single. Lhat said the Kachippo were untrained, and we would simply pick them off one by one.

We decided to rehearse our shooting strategy. That was how stupid we were. We took positions behind rocks and selected three trees located less than 1000 meters as our targets. The idea was that we had to shoot several bullets at the targets, and then we would count to see who had more shots in the target. The rehearsal turned into a competition; each one of us tried to shoot as many bullets as possible into the target to be the winner.

We started shootings, bullets echoing throughout the mountain ranges as if we were in the real battle. This was exciting. We squeezed the triggers repeatedly. Soon, Lhat's gun clicked. So did Andiria's gun. They were out of bullets. I checked mine; I only have seven bullets left in the magazine. What made things even worse was that we had not brought extra magazines with us. We realized our dilemma.

We could not pass through Kachippo territory. Without bullets in our guns, even a couple of tribeswomen could wrestle those guns out of our hands and beat the crap out of us. So, we canceled the trip and returned to Dimma. We gave a false report to Commander Machartat that the troops needed ammunition because they had hunted a lot. Thank God there were no radios or phones at that time for verification; otherwise, we would have been in big trouble with the authorities.

Fooled by a Woman

I had been to school before, so I knew the importance of education. But I did not join the rebels to become a pupil. I wanted the gun to return to my village to protect my mother and the entire village. But after the indoctrination, I now considered myself a soldier of the revolution—a soldier who could do everything through the gun's barrel—and I did not need to go to school.

My role models were higher commanders, like Kherbino Kuanyin and William Nyuon Bany. Commander Kuanyin had minimal education, and Commander Nyuon was illiterate. Yet, they had started the rebellion. Despite their lack of education, their bravery was exceptional, and this landed them in the second and third positions, respectively, in the entire movement. So, I wanted to be like them. To hell with education!

I did not see the importance of education until one day when an educated woman fooled me. I was fooled along with my good friend and battalion-mate, Comrade Agel Ring Machar (a former spokesperson for the second vice president of the Republic of South

Sudan, Taban Deng Gai). Agel is also the younger brother of Ring Machar, who accidentally shot himself in Dimma. Guess who fooled us? Agel's mother, Lieutenant Victoria Adhar Arop, was one of the commanding officers in Dimma.

In Dimma, every task force of the Red Army was commanded by one or two grownup high-ranking officers, and Lieutenant Victoria Adhardit was one of the commanding officers. If she was not the only educated woman in the entire movement, she was undoubtedly the only educated woman in Dimma. Trained with Nuur Battalion of Zalzal Two, Victoria was also a nurse and dietician by profession.

The food we ate at the camp was terrible. It mainly was sorghum. But not like the kind of sorghum we have in Sudan. No. Our Sudanese sorghum has a tasty flavor. But this sorghum was disgusting. When cooked, it looked and tasted like dirt, literally. The food was so bad that even vultures, scavenging birds that eat everything, rejected it. Hence, we nicknamed the food *arec-gon,* meaning "rejected by the vulture." What made the food even worse was that the grains were equally mixed—half sand and half sorghum. So, in addition to kwashiorkor, stomachache and diarrhea were common, affecting young boys. In other words, small boys were getting sick and malnourished because of the lack of food.

Subsequently, Victoria opened a clinic and feeding center, where the sick and malnourished boys were treated and fed. Agel, Victoria's son, and I were not interested in the clinic; we were interested in the feeding center. Extremely interested! The center served various nutritious foods: wheat, yellow-corn, beans, sardines, milk, biscuits, and other delicious foods. Our favorite food was yellow-corn flour mixed with butter oil, powder milk, egg, sugar, and salt. Very nutritious and delicious! The food was so yummy that it exploded with taste when put in the mouth. So, we named the food *athihai,* meaning "the explosive."

Unfortunately, the Feeding Center's food was meant for the sick and malnourished boys only. Agel and I were neither ill nor underweight. But that did not stop us from visiting the center regularly.

Determined to get a piece of that yummy food, we pretended to be sick every morning and headed to the Feeding Centre. We called this "the camouflage."

In Dinka culture, cheating, theft, and robbery are culturally unacceptable. So, when we went to the Kachippo and Anyuak villages to take their belongings, we were not stealing but camouflaging. That was how we justified our terrible behavior. So Agel and I went for camouflage in the feeding center every day.

In addition to being friends, Agel and I were both lastborn children of our mothers. According to South Sudanese, lastborn children are known to be nothing but "spoiled little brats" who like to get away with everything. What was next? The SPLA also spoiled us. Being the youngest in the division, we could not do heavy duties like the other big boys. We were not even allowed to stand guards at night. Indeed, we were spoiled little brats compared to our bigger comrades.

Every morning, Agel and I faked sickness and headed to the Feeding Centre to share the food with the sick and malnourished boys. The actual patients were feeding; Agel and I were feasting. Life was good. Particularly good.

Life would have been better had it not been for Comrade Adhardit, who kept disturbing us. "You two don't look sick to me," Comrade Adhardit would say when she saw us in the line, ready to get our food. "Don't ever come here again. This food is for sick people only!"

"Watch your mouth, Comrade," Agel would warn his mother, jokingly, of course. "Don't ever talk to soldiers like that. You are nothing but a recruit. Show some respect, or else I'll court-martial you!"

At that time, Comrade Adhardit was a private but retraining to be an officer. When she graduated, she would be a high-ranking officer. But now, she was just a recruit. Agel and I were not afraid of her.

The cooks in the Feeding Centre were recruits, waiting to be trained soon. It was easy for us to intimidate them into serving us, the soldiers, with the food. Recruits were expected to obey soldiers' orders. When the cooks saw Agel and me, they stood up at attention and remained standing until we told them to stand at ease or sit down. But we only told them to stand at ease after we had grabbed the food and were leaving. We continued terrorizing and tormenting the Feeding Center, mostly when Comrade Adhardit was away.

Comrade Adhardit had warned us many times not to keep stealing and robbing the sick people's food, but we did not listen. Since she was still in training, we knew there was nothing she could do to us. Or so we thought. After Comrade Victoria Adhardit had enough of our mischief, she used her education to teach us a lesson I will never forget.

One morning, she called Agel and me, wrote a letter, and gave it to us. "Take this letter to your task force commander," she said.

"What for?" Agel asked.

"I am permitting you to come to the Feeding Centre every day officially. That way, you can have all the food you want. So, take this letter and give it to your task force commander to sign it."

Agel and I looked at each other in disbelief. We could not believe our ears— completely dumbfounded. To have all the food we wanted! I pictured the explosive food *athihai* in my mouth daily. What a feeling! We did not know the contents of the letter. But, hey, Adhardit said the letter would permit us to have all the food we wanted.

Initially, the letter was given to Agel. But for some reason, he handed it to me. I did not know why. Perhaps he was a gentleman and did not want to show selfishness by keeping his mother's gift. Nevertheless, I gladly took over the custodianship of the letter. I treated the letter as a trophy. I folded the paper neatly and put it in my pocket, as we could not afford to lose or damage it. The note would take us to the most delicious food. To hell with the *arec-gon,* the sorghum mixed with the sand. We thanked Comrade Adhardit profusely, took the letter, and rushed to our headquarters to give it to Comrade Paul Anyuat.

But somehow, my gut told me there was something fishy about this letter. Adhardit had always warned us not to return to the Feeding Center, so why was she so nice? But I suppressed the nagging fear. I did not think Comrade Adhardit would mean any harm to her son and his friend.

We arrived at the headquarters and found First Lieutenant Paul Anyuat sitting under a tree listening to a radio. Agel and I uniformly marched and stamped our feet on the ground and saluted him. "Comrade," we yelled. Then, I took two steps forward and extended my right hand to hand over the letter before taking the same steps backward to align with Agel Machar. We remained standing at attention, waiting for Lieutenant Paul to read the letter. My heart was pumping with anticipation.

"I see what you two have been doing," Lieutenant Paul said. "Lie down. Now!" he yelled so loud that I thought the ground shook.

Agel and I looked at each other, puzzled. And scared! Lieutenant Paul summoned in *shurtas*—individuals selected to whip people. Before we knew it, we were being held down and given several whacks on our buttocks.

It turned out that Victoria had explained in the letter how we had been terrorizing the Feeding Centre, and she had instructed the lieutenant to give us the severest punishment possible.

We were punished and warned not to go close enough even to smell the Feeding Centre's food.

Despite the punishment, however, what hurt me the most was that Comrade Victoria Adhardit had fooled us to deliver the letter ourselves. She made us carry our own cross to the crucifixion. We were absolute fools! Armed, young, and dumb, and illiterate? What a terrible combination!

This incident changed my perception of education. I thought, "If I knew how to read and write, I would have known what was in the letter and avoided all these punishments."

The Adolescents' Foolishness

I became an adolescent in Dimma. Adolescence or puberty is a time of tumultuous transition from childhood to adulthood. Due to rapid physical changes and hormonal development, puberty is a crucial time where teenagers become interested and prepared to meet the opposite sex for the first time in their lives. But I was grossly unprepared to navigate these essential developmental changes.

Parents and society teach their children in puberty about sex, relationships, and values worldwide. And because parents and the entire community are part of these conversations, it is easy for adolescents to learn all the facts of life, including dating and sexuality. Adolescents learn by asking hard questions or copying their elders directly to take care of themselves, make decisions, and stay safe. Even if parents are reluctant to talk about sexual matters with their children, teenagers are bombarded with messages about sex and relationship online and from Snapchat and Instagram and friends, movies, songs, ads, video games, and televisions. All of these are crucial in helping the next generation pass through the magical changes from being little boys to young men or little girls to young women.

But to those of us who became adolescents in the indoctrination schools of the SPLA, we did not have the luxury of learning this transformative developmental spurt—puberty—from anyone. In Dimma, we, the Red Army, were confined in the middle of the mountains for years without parents or guardians. Our indoctrination barracks and schools were segregated from the residential areas, where the entire community (men, women, and children) lived. The idea was that the movement wanted to brainwash us in isolation, away from others who would poison our minds, making the indoctrination difficult. Boys who had relatives in these residential areas required written permission (which was not issued) to visit their relatives just for a few hours. Even our grownup commanding officers lived in the residential areas with their families, coming only every morning for inspection and returning later in the day. Remember, we were aged between eight and seventeen or eighteen, a crucial time when children need their parents the most for guidance and support. But we had no adults to ask hard questions and learn the facts of life from. There were no televisions, computers, radios, books, or social media. So, we navigated these developmental stages of puberty on our own, learning through trial and error.

In the camp, there were nearly 7,000 boys and less than one hundred girls. The girls lived in their gated compound. No males, under any circumstances, could visit the compound. At night, heavily armed personnel guarded the compound to deter such wild boys with raging hormones, who were ready to hump everything.

Subsequently, we turned our perverted attention elsewhere. Every female creature in the area became a mating target. Naturally, local tribeswomen, including Anyuak, Kachippo, Bakol, and Ngalam, were on the menu. But eventually, the local tribes migrated far away from us because of the brutality inflicted on their women by these wild boys with raging hormones and deadly Kalashnikov automatic rifles.

In 1988, I became interested in socializing with girls. My first crush was Halima, the city girl whom I met at Aramweer Cattle Camp in 1986. I was ten years old back then. Now I was twelve years old and even more interested in girls. But I did not know how or where to begin in Dimma.

My best friend, Lhat Mabor, who was fifteen years old, came to my rescue. He took the initiative and offered to help me find my first date. Lhat said he was an expert when it came to women. I believed him. He was one of the brightest fellows I knew. His traits had earned him five chevrons, the highest ranks a Red Army soldier could receive back then. In the absence of grownup commanders, Lhat Mabor commanded Task Force One. I looked up to Lhat because of his maturity in age and his seniority in the ranks. So, when he said he was an expert in women and would find me a girlfriend, I obliged without hesitation. Who would turn down an offer like that?

To demonstrate his expertise, Lhat gave me some dating tips. "You have to be direct with women," he said. "They like that." Lhat also suggested that we had to look for Ethiopian women because, according to him, they were easy to get. On the other hand, Sudanese women made things overly complicated.

I agreed with Lhat. Dating a Sudanese woman was a complicated process. I learned that from Halima. Despite the help and support I had provided her, like teaching her how to milk, the only thing I got from her was the promise to get married when we grew up. And then we had unexpectedly separated before I got anything from her. What a waste it had been!

Late in the afternoon, Lhat and I went to the Ethiopian residential areas, an hour's walk away, to look for women. Of course, our recently acquired hormones and testicles were involved in this decision. But we do not think you should blame us for this. We were just driven by the same instinct that drove ancient human beings millions of years ago—the only reason why human beings do not become extinct: the ability to procreate.

On the way, Lhat had asked me, "How do you call a woman's private part in Amharic?" I told him I do not know. Lhat did not know either. None of us were fluent in Amharic—the national language of Ethiopia. Eventually, Lhat told me not to worry and that he knew what to do.

We found our target—a woman alone in her small shop. We pretended to be customers browsing. But we scanned her from head to toe, like a bunch of hungry hyenas with prey. She was not just flawless in her bone structure; her skin was like a ripened palm fruit, and she radiated an intelligent beauty. But she was a grown woman, around thirty years old, twice our age. That did not matter to us. She was a female; that was what mattered. We had to try our luck.

I was nervous, and my voice trembled when I spoke. Also, my heart was beating hard. I always felt like that around girls, and I did not know why. Lhat, the expert, appeared nervous, too. I could smell the nervous sweat from his armpits. He blushed with his face full of pimples and acne scars. Puberty was crueler to Lhat than me.

But despite our nervousness, we were determined to talk to this woman. The hormones (chemical messengers) running through the bloodstream between our brains and recently acquired testicles gave us orders about what was needed: this woman. We used our limited Amharic vocabularies to engage the woman in a conversation. The woman talked to us politely, thinking we were just innocent boys coming to buy candies. She did not know that we were nothing but perverts. She talked to us face-to-face; we responded face-to-cleavage.

As we talked incessantly, the woman eventually asked, "What do you want?"

This question allowed Lhat to state the purpose of our visit. "We want you," he said.

"You want me?" the woman said, looking confused. "Why?"

"We want that," Lhat said, pointing directly at the woman's crotch.

The woman's face flushed with anger and rage. But she stayed calm. "Ah, you want me?" she said, calmly approaching us.

I was not an expert in women, but I could tell from her face that this woman was not coming for a kiss.

When she was at a striking distance, the woman smacked Lhat right in the mouth. Her hand was so fast that all I heard was thwack! She swung again, missing his head as we exited the shop and bolted. The furious woman grabbed stones and hurled them at us, which we dodged as we ran away.

We walked back quietly to our camp like defeated soldiers. Lhat's lower lip bled due to the slap. My dignity was hurt, too, because my first date attempt had been a complete disaster. I doubted Lhat's expertise. He said Ethiopian women were easy to get. But how come his mouth was bleeding, and we were dodging stones?

Nevertheless, in this trial-and-error learning technique, I had learned my first lesson the hard way: never point at a woman's crotch. She would hit you in the mouth.

Before I could doubt Lhat's expertise, however, he told me that our first attempt had failed because we did not use the right approach. "Pointing at a woman's crotch is disrespectful," he said. "We must know the name of the woman's private part in Amharic. That way, we can ask for it respectfully. Women like it when you are direct with them, remember?"

Lhat had such a witty personality. He was charismatic, too, so he sounded very convincing. Even if you knew he was lying, the story he told was entertaining, making him even more likable. His characters fit what the Dinka termed *alueeth*. *Alueeth* has both negative and positive senses. In the negative sense, *alueeth* means compulsive liar. But in the positive sense, it means someone who is exceptionally creative. So Lhat was *alueeth* in a positive sense.

I remember when he told a story about how he rode a hyena from Rumbek to Wau.

"How did you ride the hyena?" a boy asked.

"It's easy," he said with a straight face that showed no sense of guilt. "I had no money to buy the ticket, so I summoned a hyena, and I jumped on its back and held on tight to its ears, just like a motorbike. And off we went, reaching Wau in no time."

Boys roared in laughter. Everyone liked Lhat Mabor because he was amiable and entertaining, especially since we were in the middle of the mountains without telephone, television, radio, or social media. Therefore, we depended on *alueeth* like Lhat Mabor for entertainment purposes.

So, I believed Lhat when he said we needed to know the womanly thing in the Amharic language. We researched the female private part's name from those who knew Amharic. "*Zigzig*," a boy said was the name of a woman's private part. Perfect. We had to go back to the Ethiopian residential area tomorrow.

The following day, we hurried to the Ethiopian market with our recently acquired vocabulary, "*zigzig*." This time, we went to a different shop and found another woman. She was noticeably big and strong. Therefore, we had to be more cautious and keep a reasonable distance while talking to her. This big woman could inflict severe damage to the mouth when she slapped one of us like the other woman had yesterday. We were sure of that. This time, though, we would not point at her crotch. Instead, we knew the name of what we wanted: "*zigzig*."

Soon, Lhat, the expert, set his tongue loose in Amharic: "*Anyshii, zigzig ale?* This statement means, "Lady, is your womanly thing available?"

The woman covered her ears in disbelief at what she was hearing from these perverted little boys. Without saying a word, and before we knew it, she was wielding a machete. We bolted, and she came after us in hot pursuit, wielding the machete and calling, "*Leba! Leba!*" ("Thieves! Thieves!") The entire Ethiopian community sprang into action everywhere with sticks and machetes. We ran for our lives. Thank God it was getting dark, and we disappeared into the darkness. That was a close call.

We never went to the Ethiopian residential area again. We thought the Ethiopians would identify us, especially when that woman called us thieves. Our main worry was that the woman would complain to one of our commanders, and she would be summoned in the parade to identify us. And this could land us in prison.

You would think we had learned our lesson, but no. We were adolescents who wanted to assert our independence, explore our limits, take risks, break the rules, and rebel against authorities. In addition, we were coping with disconcerting new sexual impulses and romantic feelings. This urge overshadowed our reasoning capacities.

After those incidents with the Ethiopian women, it did not take long before we met another young fellow named Lotir. Lotir, from the Taposa tribe, said he was an expert in dating. His name was a testimony to his knowledge about women. Lotir in Taposa language means bull. Who does not know that the function of the bull is to mate? Lotir said he had love medicine that made women fall in love with you instantly. He had a combination of barks and dry leaves, ground into a light-green powder.

"You keep the powder in your pocket," Lotir advised. "And when you see a girl you like, you smear the powder onto your right hand and greet her. She will fall in love with you instantly."

After what I had been through with Lhat, I was skeptical at first.

"Does it work?" I asked the medicine man.

"*Akuj apei,*" Lotir swore. "God is one. [It works]."

Perfect. We had to get this powder. It would save us from being slapped in the mouth. We took two small bundles. And the medicine man demanded two Ethiopian birrs from us. It turned out that the love medicine was costly. So, we split the bill and paid one birr each. I had only one birr in my pocket. Let me tell you, I almost backed out of the deal because I did not want to spend the last of my money. One birr could buy me a decent meal, so I had to choose between food or woman. I chose the latter. Who would not?

Nevertheless, I had learned another valuable lesson: women are expensive.

With the powder secure in our pockets, we went hunting for the girls. We kept the powder safe like it was gold. It was the only key to women's hearts, and we could not afford to lose it. This time, we avoided the Ethiopian market because of the havoc that we had caused. Instead, we went to a Sudanese open-air market named *Suk el Keer,* meaning "the Market of Luck." Perfect. The name was very soothing and promising. Luck is what every man needs when dealing with women. Perhaps we could be lucky enough to get laid in this market.

The market was thronged with people buying and selling. We saw a beautiful girl sitting under a tree in the market, selling okra and green leaves. The marking on her face and the missing two lower teeth told us she was from the Murle tribe. She was around seventeen or eighteen years old, obviously bigger than us. No problem! The medicine would do its job.

I was fluent in the Murle language. After we were exposed to the diversity in the movement, we had enough vocabulary to conduct basic conversations in many languages, including Dinka, Arabic, Amharic, English, Nuer, Toposa, or Murle. So, it was my turn to approach the girl. I smeared the powder in my hand and went straight to the girl. I was nervous. But the urge to find a woman was strong. So, I forced myself to speak:

"*Bonanu!*" I said, extending my powdered hand. "Greetings!"

She shook my hand. Success! All we had to do now was to wait and let the powder do its job. Soon, she would fall in love with us. We sat nearby, just watching every move she made, trying to see a sign of love or something. We waited. Ten minutes. Twenty minutes. Thirty minutes. Nothing! She was just busy selling her goods. The market was full of buyers and sellers walking up and down, minding their business.

Maybe the medicine took longer than that. We waited. One hour. One hour and a half. Nothing. The girl did not fall in love. She did not even look at us.

Frustrated, Lhat wondered whether I did it the right way. Finally, he had to do it himself. He smeared the powder all over his hand and approached the girl to shake her hand again.

By now, the girl was suspicious of our strange behavior around her. She thought we were thieves, trying to poison her and steal her money and goods. When Lhat approached with his powdered hand, the girl grabbed her belongings and ran away. We remained behind like hungry lions that had caught the prey, but somehow, the quarry had just escaped.

I had learned another lesson: there was no shortcut to a woman's heart.

Sports I

It became clear that Lhat was not as expert in women as he claimed because we had exhausted every option, but we could not find even a single date. I had to try other avenues.

Surprisingly, I noticed some of my comrades had girlfriends. These comrades included Kuot Mathuch (now in Juba) Aguet Abraham (now in North Carolina). We knew each other mutually, though we were not friends. Aguet was my battalion-mate. Of all the boys in Dimma, Kuot and Aguet were the luckiest ones with girlfriends, and they became incredibly famous. How did they do it?

It did not take long before I learned their secret: they played sports. Kuot was the renowned goalkeeper in Dimma. Aguet also played soccer and volleyball. Girls were also in sports so that these male players could mingle with the female players. That was how these comrades got their girlfriends.

At first, the sport was not my thing. The first time I saw people playing soccer was when I visited Rumbek. When I played soccer for the first time in Pachong Primary School, I almost broke my toenail when I kicked the ball. It hurt so bad I never played again. But now, sports seemed to be the only way people had the opportunity to socialize with these few Dimma girls. So, I became interested in sports, and I started to attend volleyball and football games to watch.

Luckily, there were registrations taking place in 1989. The SPLA planned to organize its first sports leagues, where all the refugee camps and training centers in Ethiopia would participate. So, we had one year to prepare and train before the tournament, which would be conducted in Itang Camp, the biggest and most developed camp, headed by Commander Taban Deng Gai, the current Vice President of the Republic of South Sudan. So, I registered for both the soccer and volleyball teams.

Sports equipment was distributed in Dimma, and the competition took place weekly among the task forces. The purpose of the competition was to select the best players to prepare for the coming tournament in Itang. When the selection was made, I became the best goalkeeper for Dimma Mini Team. Kuot Mathuch was the goalkeeper for the Dimma Red Army, and David Debek was the Black Army's goalkeeper. I also qualified to be in the Dimma Volleyball Central Team and Kuot Mathuch and Aguet Abraham. Thus, I became one of the famous boys in Dimma. Even though I did not get a girlfriend, I mingled with the girls because we played volleyball together.

However, after I joined the team, I realized that the social benefits of the game were far more significant than I anticipated. In our sports clubs and teams in Dimma, I mingled with the girls and adults, officers, and even high-ranking commanders, united by their enthusiasm for the game. Remember, we, the Red Armies, were segregated in a separate camp where seeing a grownup in person was a rare treat. But the sports gave me the chance to interact with adults, including high-ranking commanders, every day.

I would never forget the first time our overall camp commander, Dr. Atem Nathaniel Riak, approached me. He had noticed me playing and that I had no jerseys. I was the goalkeeper for the Dimma Mini *(Marek-rek)* Football Team. Dr. Atem took it upon himself to buy me a goalkeeping jersey and a pair of shorts. He delivered them to me in the field, saying, "Mayom, here are your clothes." Forget about the clothes; the fact that he knew and called me by my name was mindboggling.

More mind-boggling things happened when our commander in chief, Dr. Garang, arrived in Dimma. To entertain him, we organized a match. I was the goalkeeper for one of the teams. After the game, we received our trophy, which the commander-in-chief himself handed out. Being the goalie and captain of the team, I was chosen to receive the trophy. After I stamped my foot in attention and saluted, the commander in chief saluted back, shook my hand, and handed me the award. I had shaken our chairman's hand—the most powerful person that no one else had even got closer to, let alone salute and shake his hand. I became one of the few boys who shook Dr. Garang's hand. All thanks to my involvement in sports.

Even though we could mingle with the adult commanders, protocol and discipline were still expected. Crossing that boundary and disrespecting a commander could result in severe punishment. One day, Lieutenant Suleiman Ayul punished the entire volleyball team. The incident occurred on the volleyball courts during the game.

Lieutenant Suleiman, from Shilluk, was one of our senior commanding officers who liked to joke with subordinates. And he ate with everyone. But when you disrespected him, he was also one of the meanest officers. Lieutenant Suleman was famous for the phrase *"buwuo."* Nobody knew what that meant. He added that term to every sentence, mostly when he was joking. "Watch out, soldier, *buwuo!*" Or *"Buwuo*, I will beat you up!" He sounded hilarious when he talked in a typical Shilluk accent.

Lieutenant Suleiman Ayul's front teeth were severely bent inward. Because of this, we nicknamed him *"anguaam,"* an extremely derogatory term used for people with such teeth. Since Suleiman did not speak Dinka, we called him "*anguaam*" even when he was around. When Lt. Suleiman inquired about the term, we said it meant "a powerful person" in the Dinka language.

At first, Lieutenant Suleiman was suspicious about the nickname. "Are you sure this is not an insult?" he said. "Because this term, *anguaam*, does not sound normal."

Afraid that he would punish us severely, we convinced Lieutenant Suleman the term was not an insult and that its true meaning was a strong person.

Once convinced, Lieutenant Suleiman liked the nickname. "Yes, I'm *anguaam*," he said, raising his arms, displaying his muscles. "From now on, don't ever call me Suleiman again; call me *anguaam* because I am strong. Misbehave, and I will beat you up. *Buwuo!*"

We laughed and laughed and laughed. And whenever we saw Lieutenant Suleiman, we would holler, "*anguaam, anguaam, anguaam!*" And he loved it.

Lieutenant Suleiman Ayul was our laughingstock until he discovered the truth. One day, we played volleyball when a girl named Achocha got in a fight with another boy. Achocha's teeth were also bent inward, just like Suleiman Ayul's teeth. So, when we played volleyball with the girls, Achocha overheard another boy calling her *anguaam*, and she started crying.

Lieutenant Suleiman saw Achocha crying and approached to ask, "Why are you crying?"

"These boys insulted me!" Achocha said.

"What did they say to you?"

"They called me *anguaam*," she said.

"So?" Suleiman said. "You cry because of that? What is wrong with being called *anguaam*? It is an honor to be called *anguaam*. They call me *anguaam*, too, because I'm strong!"

"No!" Achocha said. "*Anguaam* doesn't mean that. It means someone with bent inward teeth, just like yours and mine. It's an insult!"

"*Buwuo!*" Suleiman yelled.

We were gathered and hustled to the muddy river to be beaten. We were punished mercilessly for about an hour. No one ever called Lieutenant Suleiman or Achocha *anguaam* again.

In 1990, the SPLA organized a league, where all its camps and training centers in Ethiopia (Itang, Dimma, Pinyudo, Bongo, Bilpam, Tharpam, Zinc, etc.) competed in sports. The tournaments were conducted in Itang, commanded by the CDR Taban. It took us two-and-a-half days by bus from Dimma to Itang to participate in the tournaments.

In the tournaments, however, our Dimma teams did not perform well. You see, in Dimma, anyone over fifteen years old was sent to the front lines to fight, leaving us, the under fifteen-year-olds, and malnourished boys and girls. Other camps, such as Itang and Pinyudo, kept their best players for the tournaments.

Famous players like Madong William dominated the games. Madong William (now a sports director in Juba) was a volleyball player, the most feared striker. He was nicknamed "BM" because it landed like a BM bomb when he struck the ball. The other teams beat us in every game: soccer, volleyball, track, you name it. Our Dimma teams were the underdogs.

The last teams to play were the volleyball girls' teams: Dimma versus Itang. It was the most anticipated game. The Itang girls were the best and expected to win the championship. For us, though, the girls' volleyball team was our only hope, so we wanted them to win badly; otherwise, Dimma would be eliminated. Out of desperation, we decided to cheat.

The idea was that a couple of boys would play dressed as girls and mix with the real girls. That was the only way we could beat the Itang team. The two best players from the boys' team were selected, which included my best friend, Aguet Abraham, and me.

At first, I said, "Hell, no! There is no way I'm putting on a skirt like a girl!" But as they say, every scenario has both negative and positive sides. In our case, the negative side was that our friends would make fun of us for the rest of our lives. And the positive side was that this would allow us to interact with the girls. Aguet Abraham even hinted that we could spend the night in the girls' compound the night before the game. Well, this changed everything. I accepted the deal. I mean, a twelve- or thirteen-year-old boy would do anything to be around the girls. Remember, we were at that crucial moment of being allowed to socialize with girls for the first time. As previously mentioned, in Dimma, there were far more boys than girls, and they were kept in a heavily guarded compound. The message was clear: you had to dodge bullets if you wanted to talk to a girl. Now, the opportunity to mingle with the girls had presented itself to us, and we were not dumb enough to turn it down. So Aguet and I agreed to be dressed up in skirts and join the girls.

Unfortunately, the hope of spending the night in the girls' compound was just wishful thinking. The girls were not that stupid to allow a couple of hungry-looking hyenas in their compound at night. We slept in the boys' compound. Early in the morning, the girls came and took us to their compound and dressed us up with female attire: skirts, necklaces, shoes, etc. We were not given fake boobs because we were just small girls who had not developed them yet.

Aguet Abraham, a brown-skinned handsome boy, easily blended in with the girls after being dressed in a skirt. Mine was a different story. I mean, the girls tried everything they could to make me look like a girl, but to no avail. First, my cropped hair, which looked like millet grains, could not be braided. Then, when they gave me women's shoes to wear, I walked like a leper. And this was very troubling because if we were caught, the entire Dimma team could be penalized or even jailed for committing such a disgraceful or discreditable action, not to mention the embarrassment that would come with it. The girls helping us, Sarah Nyanaath (currently a South Sudanese civil rights activist), the team captain, and Nyibol Monyjith, tried their best.

Before we left the compound heading to the field, the girls gave us instructions. We had to talk less, so our male voices would not betray us. And we had to remain standing the entire time because they feared we might sit cross-legged like men. You know, men always liked to sneak a peek when a girl sat down improperly.

"Well, good luck to any perverted boy who wishes to see what is between my legs," I thought. "Trust me, pal. Do not let this dress fool you. What I have between my legs is not what you think. So, peek at your own risk!"

The girls also advised us that we should not, under any circumstances, urinate in an open area. In Africa, men were not afraid to urinate in open areas.

"Don't forget and urinate in an open area," the girls warned us. "You have to hold it until you return home to use the restroom. Women don't urinate in public."

This one rule threw me off. "Are you crazy? Hold the urine until I return home? An organ could rupture. Let us get things straight; I am not a girl, okay? So, if I want to pee, I'm throwing this stupid skirt up to my shoulders to relieve myself."

"You cannot do that," the girls insisted. "People will think Dimma girls urinate like men. They will insult us."

"Who cares?" I mean, these girls were taking things a little too far. Aguet and I were getting uncomfortable with these complicated girly things.

"Just shut up," Nyibol said as the other girls roared in laughter. "You are talking too much, like a real girl. You see, that is what skirts do; they make girls very talkative."

I had to be honest, though; being a woman was not easy. Aguet and I had spent two hours practicing being girls, and we were utterly overwhelmed about how to dress, walk, sit, talk, you name it. It was the most awkward situation I had ever experienced.

When we walked to the field, I carried a handbag in my right hand and other equipment in my left hand. The shoes kept throwing me off, so I used my hand to keep balance. On top of that, it was windy, and my skirt was being blown all over the place. The girls kept telling me to hold my dress in place. How the hell was I supposed to do that when both of my hands were already occupied, and I struggled to keep my balance because of the high heels?

But we headed to the court with confidence that we would defeat the Itang girls. Unfortunately, when we arrived, we found out we were too late because we had been so caught up trying to be girls that we had forgotten the time. The referee had waited for about five minutes, and when we did not show up on the court, we were automatically disqualified. Therefore, the Itang team won the game.

It was a disaster. We had spent our time and energy wearing women's attire, yet we did not even get the chance to play. We did not even get to spend the night in the girls' compound. Our friends mocked us for years. To this day, some of my friends still call me "Almaz," a typically female name in Ethiopia, because of that incident. All of these for nothing.

The Fall of President Mengistu

We had huddled around listening to the news on the radio held by Lieutenant Maper. A BBC reporter reported that the Ethiopian rebels, Tigrayan People's Liberation Front (TPLF) and Eritrea People's Liberation Front (EPLF), who were fighting against the socialist government of President Mengistu Haile Mariam, had captured the capital city, Addis Ababa, and that the president had fled to an unknown location, but possibly to his closest ally, President Robert Mugabe of Zimbabwe.

It was devastating news to us and the entire SPLA. President Mengistu supported the movement to the hilt. While the Arabs were slaughtering South Sudanese, the whole world turned their eyes in the other direction, except Mengistu. He accommodated South Sudanese refugees and fully supported the movement by training and equipping the SPLA fighters. He was a true friend of the SPLA, willing to share even a single peanut with the SPLA.

"Even if I have a single groundnut," Mengistu used to say, "I will share it with the SPLA."

Lieutenant Maper turned off the radio, put on his military fatigues, and headed to headquarters, his bodyguards in tow, to meet with other camp commanders.

"You must report to your respective task forces immediately and wait for further order," the lieutenant ordered.

Lhat and I looked at each other's faces without saying a word. We knew the world had gone wrong again. But instead of heading to our task force as we were ordered, we decided to follow Lt. Maper to headquarters to see what was unfolding.

By now, the news had already spread, and the camp was in disarray. All the Ethiopian workers and vendors had gone back to their respective places to be with their families. The Ethiopian markets and streets that once thronged with life stood empty. The food vendors in their brightly colored clothes were gone. The children who played amongst the crowds were gone. Gone were the stores with their windows of fine clothing or delicacies. Now, even at midday, all you found was the dusty street with only the wind for company. Littered sidewalks, empty gun shells, and broken storefronts were left—the result of desperate looters.

When we got to the headquarters, we found a convoy of about five pickup trucks had arrived, carrying high-ranking government officials loyal to President Mengistu. They were running away because they were the main targets of the Wayane rebels who wanted them killed or imprisoned. The look on these Mengistu loyalists' faces was familiar: it was the same look that I saw on the elders' faces when our village, Pachong, was attacked by the Islamic regime of Khartoum. After all, these TPLF rebels, the ousters of president Mengistu, were trained, equipped, and supported by the Khartoum Government— the same government the SPLA was fighting. Therefore, it was no surprise that the new Ethiopian government gave the South Sudanese just one week to leave the country—a deadline they did not even keep because they started attacking SPLA camps and training centers in less than a week.

Our camp commanders, Dr. Atem, Lieutenant Maper, and others, met the Ethiopian generals and their families. After a brief exchange of words, the Ethiopian generals did an unexpected thing: they surrendered their weapons, removed their uniforms, and put on civilian clothes before they mounted the trucks and took off toward the southern Sudan border. They instantly became refugees inside their own country. They were given one platoon to escort them from the camp into Sudan and finally to Kenya. From Kenya, they planned on joining their boss, Ex-President Mengistu, in Zimbabwe.

What these generals did, surrendering their uniforms and guns was mind-boggling. It was the most cowardly thing I had ever seen. A soldier could not imagine giving his AK-47 to anyone, even for just a minute. There was nothing as soothing or comforting as that smooth metal. A soldier felt lonely and miserable without a gun. I could not fathom why the Ethiopians had surrendered their weapons like that.

High Commanders Bol Madut and Gelario Modi had arrived with the Commandos' task force to oversee the operation and facilitate the movement of refugees from Dimma back to Sudan. Women, children, elderly, and disabled persons had to be evacuated immediately. Several trucks the UN had left behind were used to transport them. Everybody else had to walk. Because we were the youngest soldiers, our task force was also ordered to go with them.

All our task forces were ordered to move on foot back to Sudan. The guns that I kept were given to soldiers from the Medium task forces, especially those studying in Ethiopian schools, and returned when schools were closed. Only selected forces remained in Dimma to defend, and everyone else had to go back to Sudan. Just a few kilometers from Dimma, the SPLA was fighting the Ethiopian rebels.

Lhat and I felt belittled when soldiers from the Medium task forces remained to defend Dimma, and we were ordered to leave with the women and children.

"This is an insult," Lhat said. "We can't run away from the war with women, children, the elderly, and disabled people. Even the girls will laugh at us when we run away with them. We must fight this battle to prove we are real soldiers. Mayom, this is our moment."

I agreed. I could not run away from the war. I wanted to shoot bullets, and I also wanted to hear the hissing of incoming bullets. I had never been shot at before, and I wanted to know what it felt like to be shot at. Even though our guns were taken from us, we came up with the idea that we should remain in the camp with the armed soldiers, and when the war started, we would take guns from those who were killed or injured. We considered ourselves to be the top soldiers, and we had to fight instead of fleeing.

Lhat and I returned to our task force and found people were on the move. We intended to grab our belonging and head back to the general headquarters where those who would remain to defend the camp were. But Lieutenant Biet Wol (who passed on in 2019 in Aweil, South Sudan) saw me.

"Attention, Mayom!" he snapped. "Where have you been all day?"

Our three task forces were given a truck that would carry rations and the sick individuals who could not walk. The rest had to walk back to Sudan. Being the logistics officer, I had to oversee the food supplies loaded in the truck. Meaning I had to go to Pakhok and stay there with the food supplies until our forces arrived on foot. Lieutenant Biet hustled me up. I grabbed my bag and boarded the truck, waving Lhat goodbye. I knew he was not coming; he wanted to remain in Dimma to fight.

Vroom! We drove all day, reaching Rhad, a town located at the Ethiopia–Sudan border, late in the afternoon. And then we proceeded to Pakhok, a few kilometers away from Rhad. We arrived in Pakhok late in the evening. It was the rainy season, and the rain in that part of the world was subtle and predictable. Black clouds appeared out of nowhere, and it rained heavily. I was simply wet because there was no single shelter in Pakhok. At night, my body heat dried me off as I slept. In the morning, the sun helped with the drying process.

But the wheat flour that I brought had been soaked and washed away by the running water. The clearance where the food supplies were kept was now a pool. A few sacks of maize had soaked to germination point and were now the only food source for the sick comrades who came to Pakhok first. We roasted the soaked grains and ate them like popcorns. We called them *berenge*.

I was one of the luckiest individuals who rode from Dimma to Pakhok, where I was safe among the women, children, and disabled persons. It would be a week before our forces arrived who had trekked on foot.

But I was not happy that I was in a safe place and my comrades were in the front line where the action was.

General James Hoth Mai —the overall commander of Dimma (1988-1989).

General Anyieso Ajang—one of the leading trainers in Dimma. (Gen. Ajang passed away in 2021 when I was writing this book).

General Manyang Magom—the lieutenant who trekked with the author from Sudan to Ethiopia.

General Victoria Adhardit Arop—the woman who fooled the author and her son, Agel Machar.

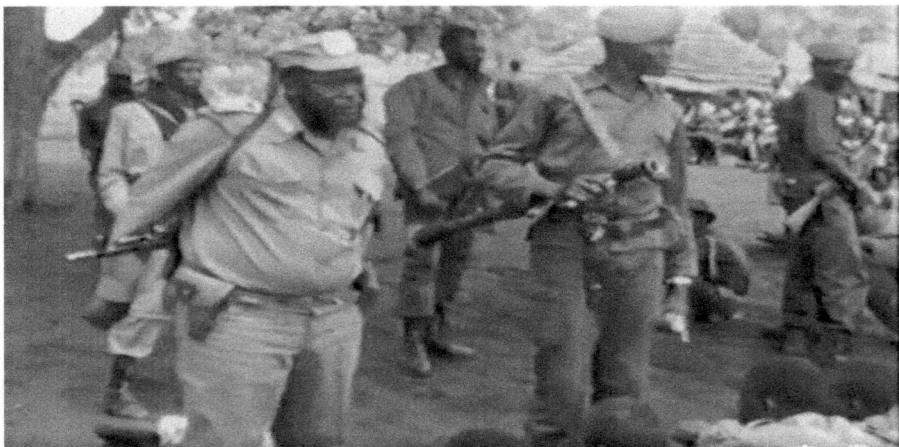

The Commander in Chief of the SPLA, Dr. John Garang, arrived flanked by heavily armed bodyguards to initiate our guerrilla warfare training in Dimma—1987.

The Red Army recruits, including the author, sitting in the parade ground, listening to the Commander in Chief. The author was somewhere in the crowd. Also, in the background were our houses.

Comrade Agel Machar (Australia)—the friend and battalion-mate who was fooled with the author by Comrade Victoria Adhardit.

Comrade Aguet Abraham (USA)—the author's friend and battalion-mate. Both Aguet and the author were dressed up as girls to join the girls' team.

The author, William Mayom Maker—Canada

PART THREE

Back to Sudan

"It was terrific how day and night worked in that part of the world. In the morning, the darkness disappeared quickly, replaced by the bright sunshine. In the evening, the sunshine disappeared quickly, replaced by darkness. It was as if Maayuäl, God almighty, sat somewhere in heaven, switching the light on and off."

Special Mission I

I was not happy in Pakhok. For some stupid reason, I wanted to return to Dimma to be with my comrades. There were forces somewhere that drove me to go ahead and make mistakes, even when intuition advised otherwise. Inwardly, I silently agreed that I was making a big mistake to return to Dimma, but I was determined to prove a point to my comrades that I was brave enough to handle crucial battles.

To be honest, the main reason I wanted to return to Dimma was to fight. Fighting was exciting for me. Because I had not known any other way, the fighting made me feel important and powerful.

It would be two days before the Red Army forces would arrive on foot from Dimma. Since the rations I brought had been destroyed by rain, I decided to return to Dimma to get more. This was just an excuse. I wanted to return because I felt this twinge of guilt, which told me I should be there in Dimma with my comrades where the action was, instead of being here with the women, children, and disabled persons.

Returning to Dimma was easy because trucks brought women, children, and disabled persons to Pakhok and returned empty to get more people. I boarded a Hino Truck driven by one of my comrades, Deng Madut. Deng was in the Medium force, but because he knew how to drive, he was given one of the trucks left behind when the UN staff fled from Dimma. We left Pakhok in the morning, reaching Rhad at around 9:00 a.m.

Things changed suddenly on our way to Dimma. We encountered Commander Bol Madut in Rhad. Commander Bol was the overall commander of the Dimma operations, but soldiers were deserting their positions and taking their families to safety. The enemy was approaching, and there were no soldiers to fight. The SPLA was losing the battle on all fronts. Panyudo, Itang, and Bongo had fallen into the hands of the Ethiopian rebels. Commander Majak Agoot's deployed forces in the Bonga area had been scattered, with many killed or captured. Now the Ethiopian troops were advancing to capture Dimma's outposts. The SPLA fighters were deserting in significant numbers, and Commander Bol had no troops to fight. Commanders who were easily defeated were frowned upon, and they had no strong voices in the movement. Therefore, Commander Bol Madut, who invented the phrase "I'm not a dumb soldier," wailed like a madman with his dignity at stake.

"What am I going to say to the commander in chief?" he cried. "That I'm a coward who runs away?"

The out-of-his-mind Commander Bol grabbed his gun, wanting to go to the front lines to fight. But his bodyguard subdued him by tying his hands and dragging him away to safety, literally. After his bodyguards prevented him from returning to Dimma, Commander Bol set up a roadblock one mile away from Rhad: soldiers leaving Rhad and heading to Pakhok had to surrender their guns to him.

"I can't force you to fight," Commander Bol told the deserting soldiers. "But you have to surrender the weapons of the SPLA and go to Pakhok as refugees."

Commander Bol gave the confiscated weapons to anyone willing and ready to fight. The idea was that any soldier returning to Ethiopia received a weapon, and any soldier crossing the border to Sudan surrendered his weapon. Many of the Red Army forces who were not armed received weapons at that moment. By now, the SPLA was desperately in need of fighters; even the young Red Army personnel who were supposed to wait for a couple of years to mature were now given guns if they were willing to fight.

I could not believe my luck. Obviously, I was returning to Dimma, and I had no gun, so I joined the line of those waiting to receive their firearms. A captain named Philip (I forgot his last name) registered our names and the serial numbers of the guns issued. I was given an AK47 with a triangular butt. And I could not have been more ecstatic.

To me, a gun was crucial. I could not be a soldier or fighter without a gun. A guerrilla soldier needs a weapon, just as a believer needs a Bible or Quran, a doctor needs a stethoscope, a carpenter needs a hammer, a mechanic needs a set of wrenches, or a farmer needs a hoe. The gun was mine to keep clean, load with ammunition, and shoot when needed. I had learned all these skills in training.

After we had received our equipment, Commander Bol made us stand in a formation to give us orders. First, he praised us for our bravery by saying, "If all the SPLA soldiers were like you, we would have captured all of Sudan by now." After his emotional speech, Commander Bol left to collect guns from other soldiers running away. He left Captain Philip in charge. We were two platoons, and rumors circulated that we were going on a *mamuriya kaaz* (special mission). We were not told where we were going.

Nevertheless, the fact that I was going on a mission under Commander Bol Madut was satisfying. I felt relieved from all the worries of being called a coward who ran away with women and children. Lieutenant Biet Wol, who wanted me to go to Pakhok and wait there until all our forces arrived, would not say anything because Commander Bol had sent me on a special mission.

At the ration store at Rhad, Captain Philip talked with a store-keeper. Each one of us was given five cans of sardine and a box of biscuits. We boarded the truck and left, heading toward Dimma at night. The ride was slow and bumpy. It was a quiet ride, partly because of the uncertainty of what we would encounter and partly because we did not know each other. The captain tried to converse by asking everyone which division they belonged to. It was then that I realized many of my platoon-mates were from Ariathdit, a recently graduated batch. The captain was from Muormuor, another young fellow of the Kazuk Division. Another young man and I were from Zalzal. The four of us were the only senior soldiers. The guy from Kazuk was put in charge of the first platoon, and the guy from Zalzal oversaw the second platoon. Being the youngest worked against me, so I ended up being one of the captain's personnel.

As we rode, I thought back to when I had visited Rumbek and saw soldiers riding by in a truck. I had admired them. Now, here I was, a soldier riding in a truck myself. How far I had come in the last five years. I had begun this adventure as a devoted eleven-year-old boy who wanted a gun to protect his mother, and now I felt like a man and a soldier holding a weapon that a frightened soldier had surrendered. I was going on a special mission. I felt an incredible sense of extreme pride. I felt particularly honored and privileged to be among fighters that Commander Bol Madut praised: "If all SPLA fighters were like you, we would have captured Sudan by now."

We arrived in Khor Deng Majok at midnight. Many of the Red Army forces trekking on foot had already arrived there and slept for the night. We passed through without stopping. I thought about my friend, Lhat Mabor. I knew he was in Dimma, unarmed, but waiting for the firefight to start before he could grab a gun from a dead or seriously wounded soldier. My other friends and sports teammates, including Kuot Mathuch, were officially armed to remain in Dimma. They thought I was in Pakhok, unaware that I was now on a *mamuri-ya kaaz*—a classified secret operation.

We came to Marketh early in the morning. We gobbled our sardines down and drank water before we left on foot, heading northwest. The truck turned around and headed back to Rhad as soon as we left. Deng Madut, the driver, stuck his hand out to wave me goodbye before he drove away. That was the last time I saw Deng. I heard he was killed in the Equatoria region in 1996.

The captain shouted us into columns, one on each side of the path. We started a slow, agonizing walk down the bushy path. It was a surprise to find a narrow footpath that cut into the side of the hill. Typically, the jungle was nothing but wilderness. But this was a secret path that the local tribesmen used to avoid passing through Dimma when they went to mine for gold.

We learned we were heading to set up an ambush on the Koi Road, the only road that connected Dimma to the rest of Ethiopian cities and towns. Two or three days earlier, a landmine team headed by Isaac Majak Roor (currently in Rumbek) had set up a mine blowing up a Wayane's truck. The impact had forced the convoy back to Aman to regroup. Now we were going to hold back the Wayane troops so that Dimma was evacuated.

As we advanced, the jungle thickened, and the path narrowed. We walked in a single line, paced about fifteen feet apart. Walking with enough distance between us minimized how many of us could be killed or wounded if someone hit us with a burst of machine gunfire. We moved slowly and deliberately, periodically stopping and listening before moving on.

As I walked, the backpack and gun quickly wore me down. I hunched and constantly bounced the backpack up off my shoulders. It helped, but not for long. The impact of the load forced me and everyone else to walk bent over.

My stomach jumped up into my throat. This was it; I was going into battle, not dreaming. I was filled with mixed emotions. Half of me wanted to taste my first war experience. The other half wanted my mother to come and take me away from this madness and warn me not to repeat this stupid mistake. I knew the latter was wishful thinking now.

We continued forward, moving slowly, cautiously, silently—well dispersed. We came to a stream—one of the Dimma River's tributaries. We crossed a shallow stream, drinking as we did. I flopped down beside the captain, and I watched as the rest of my comrades closed in behind us. Finding a spot, I sat on a rock on the jungle floor and leaned against a tree for a backrest. The Kazuk sergeant staggered into the clump of trees next to me and dropped to the ground, exhausted.

"*Harak!*" the captain ordered a few minutes later. "Move!"

We started up again, trudging slowly through the scrub. About several meters from the stream, the terrain changed drastically, and the jungle seemed to engulf us. About 150 meters ahead of us were tall trees running along the Dimma River; the trees were festooned with hanging and mosses,

I recognized the terrain. It was the area where Lhat Mabor, Andiria Buoth, and I wasted eighty-six bullets when we practiced our shooting strategies. To the north was Koi Town. To the south was Dimma. And to the east was the temporary camp where we spent the summer hunting and gathering building materials.

In about forty-five minutes' walk from where we were standing, we would go to the camp where my friend Ring accidentally shot himself to death. The memories flashed into my mind. I remembered how he was lying prone, with a bullet wound in his head. How the big, greenfly came and sat on the twig, looked at me, looked at Ring's lifeless body, and looked at me again before shaking its head and flying away as if it could not believe why these skinny human kids had such a short lifespan. Thinking about the death of my friend brought a chill to my body. Now I was heading to set up an ambush. Would I survive or die like my friend? What worried me the most was that I would die among strangers instead of my comrades and friends, including Lhat Mabor.

Nevertheless, I was a soldier trained to kill or get killed, end of the story. No one would remember who I was and why I joined the movement in the first place. I was just a number. "Two platoons were sent on a special mission, and they were all killed," Commander Bol Madut would say. "This is the cost of war. We are dying for the freedom of our people."

But the truth was Commander Bul Madut had personal bodyguards who dragged him to safety, even if he intended to fight. The commander in chief, Dr. Garang, was touring foreign countries, making speeches and generating weapons. These weapons would be given to the children of poor people, like me, to fight; meanwhile, the children of big men (high-ranking leaders of the movement) were sent to safety abroad. The indoctrinated children of the poor South Sudanese would admire the powerful and charismatic leaders and volunteer to die, even if they were told they were too young to fight.

"Take cover!" the captain yelled, disrupting my daydream. Before I knew it, I was lying flat on my stomach, all senses on alert, my heart racing a thousand miles an hour. The air stood still, and there was no movement in the bush; it was quieter than normal. My heart was pounding in my chest like an Agaar drum.

Trrrreeee! Trrrreeee! A couple of quick bursts of small-arms fire erupted from the jungle to the right. The captain kneeled behind the rock, and I did the same thing. The Kazuk sergeant was on my left and the captain on my right.

Trrrreeee! Trrrreee! Sporadic gunfire echoed from somewhere up ahead, bullets whining past me like bees. The recently discharged recruits who had not even shot a gun before had frozen. Others were running around like madmen, despite the captain's attempt to make them take cover and get ready to return fire.

The captain and the Kazuk sergeant had already opened fire. My Kalashnikov had sprung into action; its butt kicked my right shoulder as the bullets spewed out. We could not see enemy soldiers with the jungle so thick, so we fired in the direction the gunfire came from.

The enemy fired back rapidly. I heard artillery round, perhaps a howitzer, whoosh over my head as it passed by, then exploded behind us. Turning my head, I saw a cloud of smoke behind me, and I smelled the odor of detonated high explosives. There was screaming, shouting, and groaning.

I buried my head down and continued squeezing the trigger. The five minutes or so under gunfire felt like five hours. We only felt hesitation was when a bomb landed. The time seemed never-ending with all the noise and smoke. We kept firing many rounds; the grass in front of us seemed to drop as if cut with a sickle.

I buried my head in the grass behind the rock and squeezed the trigger. The gun clicked empty. I had shot my first magazine of thirty-one bullets, including the one that was in the chamber.

"Let's go!" I heard the captain yell over the bursts of fire.

Remembering my training, I thought we were launching an assault. In training, we were taught to shoot, get up, and run forward while shooting. But that was not what the captain meant. We were running away.

When I looked up, I saw the captain and the sergeant disappearing into the grass in the direction we had come from. I got up to run, and my foot landed on unstable rock. I fell, breaking the fall with the gun in my right hand. At first, I thought I was shot. But when I got up and ran normally, I know my bones were intact.

We ran up and down the hill, heading toward Marketh, the same route we had come from. The two-platoon members had scattered in different directions. Ahead of me was the captain, his bodyguard, and the sergeant from Kazuk. We came to the stream. Bullets whined in the air just above my head, ricocheting from the rocks on the other side of the stream. We had no time to find the shallow point where we had crossed a few hours ago. Here we had to jump several feet down into the stream.

The captain and sergeant made leaps of faith, jumping at full speed without looking to see where they would land. Amidst the bursts of gunfire, I ran at full speed and jumped, feeling the air hissing as I landed.

I misjudged the height, and the backpack on my back and Kalashnikov on my right hand prevented me from landing feet first. Instead, I landed prone. It felt like I had landed on cement: the impact smashed the air out of my lungs for a few seconds. The pain was unbearable in my face, chest, and groin. I lost my gun in my panic and pain. I tried to stand, but it was too deep. The backpack, clothes, and the Adidas shoes I was wearing prevented me from swimming. I pulled my head up and saw the captain and other comrades disappearing into the grass.

In my mind, the Ethiopian fighters were approaching to shoot me, and I would die in the river like a fish. The panic mechanism in me kept sounding the alarm. The first struggle was to release me from the false hope that my comrades would help me. None of them had brought me into the bush. I had jumped into the bush alone. If I did not try harder to save myself alone, I would die alone.

With the weapon gone, I let go of the heavy backpack full of water, kicked my legs, and swung my hands harder to swim. Soon my hands touched the rock on the other side. The gunfire had quietened down, and I ran on the trail empty-handed, with no gun and no bag. I solely depended on my legs to take me to safety.

I thought I was heading to Marketh. But the trail led me straight to Khor Deng Majok. To this day, I still do not remember how I ran that distance without getting tired. I was a survivor deserted by hunger, thirst, and exhaustion.

At Khor Deng Majok, I met hundreds of refugees and soldiers heading to Rhad. The Ethiopian rebels had captured Dimma and Marketh, and many South Sudanese were killed. Among them was Kuol Piom, from Gogrial, who commanded the Red Army fighters defending Dimma.

That was that. I had fought and survived my first battle. I had been shot at, and I had shot back like a soldier. I was a veteran SPLA fighter.

On the other hand, the fact that I had lost my weapon overshadowed my accomplishment. We were told that a guerrilla fighter was only separated from his gun when he had died. Losing a firearm for any reason was a disgrace. Even in training, if you lost your dummy guns, you were arrested and mercilessly punished. Also, losing a gun was a punishable crime, so I thought Commander Bol Madut would arrest me for losing my weapon. Even though I had volunteered for this special mission and fought courageously, the fact that I had lost my gun made me ashamed of myself. I did not even mention my participation in this battle to my friends, fearing they would either laugh at me for losing a gun or criticize me for my stupidity in joining the battle I was not supposed to be in. So, I kept that secret to myself, and this is the first time I have openly talked about that ambush.

Years later, I learned that Lhat Mabor had a secret of his own. In Dimma, Lhat was able to grab an MK46 gun from a seriously wounded comrade. After firing rapidly, the Ethiopians overwhelmed them; he left the artillery behind and fled because it was too heavy for him to carry. I also heard the same story from my comrades who had lost their guns in the rivers in Dimma and Rhad. They could not swim across the raging rivers with heavy guns. The best bet was to discard everything and use both hands to swim across. Countless people and guns had been lost in rivers. But no one wanted to remember those painful memories of war.

Special Mission II

After the ambush, I arrived in Khor Anyuak at dusk, the last outpost before Rhad, where I found my brother, Makis. We were glad that we had found each other alive. Being in a war zone, you cherished every moment you spent alive, knowing tomorrow could be it.

Lieutenant Maper Manyiel now commanded Khor Anyuak. Neither my brother nor Lieutenant Maper had asked me where I came from. They knew I had gone to Pakhok three days ago, but none of them asked why I had returned. I did not tell them about the battle that I had participated in yesterday, for I knew they would blame me for my stupidity.

I was hungry. An Ethiopian woman named Kadiji (now in Connecticut, USA) who had married an Agaar man named Paul Marol was in Lieutenant Maper's headquarters and noticed how hungry I was. She prepared me some food. It was the first hot meal I had eaten for one week because I had survived on sardines and biscuits.

I ate and then went to sleep right away. Despite being completely exhausted, I did not sleep well because the nightmares of the battle kept flashing in my mind: the shooting, the screaming, the drowning, the running, you name it.

In the morning, Lieutenant Maper blew a whistle and hustled us into a formation. Orders had arrived from Commander Bol Madut; Lieutenant Maper had to go to Tula, an outpost located about three hours' walk from Khor Anyuak. An eighteen-year-old sergeant commanded one squad of the Red Army in Tula. They needed a grown commander, and Lieutenant Maper was chosen. It was Commander Bol Madut's last attempt to protect Rhad after Dimma and Marketh were captured.

Lieutenant Maper had sent his bodyguard to take his family to safety yesterday. So, he asked my brother Makis and me to escort him to Tula as his bodyguards. Lieutenant Maper confiscated two Kalashnikovs from soldiers going to Pakhok and gave them to us. I was glad to get another gun after I lost my first gun during the ambush. I promised myself not to lose this again, no matter what.

I liked this second special mission because I was with my brother and Lieutenant Maper Manyiel. If something happened to me, they would message my mother to tell her how and where I died. If something happened to any one of them, I would take a message home as well.

Locked and loaded, we left Khor Anyuak at around 7:00 a.m. The first lieutenant oversaw the mission with his deputy, Second Lieutenant Deng Makeny. It was a platoon of twelve people in our group.

After walking for about one hour, the path led us to a hut with a grass-thatched roof built between two big and shadowy trees. Suddenly, we unknowingly emerged into the compound and found about fifty Anyuak militiamen, all armed, some of them wearing SPLA uniforms. They were in a meeting. We completely caught them off guard as they just sat there staring, unsure of what to do.

Without hesitation, Lieutenant Maper ordered in Dinka, "Anyone who unlocks a gun, shoot him."

The Anyuak militiamen just sat scared; no one even moved or spoke.

Lieutenant Maper went straight to them and greeted them in Arabic. "*Salam Aleikum!*"

The rest of us moved around them, leaving Lieutenant Maper and his deputy Deng Makeny with the Anyuaks in the middle; we were all watching to see who would unlock his gun.

"*Aleikum, Salam*, Comrade Maper," one of the Anyuaks who presided over the meeting said.

We were surprised that he knew Lieutenant Maper by name. Lieutenant Maper knew him too because they were in shield three together before he deserted the SPLA and joined his people, the Anyuak.

When the lieutenant asked why they had gathered there, the Anyuak leader said they had nothing against the SPLA and that they were preparing to attack the Kachippo tribe, who had attacked one of their villages and killed people. We knew he was lying. The Anyuak had collaborated with the Ethiopian rebels; they showed the Ethiopian rebels where the SPLA camps and training centers were. They were preparing to attack either Tula or Khor Anyuak, where we had come from.

While Lieutenant Maper talked to his counterpart, the Anyuak militia started getting up and leaving one by one. We stayed, thinking they would turn around and fire at us, but nothing happened. They all left us with their leader, who appeared scared, thinking the SPLA wanted him for deserting.

We left that place quickly to avoid being surprised by the militia who had disappeared in the jungle. We thought we would fall into an ambush, but nothing happened until we reached our destination, Tula.

When we reached Tula, we found the squad stationed there with low morale. Their food and ammunition supplies were low. They were armed with light machine guns, not artillery or RPG. We were supposed to stay there in Tula, but Lt. Maper suddenly changed his mind. He decided we should return to Khor Anyuak the same day to find an artillery gunner.

We left late in the afternoon and went back to Khor Anyuak. Lieutenant Maper wanted to mobilize big gunners before returning to Tula to stay there until further notice. But Lieutenant Maper's quick change of mind had saved us from death. Because just one hour after we left, the Ethiopian rebels surrounded Tula, killing the entire squad. Only the squad leader survived, and he ran after us to Khor Anyuak to tell us what had happened. According to him, the Ethiopian rebels came just half an hour after leaving, and they killed his entire squad except him.

The following morning, Lieutenant Maper gathered up some soldiers to go and recapture Tula. He intended to go and retrieve the bodies of those young comrades that were killed there. By now, Lieutenant Maper's bodyguards, Muothich Jalla (now in Rumbek), Madiria Kachuol (in Juba), and Mayiel, from the Nuer, had arrived. They went with Lieutenant Maper. The artillery gunner named Mayom had also come from Rhad, sent by Commander Bol Madut. Mayom joined them. Makis and I remained to defend Khor Anyuak.

Since I was not selected to return to Tula, I would not volunteer to put myself back in harm's way. I had already learned my lesson the hard way when I volunteered in the first ambush, which almost took my life.

A few hours later, Lieutenant Maper returned, utterly exhausted. His troops had been scattered; others were killed, including the MK46 gunner, Mayom. Now the Ethiopian rebels were advancing from both Tula and Dimma. We fled to Rhad.

When we arrived in Rhad, the place was a mess. The river was full, and the current was uprooting and carrying big trees away. Thousands of refugees and soldiers who did not know how to swim were stranded on the other side.

Since I had almost died when I crossed the river in Jonglei, swimming had become my priority in Dimma. After we had completed our training, we did nothing but swim all day. I could cross any river, no matter how intense the current was. But swimming with a load was another thing. My sixteen-year-old skinny body could not carry a gun with one hand and swim with another because the gun was too heavy. That was how I lost my gun during the ambush. However, I learned the trick on how to cross with a heavy load from Muothich Jalla in Rhad. You placed all your belongings in a plastic sheet and tied it securely, so no water entered inside. Then you put the content to float on water, and you just pushed as you swam across. That was how I crossed the river with my belongings in Rhad, with guidance from Muothich Jalla.

Muothich Jalla had helped many people across the river. He was going back and forth, helping friends who did not know how to swim. But at one point, Muothich was overly confident, and he tied seven guns in a plastic sheet, trying to take them across. At first, the load floated. But when he reached the middle of the river, the heavy load sank. The seven guns had been lost. Muothich shushed me not to mention this to anyone. This is the first time I am mentioning this incident.

There were thousands of people waiting to cross. None knew how to swim. They were waiting for the river to subside before they could cross. But it was the rainy season, and the river kept increasing instead of reducing. And the Ethiopians were advancing.

When we came to Rhad, the soldier from whom Lieutenant Maper had confiscated a gun and given it to me when I was going to Tula came to ask for his gun back. Lieutenant Maper told me to give him back his rifle. I went to a gun store, hoping I would get a gun. The store was wide open, and people were serving themselves. There were no guns, but I ended up grabbing six pairs of uniforms. In the uniform, I found a pistol, PT 92, fully loaded. This was a jackpot. Pistols were extremely valuable; only high-ranking commanders had them. I kept the pistol always hidden, only bringing it out at night or when there was no one around.

I sat next to Lt. Maper, narrating the events during the failed mission to retake Tula when a bomb landed on top of Rhad mountain, where heavy artilleries were deployed. The Ethiopian fighters had attacked us. The thousands of people, mostly refugees who did not know how to swim, panicked. They knew they were in a death trap. The river was raging, and the Ethiopians were attacking. Soon, we on the other side would shoot back, and they would be caught in the crossfire in the middle.

I saw Lt. Maper diving into a trench next to a big tree. I dove into another trench next to him. We watched as the refugees running up and down the bank like madmen.

Soon the gunfire erupted. The Ethiopians opened fire, and the

SPLA on the other side responded. The refugees, thousands of them waiting to cross, were caught in the crossfire. Looking in the river, all I saw was the chaos of waves and flailing limbs, popping heads as non-swimmers grasped for anything that floated past, be it wood or dead bodies.

Lt. Maper was shouting, telling people not to shoot because our people were on the other side of the river. But others continued shooting.

A pregnant woman was dangling on the other side of the bank. She was holding some grass, her feet flailing. If she let go of the grass, she would fall into the raging river. If she pulled herself up, the Ethiopians would spot and shoot her. She was screaming frantically.

"Keep your head down and stay calm," Lieutenant Maper kept shouting at the woman. "But don't let go. Hold on."

The same scene was happening everywhere. At one point, so many people jammed into the river so that even those who did not know how to swim walked over the other people to cross.

Luckily, the Ethiopians were defeated. They returned to Khor Anyuak. Many of the people who panicked and jumped into the river had disappeared with the current. When the river subdued, a bulldozer was used to bring survivors stranded on the other side. Many of them were wounded.

The pregnant woman was lucky; she was not shot. But she had a miscarriage right there where she was dangling on the riverbank. Blood was still dripping from her legs, but she had no time to recover before she walked to Pakhok. My brother Makis and I fled to Pakhok, too. Lieutenant Maper also joined us in Pakhok.

Special Mission III

From Rhad we came to Pakhok. Pakhok was first called Khor-cum; it was a training center located less than fifty kilometers from the Ethiopian border, where battalions of Zalzal Two, including Gerger, were trained. In 1988, however, Ugandan rebels named Aringa re-belled against President Museveni and came to the SPLA for support and training. Back then, President Museveni and his government did not support the SPLA yet. But when President Museveni realized that his opposition was seeking support from the SPLA, he pledged to support the SPLA as well. In return, President Museveni asked the SPLA not to equip the Aringa rebels. President Museveni's tactics worked. The SPLA kept the Ugandan rebels in Khor-cum, not arming or allowing them to travel anywhere, even though they were trained. That was the end of the Aringa movement, and President Museveni became a permanent ally of the SPLA.

After the SPLA suppressed the Aringa rebellion, another Uganda rebellion started, The Lord's Resistance Army (LRA), led by Joseph Kony. Knowing the relationship between the SPLA and Museveni government was strong, LRA sought support from the Khartoum government instead. But the LRA adopted the Khartoum doctrine of killing. The LRA committed heinous atrocities against its people in northern Uganda. And because they depended solely on brutally killing and ab-ducting people, the LRA could not gain support locally or internation-ally. The movement eventually failed without achieving its objectives.

Unfortunately, the SPLA movement was falling apart when we were in Pakhok. The movement had lost its only ally, President Mengistu of Ethiopia. Commander Riek Machar and Commander William Nyuon had broken away from the SPLA, splitting the move-ment into two. The Khartoum government had taken advantage of this division and had launched major offenses, vowing to finish off the SPLA. The Ethiopian rebels, who ousted President Mengistu, were supported by Khartoum, so they evicted the SPLA from their borders to appease their main ally: Khartoum.

All the refugees who fled from Dimma were in Pakhok; those who fled from Panyudo and Itang were in Pachalla. The refugees were in danger. A report came that Khartoum troops, mixed with the Ethiopian forces, who dislodged us from Ethiopia, were advancing to clean the SPLA away, starting from Pachalla and going to Pakhok and

Kapoeta. Ismail Konyi's militias, armed and equipped by Khartoum, were lurking in the area. Anyuak militias, supported by the Ethiopian rebels, had gone insane. But the weakened SPLA had no fighters. The fighters from the Black Army who were at the border had deserted; each soldier said he was taking his family to safety but never returned.

Subsequently, the entire Red Army forces, including those supposed to wait for a few years to mature before being armed, the *Marek-rek* forces, were now armed to protect themselves and the refugees. The Red Army forces from Dimma became the only hope of the SPLA on the border.

The report came that refugees who had fled from Panyudo and Itang to Pachalla were about to be attacked by Anyuak militiamen. There were no SPLA soldiers to protect them. Some of the Red Army forces remained in Pakhok, and others were taken to Pachalla to go and rescue the refugees. The author was among those who were sent to Pachall under the command of Lt. Maper Manyiel.

We walked from Pakhok to Pachalla, where we were immediately deployed on the perimeter of the town. We dug our trenches, where we spent our days and nights. During the night, squad members had to pull guard at night in the hole for about two hours. The squad leaders worked out systems so that everyone took a turn guarding. Meanwhile, the entire town slept well because they were well protected.

However, our commander, Lt. Maper Manyiel, was fuming with anger. To begin with, he had been the only officer who had led every operation since we were dislodged in Ethiopia three months ago; meanwhile, his fellow officers did not want to participate. In Pachalla, Lieutenant Maper could not believe what he was seeing. Some of the so-called refugees we were protecting were grownups who had laid down their weapons and pretended to be refugees because they did not want to fight.

"Why should I put these children (pointing at us) in harm's way when grownups have refused to fight? Children should not protect the adults; it should be the other way around."

143

Also, Lieutenant Maper was angry because thousands of the Red Army forces in Pachalla were not armed. Instead, they were known as *teirab*, meaning seeds of New Sudan. Lieutenant Maper thought it was unfair for him to force us into numerous battles when our agemates were called *teirab*. Lieutenant Maper had a lot to be angry about.

But the last straw came when Lieutenant Maper met with Commander Jurkuch, who commanded Pachalla. Commander Jurkcuh was senior in rank to Lieutenant Maper. I was not at the meeting, so I do not know what transpired. But Lieutenant stomped out of the meeting and blew a whistle. "Pack up and move," he ordered. "We are returning to Pakhok. This is an order!" That was the end of our tour of duty. We returned to Pakhok immediately.

In Pakhok, we landed in hunger. The Ugandan rebels in Pakhok had grown maize, groundnut, yam, and cassava for their consumption. But we, the South Sudanese, who fled from Ethiopia, did not have food. The Ugandans' farms became the only source of food for both the Ugandans and South Sudanese. But it did not take long before the farms were prematurely harvested and depleted. Hunger struck.

When we returned from Pachalla to Pakhok, we found the hunger had turned into full starvation. Pakhok was a vast savanna with tall elephant grass and scattered trees, so there were no animals to hunt. Even if the animals were there, we could not find them in that thick elephant grass. There were no edible wild leaves or fruits either.

When the hunger turned into starvation, we turned to our last resort: cows. In 1989, the SPLA collected cows somewhere in Southern Sudan and sent them to Dimma, Ethiopia. I do not know the exact number of cows, but the cows were enough to supply the entire camp with milk. Those cows saved our lives in Pakhok. Without them, we would have starved to death.

Several months later, after we had slaughtered all the cows, our survival mode jumped to the next level. As the grass was drying, we discovered a treasure hidden beneath the earth. There were wild tubers, which we dug and ate. However, unlike any other tubers, these wild tubers were unpalatable: they tasted extremely bitter, produced inflammation, and showed toxicity. We named them "hot ones." Despite being toxic, hot ones became our only diet in Pakhok.

The preparation of the hot ones took several hours. After digging, you cleaned and washed the tubers thoroughly. Then you boiled them for an hour or so, drained the water, and rinsed them in clean water before boiling them again. You repeated the boiling, draining, and washing several times to reduce the toxicity. Finally, after over six hours, it was ready to eat. It was crunchy and still bitter. That was how the name the hot ones came about. But a little thing like bitterness could not stand in our way. We survived on hot ones for months in Pakhok.

We supplemented the hot ones with wild meat. Any wild animals that we encountered in the bush were shot and eaten. Even animals such as monkeys that were culturally unacceptable to eat were on the menu. We ate them not only because we were starving but also because we were trained to believe guerrilla fighters ate anything. As stated earlier, the more disgusting things you ate, the better soldier your peers and commanders considered and respected you.

One day, my friend Lhat and I ventured into the wilderness to hunt with three other comrades. At this moment, we did not even care about Ismail Konyi or Anyuak militiamen who were in the area; we just roamed in the bushes, hoping to find an animal to shoot or fruits to eat. After hunting for several hours, to no avail, we came to a stream with tall trees alongside it. Looking up, we saw a Columbus monkey sitting comfortably on a branch. The Columbus monkey looked down on us as if it were wondering where in the hell these anorexic creatures on two legs had come from? We would be dumb to let this monkey escape.

Remember, it was culturally unacceptable for Dinka to eat a monkey. But cultural norms and taboos were frozen. We had to prove to ourselves that we were guerrilla fighters who ate everything without being disgusted. Most prominently, this Columbus monkey would provide us with the calories we needed so severely.

Usually, we would argue as to who would shoot first. But not this time. It was not a game; it was a serious matter. We needed someone who would not miss this animal; otherwise, we would not even have enough energy to walk back to the camp.

Lhat Mabor, the senior in age and ranks, took the initiative to choose the shooter: me. The responsibility was placed on my bony shoulders. I had to shoot the Columbus monkey. I was the best shooter, and all my comrades knew that. I accepted the task. I was extremely nervous because all the eyes were on me. I unlocked the AK-47, which was already loaded, and removed the magazine. My sixteen-year-old skinny hands could not aim properly, so I removed the magazine to make the gun lighter.

I stood straight and aimed with only one bullet in the chamber; the butt of the gun rested on my right shoulder, and my neck was crooked and relaxed to let the cheek fall naturally to the stock. This ensured that my eye aligned naturally to the sight. I adjusted and steadied my grips; my index finger curled around the trigger. When the monkey's head was inside the crook (*kurum tanshin*), I relaxed my muscles, held my breath, and gently squeezed the trigger.

Bang! The Columbus monkey came tumbling down before I even heard the gunshot. We high-fived each other. Even though we considered ourselves as true guerrillas who ate the most disgusting things, the first thing we did was cut off the monkey's hands and threw them away because they looked like human hands. We started a fire and roasted the animal right there. While eating, Lhat Mabor composed and sang the following song:

Aye cɔɔl agɔɔk, aba ye weŋ.
Marial (agang-rial) aba ye weŋ!

People called it a monkey,
But it is a cow.
Columbus monkey is the cow!

In 2015, twenty-five years after we ate that Columbus monkey, I spoke to a guy named Johk Atuer. I was in Canada, and Jhok was in Perth, Australia.

Johk and I had not seen each other since Pakhok in 1991. When I called Jhok and introduced myself to him, he said, "Is this Mayom who shot the Columbus monkey?"

We both laughed as we reminisced about our days in the liberation strug-gle when living in the bush forced us to disregard some of our cultural norms and taboos temporarily. You see, when a condition pushes you to the limit, the survival instinct, which prevents every living creature from extinction, will au-tomatically kick in. Our survival instinct did not fail us: we did all we could to survive as guerrilla fighters, despite our tender age.

Helping Vulnerable Family

In 1991, I met a young mother named Adut Machar Dak with her two infant children in Pakhok. Adut Machar, from the Atuot, was married to Manyang Majok Duop, from the Agaar. I did not know Adut personally, but I knew her husband's family back home.

Majok Duop's family members were traditional bonesetters, re-nowned for treating bone injuries—knowledge verbally passed from one generation to another without formal documentation.

By now, Pakhok was a death trap. The starvation was at its peak. The Ethiopian troops who evicted us from Dimma were reported to be crossing the river to push us away from the border. Khartoum troops were also said to be on their way to wipe out the weakened SPLA from the border. Ismail Konyi's militias, equipped and support-ed by the Khartoum regime, were lurking in the area. Anyuak mili-tiamen were armed to the teeth. Pakhok was a living graveyard, and everyone wanted to get the hell out of that place.

With her two infant children, the young mother (Adut Machar) wanted to go to Kapoeta. But there were no vehicles. The few avail-able trucks were being used to carry commanders with their fami-lies. Everyone else had to walk hundreds of miles from Pakhok to Kapoeta. There was no way Adut could take her two children, Majok and Mayom, who were three and one, respectively, and walk hun-dreds of miles. Also, lions had attacked and devoured several people between Pakhok and Buma. Not to mention that local tribespeople and some perverts within the movement had sexually abused unaccompanied females on the way. The young mother who was stranded in Pakhok knew traveling alone was suicidal.

The desperate young mother (Adut) came to me one day. "Mayom, please, you have to help me with my children. Take me to Kapoeta."

Even though I sympathized with Adut, I told her it was impossible to escort her to Kapoeta because my commander would not allow me to leave. We, the Red Armies, were the only hope for the SPLA in that area. All the Black Armies had left with their families. The Red Armies had no excuse to leave the front lines because we had no families. We only moved under the direct order from the commander in chief, Dr. Garang; otherwise, we stayed put to face the looming dangers in Pakhok.

After I told Adut that my commander would not allow me to escort her, she went to my task force commander, Lieutenant Maper Manyiel. I do not know what Adut told Lieutenant Maper. But Lieutenant Maper called me that evening to talk to me.

"You must help this woman with her children," Lieutenant Maper said, speaking more like an elder than a commander.

I was not interested in going to safety with Adut. I did not want to leave my comrades and go to safety. I wanted to be on the front line with my comrades, where the action was.

After Lieutenant Maper sensed resistance, he said. "Mayom, these are Agaar children, and if they die here, their blood will be in our hands. Remember, we will go back to the Agaarland one day, and the society will blame us if we don't do something to help this vulnerable Agaar family."

After I heard that, I agreed to take Adut to safety with her children. I told Adut that evening to prepare for our departure in the morning. That night, I was approached by another man from the Agaar named Mathiang. I later nicknamed him "Mathiang Rilpuou" (Tenacious Mathiang) because he was that. Looking at him, I wondered how the hell did he get here? Mathiang was unique. Standing less than three feet tall, he was a little person (dwarf). He looked like a three-year-old child. The only way you could tell Mathiang was an adult was the six scarification marks on his forehead. I had no idea how Mathiang managed to walk for months across the savannah, the desert, and the mountain ranges from Rumbek to Ethiopia. Or how Mathiang had made it out alive in Ethiopia, where thousands of people had died. That is why I nicknamed him Tenacious Mathiang.

"Mayom, I hear that you are going to Kapoeta," Tenacious Mathiang said. "Please don't leave me here. You are the only Agaar I know."

I let Mathiang join us. An older woman (I have forgotten her name) from the Atuot also joined us. Now I had five vulnerable people I was responsible for: the young mother with her two infants, the disabled person, and the old Atuot woman. Remember, I was only sixteen years old. I did not even know what I was doing. It was desperation in a desperate situation.

Soldiers were not allowed to leave with weapons, so I left mine in Pakhok. But I had my concealed weapon, the PT92 pistol, which I found in a store in Rhad. I kept the handgun hidden because I did not want it confiscated by high-ranking officers. Even Lieutenant Maper did not know I had it. Only my trusted friend, Lhat, knew I had the gun.

With the pistol securely tucked by my groin, I left Pakhok with my vulnerable crew. I put the three-year-old Majok on my shoulders, his butt resting on the backpack on my back. Adut was carrying a load on her head and the child on her back. The old Atuot woman carried her belongings. Mathiang carried our food supplies, raw lentils, and maize. On the way, we were joined by another armed man called Agondong (currently in Rumbek). Agondong, from the Black Army, was armed with an AK47.

We went from Pakhok to Khor Bulldozer, reaching Nyalong-goro at midday. Nyalong-goro was then commanded by Lieutenant Marial Manyuon (killed in Juba in 2011), who later became a renowned teacher at Nafata Secondary School in Kakuma, Kenya. Lieutenant Marial commanded rigorous order.

"From here to Khor-Ghana," he warned every soldier that passed through, "I don't want to hear a gunshot. I know you, *Jesh Amer,* shoot randomly like madmen."

We left Nyalong-goro late in the afternoon. Another soldier had told us to be vigilant on the way because lions had killed two people yesterday. I did not care, nor was I afraid. You see, a teenager with a gun felt like he had an extra set of testicles, even though the two testicles he already had were not mature yet.

We walked along a very narrow path planked by the tall elephant grass on both sides. The road was so narrow that one had to step off the road to let the other go by when two people passed each other. And the elephant grass was so thick that visibility was limited.

At around 5:00 p.m., we came to Khor-gana. Looking around, I discovered Mathiang was not in sight. I was leading, and Agondong was behind; our vulnerable crew was in the middle. Because of the thick tall grass, you just walked, thinking others were just a few yards behind. Agondong said Mathiang was just behind him. So, we thought Mathiang had lagged and that he would show up in a few minutes.

We waited for about thirty minutes, but he did not show up. The sun was setting. The children were now crying because they were hungry. But Mathiang, who carried our food supplies, was missing.

I asked Agondong to go with me to look for Mathiang. But Agondong said he was exhausted. So, I took the AK47 from him and went to search for Mathiang alone. I thought I would find Mathiang just on the outskirts of the outpost. But that was not the case.

Soon it was dark already—pitch black. It was terrific how day and night worked in that part of the world. In the morning, the darkness disappeared quickly, replaced by the bright sunshine. In the evening, the sunshine disappeared quickly, replaced by darkness. It was as if *Maayuäl,* God almighty, sat somewhere in heaven, switching the light on and off. I looked and saw the artwork of *Maayuäl* in heaven above, the constellation, the recognizable patterns dominating the universe. Back home, I would have enjoyed such meticulous work of the Creator. But not here in the darkness.

I loaded the pistol and stuffed it inside my pants. In my hands was the loaded and unlocked AK47; my grip on the gun's handle was firm, and my index finger curled around the trigger, ready to fire. I thought that if a lion knocked me down and I parted with the AK47, I would still use the pistol to defend myself before the beast broke my neck.

After walking for a while in the absolute darkness, I was completely crippled by fear. My heart was thumping in my ears. The testicles which had misled me in the first place were now gone. That is what testicles do; they mislead a man, and when he is in a serious problem, they shrink, leaving you on your own.

I had been walking for about an hour in the darkness, but Mathiang was nowhere to be found. I gave up. I did not know whether Mathiang had returned to Pakhok or a lion had attacked and devoured him.

When I was about to make a U-turn, something fell with a "thud" just a few yards away. I squatted and aimed in the darkness to where the sound came from. My heart raced. My index finger was shaking but firmly pressed against the trigger with the lever switched to automatic. With one squeeze, several bullets would spew out, burning everything in their way. Even if I missed the beast, the sound of the gun would scare it away. I thought.

I heard a sigh, like someone lifting a heavy load. I knew this was Mathiang; he had tripped and fallen and now was lifting the load again.

"Mathiang, is that you?" I called.

"Yes," he replied, sounding scared out of his mind. "It's good that you've come, Mayom."

It turned out that Mathiang barely saw in the daylight, but he was completely blind at night. Additionally, Mathiang had warped legs and feet; his knees were curved inward, and his feet had grown outward, making it harder for him to walk in the narrow path because the grass easily tangled his feet. Also, the loads (the backpack on his back and food supplies on his head) were too heavy for him. That was why he could not keep up with us.

We returned to Khor-gana. By now, I was outraged—a combination of fear, hunger, thirst, and fatigue. I no longer cared about the earlier orders made by Lieutenant Marial, who said, "From here to Khor-gana, I don't want to hear a gunshot. I know you, *Jesh Amer,* shoot randomly like madmen." I was a madman now. Every rustle in the bush was met with a bullet or two.

We came to a dry stream surrounded by bamboo bushes. It was because of this the place was named Khor-gana, meaning bamboo stream. It was the place lion hid and attacked people.

As we ascended down the stream, Mathiang slipped and fell. While grunting and groaning in pain, Mathiang tumbled down the stream with the load he was carrying. I thought a lion had grabbed him, so I shot several bullets in the air.

A few seconds later, Mathiang yelled from the bottom of the stream. "Mayom, don't shoot me! I'm down here!"

When we came to Khor-gana, the commander named Makur wanted to arrest me for the shooting. I lied to the commander that "something had jumped over our heads in the darkness, so I had to shoot it." The commander asked Mathiang whether what I said was true, and he said it was. They did not arrest me.

We left the following morning. But fatigue had set in, and Majok was too heavy for me. My skinny neck, where Majok had sat for two days, was stiffened to the point that I could not even turn my head. Adut was also in bad shape, and so was the old woman. Mathiang was the worst among us. But we pressed on.

Luckily, we arrived at Khor-chuei, where we found a truck going to Buma. I talked to the driver, and he was kind enough to take my vulnerable crew: Adut with the children, Mathiang, and the old woman.

Since my vulnerable crew had found a ride, I wanted to return to Pakhok. But Adut hated the idea, and she begged me not to return. She feared that maybe the truck would break down on the road. Adut ensured me that she would wait for me in Buma, where the truck was heading. She took my bags with her, saying it would be easier for me to walk without a heavy load. But I knew she took my bag as collateral, knowing I would not return to Pakhok without my belongings. She was right, though. I would have returned to Pakhok had she not taken my bag.

Nevertheless, Agondong and I walked to Buma. Without loads, we cruised along luxuriously. We arrived in Buma at around 8:00 p.m. It was dark, and I could not find my crew. Hunger was not my main concern. I had nowhere to sleep because my bag was with Adut.

While searching, I met another comrade called Lodionga, one of the few Red Army who had escaped from Pakhok, going to his homeland, Torit. People were starving in Buma too, and Lodionga and the squad had been in Buma for two days without food. Lodionga offered to share his blanket when I could not find my crew.

Soon, Commander Bol Madut arrived, flanked by his bodyguards. I had not seen him since Rhad when he sent us to that ambush. Thank God it was night, and he would not recognize me. My biggest fear was Captain Philip; if he saw me, he would recognize me even in the darkness. But I knew Captain Philip did not know I had lost my gun in the river during the ambush. So, my plan was, when asked, that I would say I had left the gun in Pakhok.

But Commander Bol was coming to encourage the starving people to go to Kapoeta.

"I am sorry, *Jesh Amer*," he said in Arabic. "I have no food to give you. The little food that I had was given to the women and children. You must proceed to Kapoeta. There you will get enough food."

Commander Bol Madut liked to say, "I am not a dumb soldier." He liked to surround himself with his tribe members. Most of his bodyguards were from Tonj, mostly his close relatives and friends.

At the end of his speech, Commander Bol Madut switched from Arabic to Dinka. "I have slaughtered a small goat in my house," he said. "So, if you can hear what I am saying, you sneak into my compound to get yourself a piece of meat with broth. But don't tell anyone who does not understand this language."

Commander Bol Madut intended only to invite Dinka to his house. He did not know that *Jesh Amer* was not that easily fooled.

After having been together as one family for years in Dimma, *Jesh Amer* spoke almost every South Sudanese language. You could never insult or speak contemptuously against them in any language and get away with it. CDR Bol was about to learn a lesson the hard way.

As Commander Bol spoke, Lodionga poked me. Lodionga was not a Dinka; he was from Lotuko. But he was fluent in Dinka. That was why he poked me; to tell me that he had understood what Commander Bol Madut was saying and that he was going to Commander Bol's compound to get himself a piece of meat with the broth.

After Commander Bol Madut left, we started sneaking out to his compound one by one. And, indeed, there was food. Each of us had a piece of meat with broth and boiled maize.

After eating, Commander Bol came to chat with us. He asked us to introduce ourselves. We all introduced ourselves, name, and sub-tribe—all Dinka.

When it was Lodionga's turned to introduce himself, he said, in Dinka with an accent, "My name is Lodionga. I'm from Lotuko."

"Lotuko?" CDR Bol asked, surprised. "How did you get in here?"

"Well," Lodionga said, "Comrade Bol, you said you had slaughtered a small goat in your house and that anyone who heard it was welcome. So, I heard what you said, and here I am, having my broth."

We all roared with laughter, including Commander Madut.

"Oh! *Jesh Amer, Jesh Amer!*" Commander Boldit said, laughing. "What can I say? You are truly the faces of the New Sudan we are fighting for."

I found my crew in the morning. Adut was relieved to see me. She said that she had found another truck heading to Kapoeta. Since she had found a truck to take them to Kapoeta, where her husband was, I told her I would return to Pakhok. I did not want to walk in the desert of Magos between Buma and Kapoeta. But Adut did not want me to return to Pakhok; she had already convinced the driver to take all of us, including Agondong and me. She feared that if the truck broke down on the way, there was no one to help her.

We boarded the truck and left Buma in the morning, reaching Kapoeta at around 7:00 p.m. I found my brother, Manyang, in Kapoeta, and we were happy to see each other alive. It was the third time we had met. The first time was when we traveled from Dimma to Itang for sporting events. Manyang was wounded in the front line and was taken to Itang for treatment. He had stepped on an antipersonnel land-mine, which had broken his right leg just above the ankle. Fortunately, the major artery was not damaged, and he had avoided an amputation. And when he was transferred from Itang to Kapoeta for treatment, he had passed through Dimma, where he spent two days with me. Now Manyang lived with one of our distant relatives in Kapoeta, so he took me to live with him. I was happy to unite with him.

In Kapoeta, Adut learned her husband was in Torit. So Adut want-ed me to go to Torit with them. From Kapoeta, we found a Toyota pickup which took us to Torit, where Adut was finally reunited with her husband, Manyang Majok Duop. Adut narrated everything to her husband and said they would not have made it out alive without me. Manyang thanked me profusely for saving his family's life. But he thanked me in a typical Dinka way, "I will give you my daughter for free in the future. If I do not have a daughter to give you, I will pay my share of the bride-price when you marry."

In Torit, we stayed at Commander Samuel Ater Dak's home, who was Adut's uncle. Subsequently, Commander Ater wanted me to be his bodyguard. But I told him that I was returning to my unit in Pakhok.

In Torit, I met Madhieu Makuach Adhil (now a member of par-liament in Rumbek). Madhieu took me to his place, where I met Lieutenant Mabor Meen Wol (now an MP in Rumbek). Lieutenant Mabor also wanted me to be his bodyguard. I do not know why every officer I met wanted me to be his bodyguard. I did not like being a bodyguard either. But Lieutenant Mabor Meen did it smartly. Instead of approaching me himself, Mabor told Madhieu to convince me to be his bodyguard.

Mabor was a signal division staff responsible for policy, control, and management of all SPLA communications. Because of this,

Madhieu said being Mabor Meen's bodyguard would allow me to learn. Madhieu had a point, though. Signal staff members were the most educated individuals in the SPLA because they always wrote, read, and even took courses. So, I became Lieutenant Mabor Meen's bodyguard in Torit. But I quit three days later because being a bodyguard was not my thing.

I returned to Kapoeta. That was the last time I saw Adut, with her two children, Mathiang and the old Atuot lady.

Adut Machar is currently in Yirol. Majok and his little brother, Mayom, are in Juba. In 2020, I wrote and posted this story on Facebook, and Majok and Mayom tracked me down and thanked me for saving their lives. Majok, the boy that I carried on my shoulder, is a police officer. I learned from them that their father had passed away years back. Majok and Mayom now follow me on social media.

Kapoeta

After taking the young family to reunite with their father in Torit, I went to Kapoeta, intending to return to Pakhok to be with my unit. I had to wait for a truck going to Buma or Pakhok, although no trucks were heading in that direction.

In the meantime, I enjoyed spending time with my older brother, Manyang, in Kapoeta. On the front line, a moment like this was precious to share with loved ones. So, we cherished every moment, talking about our mother back home. My brother left home in 1986, and I left in 1987. Being the last one to leave home, I always had a lot to say about our mother. So, we rekindled our broken childhood memories.

We talked about our village, our mother, our people, and the bounty we had given up for the sake of our country. We had been seven children; three had died, leaving three boys and one girl. The three of us, Mabor, Manyang, and I, in addition to our half-brother, Makis, had joined the movement, leaving our sister, Yar, with our mother. Our sister died later in 1996.

We had a reason to love our land and its bounty. As mentioned earlier, the Agaarland, which we had left behind, was full of unspoiled natural beauty. We had endless savannahs, inspiring jungles, and breathtaking swamps inhabited by animals, birds, reptiles, and amphibians. There was nothing fake or unnatural in the Agaarland, and my brother and I took comfort in all of this before the war arrived.

We grew up poor, but we did not notice it. Happy children do not always know how poor they are. We had our parents; even after our father passed away, we still had our mother, uncles, and aunts take care of us. We cultivated our land, reared our animals, fished our rivers and lakes, and hunted all we wanted. That was the definition of having plenty.

But all of that had changed when strangers arrived in our land. As perfectly stated in the book, The Proud People:

Since foreigners arrived in our beloved country, Sudan, centuries ago, our culture and history have been stained with blood, pain, and suffering that multigenerational colonization and Arabization had caused. This had created enormous destruction of our land, our people, and our way of life. Our ancestors called these devastating effects of oppression the "ruin of the earth." Indeed, our land was ruined because the foreigners brought their alien cultures, such as guns, religions, laws, and regulations, which they imposed on us. These cultures, especially the guns and religions, appeared toxic, and they ultimately poisoned our pure and natural ways of life—the critical components which defined our humanness. Subsequently, the proudest people of Jieng, particularly the Agaar, were turned upside-down and inside-out until they no longer recognized themselves, their lived environment, and their creator—Nhialic God.[1]

So, there we were, my brother and I, in Kapoeta, the land of Taposa, thousands of miles from our home, our mother, and our dreams. Manyang had been wounded, and he walked with a limp. My sixteen-year-old mind had been severely wounded, too. I did not mention to

---

1   Maker, W., *The Proud People*, Perth: Africa World Books, 2020, p. 23

my brother that I had volunteered to go to an ambush, as I knew he would criticize me for my stupidity. I did not even tell my brother about the concealed pistol hidden in my bag, for I thought he would convince me to surrender it to the authorities to avoid being arrested. I kept everything from my older brother, but now he can read about them.

Nevertheless, we could not fully enjoy our companionship because of aerial bombardments in Kapoeta. By now, the Sudan government had tripled its aerial campaign. Knowing the refugees fleeing from Ethiopia were in Kapoeta, the aerial bombardment was a deliberate attempt to terrorize the civilian populations. Antonovs bombed the town three times a day, morning, noon, and evening.

The aerial bombardment was new to me because we did not experience it in Ethiopia. I had fought the ground assault, where I had the advantage of shooting back. But this aerial assault was a different story.

I first heard about the aerial bombardment when I arrived in Kapoeta from Pakhok. At the checkpoint, before entering the town, a guard laughed sarcastically. "You are lucky," he said. "You've just missed the supper. But do not worry; you will get the breakfast first thing in the morning, delivered straight from Khartoum, fresh and hot. And just between noon and 2:00 p.m., you will get your lunch, plenty of it. Welcome to Kapoeta!"

The soldier was talking about aerial bombardment. Antonov bombed every day, three times a day here in Kapoeta. In a warzone, veterans tried to see the humor in anything and everything, just for laughs. This soldier had decided to make us, the new arrivals, his sources of entertainment; we were the joke and the punchline.

The guard was right; I received my breakfast first thing in the morning, delivered directly from Khartoum. Exhausted from the long truck ride from Buma, I slept in. Suddenly, my brother woke me up. "Mayom, Mayom," he said, slapping me so hard that it hurt before dashing outside. At first, I did not know what was happening or where

I was—the feeling you often have after sleeping in an unknown place. Then there was a plane flying overhead, accompanied by the low growl of its engines. I remembered what the guard had told me at the checkpoint yesterday about the Antonovs: I had received my first breakfast hot and fresh straight from Khartoum.

I ran outside, but I could not get to the bunker. Then there were three or four terrifying bangs. The bomb landed on the other side of the river at New Kapoeta, killing three soldiers and wounding several others, including civilians. The Antonov kept circling the town, but it did not drop any more bombs. It was cloudy, so it could not see its target.

I did not want to be in the same place as my brother, risking being killed by one bomb, so I went to the airport. Most of the soldiers deployed in Kapoeta were from Dimma, and I knew many of them.

At 2:00 p.m., the Antonov returned to deliver a special lunch. The weather was clear, and I saw and heard the plane making that awful sound. When it made a buzzing sound, you knew you were safe. But when the sound stopped, and the aircraft lifted its nose and lowered its bottom, you began to worry, for the crew was rolling the barrel bombs out of their cargo hatch. Again, if you heard the barrel bombs landing and the ground shaking, you knew you were alive, for the bombs had not fallen directly on you. I endured this aerial bombardment for two months.

The last time an Antonov bomb fell a few feet away from me was in the middle of 1992. By now, my other brother, Makis, had joined us in Kapoeta. We were staying at the airport, from where the antiaircraft bomber was deployed. At the airport, we became the main targets because the Antonovs wanted to destroy the antiaircraft bomber.

An Antonov came over that day at around 2:00 p.m. There was not a single cloud in the sky. I ran into an open trench with a group of people, including my half-brother, Makis (now working in the South Sudanese embassy in Zimbabwe), Muothich Jalla (currently in Rumbek), and Kadiji, the Ethiopian woman who left with us from Ethiopia (now in Connecticut, USA). The plane traveling from north to south dropped three bombs, which fell inside the town center.

Because of the presence of the UN in Pakhok, the Red Army forces were disarmed and allowed to move with the refugees to Narus. Out of the eleven task forces of the Red Army from Dimma, only two task forces came to Narus. The two disarmed forces were under Lieutenant Gordon Maper Manyiel, who was still armed with his bodyguards. Under the direct orders from the commander in chief, Dr. Garang, these two task forces were told to stay in the refugee camp to mature physically and mentally before being sent back to fight.

On their way to Narus, Lieutenant Maper found me in Kapoeta. He asked me about Adut and her children. I told him that I had successfully taken them to her husband in Torit.

"Well done," he said. "Of course, now that they are with their father, their blood will not be in our hands even if something happens to them." The lieutenant did not even ask me where I lived. Instead, he just ordered, "Grab your bag and report to your task force immediately!"

So, I grabbed my bag and said goodbye to my brother, and left Kapoeta for Narus. In Narus, our two task forces were isolated from the camp; we lived on the camp's outskirts. I was delighted to be with my comrades again. After spending three weeks in Narus, Kapoeta was captured by the Khartoum government. As I mentioned earlier, the Red Army was the only hope of the SPLA at the border. But since the UN, who accused the SPLA of recruiting children, had arrived and the Red Army forces were disarmed, the Arab convoyed passed freely, capturing Kapoeta and Torit, respectively.

Simultaneously, the SPLA had split into two: Commander Riek Machar (now Vice President of the Republic of South Sudan), with his forces, which the Khartoum government was supporting, fought the main SPLA under Col. Garang's leadership. The division had weakened the SPLA, and the towns controlled by the SPLA were falling into either Dr. Riek's or Umar el Bashir's hands.

To rectify the situation, the SPLA wanted to recapture Kapoeta from the Arabs. But there were no fighters. Finally, High-Commander Dominic Dim Deng, who later became the minister of defense of

Then it circled again, coming from east to west. It was a heavy war bomber. On the front of its wings were four black propellers, and at the back were twin elliptical fins and rudders. It was right above me.

Suddenly, the noise stopped, and the plane lifted its nose and lowered its tail. Then I heard a jingling sound, like rolling a drum full of nails. At that, I buried my face down in the trench as three terrific bangs shook the ground. First, one bomb landed in the courtyard, destroying the house we had been in a few minutes ago. Next, a big piece of hot iron flew over us and landed on the trench barrier, still smoking. If we were not lying in the trench, the shrapnel could have killed or injured us badly.

After Antonov had left, I saw the casualties from the bombing. The house that we stayed in was destroyed, and only the frame was left standing. The dog that had been playing in the backyard was killed instantly. Birds that had nested in the tree in the courtyard had died, killed by the noise, not the bomb. Seven people were killed in the airport, with many others wounded, including a woman who had one breast cut off by shrapnel.

After two months in Kapoeta, refugees in Pachalla and Pakhok started arriving in Kapoeta on their way to Narus at the Kenyan border. After we had deserted our position in Pachalla, the refugees became vulnerable, so they had to be moved to the other border between Sudan and Kenya. The Red Cross had provided a few trucks to transport men, women, children, elderly, and disabled persons. Most people trekked on foot, though they were supported by the Red Cross staff members, who provided them with food and water throughout the journey.

By now, the UN had landed in Pakhok to help move the stranded refugees in Pachalla and Pakhok. Unfortunately, the Red Cross did not have enough trucks to transport the refugees. But it provided trucks and tankers that delivered food and water to the refugees trekking on foot from Pachalla in the Ethiopian border to Narus in the Kenyan border.

South Sudan and then died later in a plane crash, came to Nairus to mobilize fighters. Any soldier who had joined the refugees was wanted. Our two task forces were on the top of the menu.

Despite the presence of the UN, the forceful mobilization, the *kasha*, took place anyway. The troops came in the middle of the night and encircled the entire camp, going from house to house, taking all males, trained or not.

A group of heavily armed men, led by a captain named Kur, came to our residential area and started to round us all up. Since we had no guns, we had no choice other than to obey. Our commander, Lieutenant Maper, and his three bodyguards had their guns, but they lived one block away from us with their families. So, we were mobilized in our commander's absence.

But Lieutenant Maper had heard a commotion and came with his bodyguards to investigate. He found Captain Kur talking as we stood at attention.

"You must march in one line to where I will tell you. If you move out of the line or try to run, you will be shot. Understood?" Captain Kur barked.

Lieutenant Maper arrived, fuming. "Who are you? And what are you doing here in the middle of the night?"

The captain was caught off guard because he did not expect armed officers in that part of the camp. "I'm Captain Kur," he said. "And who are you?"

"First Lieutenant Maper, the commander of these two task forces."

"Well, Lieutenant," the captain stammered, "Commander Dim has ordered me to conduct *kasha* in Narus. Whether trained or not, every male must report to the headquarters where Commander Dim is."

"Well, Captain," Lieutenant Maper said. "You can't just come into our camp and order soldiers around without consulting their commander."

"These are orders from Commander Dim," the captain said.

"I don't care even if the orders come from the commander in chief himself. He has to consult me first before taking my soldiers away."

By now, we had encircled the captain with his five soldiers. They were nervous. It was dark, and they did not know what we had. So, the captain left with his soldiers saying: "You will regret this, Lieutenant, for disobeying the orders from the high commander."

The *kasha* was conducted in the entire camp, except our area. Those who were caught slept in the cold night at the compound until morning. In the morning, Lieutenant Maper blew a whistle, and we gathered. He marched us to the headquarters where Commander Dim was. He stood us at attention, saluted, and gave the report to Commander Dim Deng.

"I heard you had disobeyed my orders last night, Lieutenant," Commander Dim said.

"I didn't obey your orders, Commander Dim," Lieutenant Maper said. "All I said was that these are trained soldiers, and I'm their commander. These are the Red Army from Dimma. They were recently disarmed under orders from the Commander in Chief, Dr. Garang, who said they must wait for a couple of years to mature before they are armed. And if you decided to arm them, you must come to me first. So here they are now; no need for *kasha*."

After listening attentively, Commander Dim finally said, "You are right, Lieutenant. I did not know there were organized forces on special orders from the Commander in Chief. We are looking for soldiers who are hiding among the refugees. Therefore, take your forces and returned to the camp until further notice."

That was that. We returned to our camp.

On the same day, the UN decided to move refugees to Kenya because Khartoum forces had captured Kapoeta, and the refugees were at risk. So, our two task forces joined the refugees heading to Kenya. We walked all day and night, reaching the Kenyan border in the morning.

At Key-base, Lieutenant Maper finally surrendered his weapons, an AK47 and a pistol, which he gave to the SPLA soldiers at the border before crossing into Kenya. I had a final ritual to make before crossing the border. First, I had to get rid of my concealed pistol. But instead of surrendering it to the soldiers, I wrapped it up in a piece of cloth, wrapped the entire contents with a plastic bag, and then buried it under an *ashab* tree located several meters away from the man road. Next, I carved my initials "WM" on the tree bark where I had buried the weapon. Finally, I crossed the border to Lokichogio, Kenya.

I still remember the ashab tree, standing on the bank of a dry stream. No matter how long it takes, I will visit that area to look for that pistol one day.

The author escorted the young family (now grown-up) to safety: Adut Machar (center), Majok Manyang (in uniform)—the three-year boy the author carried, and Mayom Manyang.

Comrade Gordon Maper Manyiel—the author's commander.

PART FOUR

Kenya

<hr>

"The moment we had crossed the border, we were known as 'refugees'—a brand that did not only degrade our status but limited our basic human needs. I was in a new world with strange laws and regulations, boundaries, stories, and histories. Governed by the UN and the humanitarian agencies, it was the place where people survived, not thrived."

Kakuma Refugee Camp

I n 1992, we crossed the Kenyan border to a small town called Lokichogio. From there, we were packed in trucks like sardines and headed to the Rift Valley Province. After driving for about ninety kilometers through the arid desert, the truck stopped at a little town with three iron sheet buildings surrounded by igloo–like twig houses with thorn enclosures. The houses were called *Manyattas*.

Our vehicle suddenly stopped on the crumbly ochre road where bored police officers glared down the hot road. The road leading to the interior of Kenya was blocked with spiked metal. We were not allowed to go through. The moment we had crossed the border, we were known as "refugees"—a brand that did not only degrade our status but limited our basic human needs. I was in a new world with strange laws and regulations, boundaries, stories, and histories. Governed by the UN and the humanitarian agencies, it was the place where people survived, not thrived.

From the checkpoint, we turned left onto a dirt road where we stopped at a heavily fortified compound, housing the operations of the United Nations Commissioner for Refugees (UNHCR), the World Food Programme (LWF), the International Community for Red Cross (ICRC), and many other aid agencies that facilitated our migration and would supply the camp. Each aid agency had tents with its logos.

Our truck slowed down, but my heart sped up. I glanced to the left and saw a signboard with white lettering on a simple blackboard with two metal frames hammered into the ground. WELCOME TO KAKUMA, the sign read.

Welcome? The place did not appear that welcoming. The word Kakuma means "nowhere," and indeed, the area lived up to its name. This name resonated with the arid desert; the land was naked, without even a single blade of green grass. It was just red and tan-colored soil with scattered anthills and shrubs. Rain was a foreign concept in Kakuma. A cloud of dust rose to the sky and rained down on us with the finest particles of dust, coating the land and its inhabitants. The place was known for its dry river full of sand—there was no water on the surface. The natives of this land, the Turkana people, had adapted and bathed with the dry sand. Because of its scarcity, water was so sacred that a woman only bathed when mourning her husband's death to wash away the death spirit. The land had nothing to offer. It looked as if God had been absentminded when he created this part of the world.

In addition to the unwelcoming land and climate, the Turkana local people did not seem impressed to see us in their land. The UN had paid a fortune, millions of dollars, to the Kenyan government to secure an area where we could be accommodated. But the money had gone into the pockets of corrupt politicians in Nairobi. Not a penny had gone to the local people, the Turkana, who their government had grossly neglected. Their territory had remained the way it was thousands of years ago, and the locals still wore clothing made from animal hides. The Turkana did not understand why their government, which had neglected them, was suddenly keen on helping foreign refugees. Additionally, the Turkana had feuds with the Toposa people of South Sudan, so they considered all South Sudanese as their enemy. So, the sign WELCOME TO KAKUMA was misleading because nothing welcomed us in that part of the world.

The convoy of trucks veered northeast amidst the spiraling red dust from the compound. We drove for about ten minutes. Finally, we came to demarcated pieces of land; each piece was about the size of a football field. One piece of land formed a group; several groups formed a zone. Each group had between one hundred and three hundred members, and between ten and fifteen groups formed a zone.

The demarcated pieces of land would be our residential areas for the next ten years.

I thought Kakuma would be like Dimma, Ethiopia, where we had AK47 automatic rifles and pens—for studying and soldiering at the same time. The President of Ethiopia, Comrade Mengistu, had given us the freedom to do what we wished. But President Moi of Kenya was not fond of the SPLA. So, we were not allowed to conduct military drills, sing revolutionary songs, or even call each other comrade. So instead of the Red Army, we were now called "unaccompanied minors." Later, the phrase was replaced with the more derogatory name, the "lost boys." And yes, we were minors and lost boys in all senses. We were little skinny boys living in a state of abject poverty and without parents or guardians.

Our commanders turned into teachers and caretakers. So instead of Lieutenant Maper, he was now *Ustaz* (Teacher) Maper. Taskforces became groups; companies and squads were villages and sub-groups, respectively. Company or squad leaders became head-boys. It was a mess I had never seen before.

Out of the 7000 boys in Dimma, only 700 (two task forces) arrived in Kakuma. The other Red Army forces from Pachalla were seventeen groups. Our two task forces, now known as Group One and Group Two, lived side by side. Each group had 350 boys, and each group was divided into seven sections called villages. Each village had thirty-five members. Kuot Mathuch was the head-boy of Group One, and my friend, Lhat Mabor, was the head-boy of Group Two. And I was the head-boy of Village Seven, Group Two, in Zone One. I reported to my friend Lhat, the head-boy, and Lhat reported to a grown-up teacher or caretaker.

The same trucks that brought us to Kakuma delivered building materials, such as poles, nails, and palm leaves called *makuti* used for roofing. The *makuti* roof was not durable, so we eventually used tins roofs. We built our houses, and four people shared one house. I shared a house with my friends, Lhat Mabor, James Dhuor Anok, and Daniel Thuch Achiek.

Registration was made, and everyone was given a ration card. The white card had digits from one to twenty-four. Every time you visited a distribution center, which was twice a month (the beginning and middle of the month), a hole was punched in the card so that at the end of the year, you had a total of twenty-four punches before being given a new card. If you lost your card, you would not have food rations until the next annual headcount; you had to share it with friends.

Each zone (nearly 10,000 people) had one distribution center. The Zone One distribution center was in an open field next to a hill. The center was a barbed wire complex with one exit and one entrance. The narrow exit and entrance were guarded by Kenyan policemen armed with guns and sticks. As a result, the place looked more like a concentration camp than a distribution center.

Because of the corrupt UN staff who stole and sold refugees' food, food rations often ran out, leaving others without food. Because of this, everyone wanted to be the first in line to receive their allocation before the food ran out. So, the strongest trampled the weakest to enter the distribution center first. This allowed the police to swat people like donkeys. It was a routine humiliation.

The night before food distribution, some people slept in the lineup at the gate. The food trucks came with World Food Programme staff in the morning, escorted by a police squad or two. People swamped the gate, pushing and shoving, each person gripping both an empty sack and the white ration card with its days and distributions marked out like a calendar. People were elbowing, kicking, and shouting, their voices echoing like a swarm of bees. Finally, thousands of people stampeded through a narrow-barbed gate under the baking sun of Kakuma.

When you entered the gate, you presented your ration to a UN staff member that checked the card for date and validity. A police officer stood there, ready to swat anyone accused of having a fraudulent card. After your card was verified, you entered the vast warehouse where a man coated with white stuff from head to toe scooped up two *bakulis* (bowls) of maize or sorghum flour and dumped them in your sack. Next, you proceeded to another woman to get two cups of beans. At the third, a woman with oily hands and feet dipped a mug in a barrel and poured oil into your container. The next corridor yielded a spoonful of salt and occasional sugar. But you were not done yet.

From the barbed warehouse, you emerged into a compound where you grabbed a bundle of firewood or a heap of charcoal. Before you exited, you surrendered your ration card to another UN staff to punch the next hole on the card, indicating it had been used that month. Occasionally, staff would be distracted, and you would sneak out with your card unpunched. Finally, you hit the jackpot, for you would make a U-turn and kick and elbow your way back into the line for a second ration run. But the chance of leaving with the unpunched card was exactly like winning a lottery; the chance was extremely slim.

Finally, you exited into the blinding midday sun with your two-week rations: four kilos of maize, one kilo of beans, half a liter of oil, a cup of salt, and a bundle of wood. Everyone got the same amount of food, be they young, old, or infant. This ration had to last for fifteen days until the next distribution cycle.

To last longer, five or more people pooled their rations together. Even so, no one ate twice a day in Kakuma. If you did, your ration would finish in one week, leaving you hungry for another week before the subsequent distribution.

Water shortage was another major problem. A pump was dug hundreds of meters deep in the ground, where a generator was used to pump water. A network of pipes ran throughout the camp, with two or more groups sharing a tap or two. The generator ran three times a day. But in most cases, there was no fuel to run the generator. Water ran three times a day, from 6 a.m. to 8 a.m., noon to 2 p.m., and finally, from 6 p.m. to 8 pm. The water was used mainly for cooking and drinking. Forget about bathing or doing laundry; these were luxuries we rarely enjoyed. Because when you were a refugee, someone dictated when you could drink, cook, bathe, or do laundry.

When we, the refugees, complained that the food and water were not enough, we were urged to be patient. Patience for what or for how long was never explained. As the Dinka say, "A beggar's pot is always dry." When you survived on the UN's handouts, you had to be patient.

About sixty community groups were men, women, and children, and nineteen groups were unaccompanied minors, the Red Army. Unlike the minor groups who were mixed, the community groups were segregated in tribal lanes. Each tribe, such as Dinka, Nuer, Lotuko, etc., had separate groups and zones. Each tribe was further divided into sections and sub-sections; each had different groups. The tribal conflict became prevalent, and insecurities peaked in the camp. The Kenyan police were quick to come and swat people at distribution centers, but they never showed up when refugees were killing each other mercilessly.

Kakuma initially held about twenty thousand South Sudanese refugees fleeing the civil war. But the camp eventually multiplied as more waves of Sudanese, Congolese, Ethiopians, Ugandans, Somalis, Rwandans, Burundians, and Liberians sought asylum. As time went by, the refugees had children, and more asylum seekers continued to arrive. So Kakuma turned into a big cosmopolitan city of tin-roofed houses and muddy walls. Since we first founded it in 1992, Kakuma is now one of the biggest refugee camps in the world.

The only good thing in Kakuma was that, unlike Ethiopia, where we, the Red Armies, were segregated, we were finally allowed to mingle freely with the rest of the community (women, children, and adults). Both minors and community groups lived side by side. So, boys who had relatives had the option of leaving minor groups and reintegrating into their respective community groups.

But by then, we were already different species. We were more comfortable with each other and could not function appropriately in a community setting. Moreover, the years we had spent in isolation had altered our behavior. The adults found our behavior to be odd. The boys who grew up under parental control were cute and engaging. Those who grew up with the constant brush of near-death experiences were strange and often seemed sullen or irritated.

An elder once said, "These children (referring to us) are getting more stupid. So, integrate them back into the society to learn decent manners and the right way of doing things."

The elder was right. We lacked social skills and decent manners. Children learn facts of life (through observation) from parents, relatives, and adults. But *Jesh el Amer,* who had trekked to Ethiopia during the liberation struggle, had left their parents and communities. When we were in Ethiopia, we were segregated and not allowed to mingle with adults to maximize our indoctrination. Remember, we were aged between seven and seventeen, which is critical when children need adults the most. But we were not even allowed to visit residential areas where adults lived. Even boys who had relatives in the residential areas had to seek written permissions (which were not issued) to visit for an hour or two. We had no adults, no radios, televisions, computers, phones, and social media. Nothing! We were completely cut off from the outside world. That was why they eventually nicknamed us the Lost Boys of Sudan.

Without adequate social skills and no adults to learn from, we had depended on each other for survival. We made decisions, wrong or right, collectively. We all learned the facts of life through trial and error, often the latter. The isolation and vulnerability had bonded us together. Like a shoal of fish or a herd of wildebeests, we pooled together for survival. We dodged bullets and bombs together, leaped over landmines together, crossed crocodile-infested rivers together, and endured hunger and thirst together.

It was in Kakuma that I finally reconnected with my older brother, Manyang. He was living in Group Eighteen with Aunt Diing Manyol, currently in Perth, Australia. Group Eighteen belonged to the Agaar tribe, my people. Manyang and Aunt Diing wanted me to go and live with them to provide guidance and protection.

At first, it seemed like a good idea to go and live with my brother, aunt, and the entire Agaar tribe. Living in the community meant I would learn all the facts of life from the elders. And most importantly, I would eat good food prepared by women. I had not eaten hot meals prepared by women since I left my mother over ten years ago. So, I packed my belongings and moved to Group Eighteen to live with my brother and aunt.

But it did not take long before I realized I did not belong to that society. I could not function in our normal society with women, children, and adults—a place where I had to watch what to say or do. I missed my comrades. Subsequently, I felt utterly lost and isolated. Do not get me wrong; I was not dumb or anything. Back in our group, I was a leader, a head boy. At the camp level, I was one of the volleyball superstars. I also coached junior teams of boys and girls. And in school, I was also a straight-A student who rarely missed the top position in the class. So, I was a very bright young man. But I could not function in a place where adults, women, and children were. I did not make a solid emotional connection with the people, and I had a gaping hole where proper security was. In less than a week, I packed up my belongings and moved back to the minor group to be with my comrades.

School

I knew I had to find a way to settle in this world of refugees. I was once a naked herd boy, but I had adjusted and become a soldier. Now that I was an unaccompanied minor or a lost boy, I had to find other ways to find myself. To do that, I had to go to school, which was the only thing available to do at the camp.

I first began my schooling in Pachong Primary School in Rumbek, Sudan, where I completed my third grade before the war broke out. In Pachong, classes were taught in Arabic. I began my English classes in Dimma, Ethiopia. But again, after I completed my third grade in Dimma, war broke out, and we moved to Kenya.

In school, I was motivated by the incentives I got when I work hard. For example, in Sudan, pupils who topped their classes received gifts. This system began when the British first introduced modern schooling to Dinka during the colonization. Because Dinka parents did not want to send their children to school, the British used to reward students who worked hard with incentives such as cows, goats, or sheep to motivate the students to stay in school and work hard and, at the same time, allow the parents to keep their children in school and encourage others to send their children to school. Since then, it became a habit that pupils who topped their classes from number one to ten received gifts and standing ovations in every class.

I liked to receive gifts and standing ovations; these were the only motivators for working hard in schools. I was a very shy boy, so the only way I grabbed students' and teachers' attention was to be smart. In other words, what I lacked in verbal communication, I made up for in writing. In Pachong, for example, I topped all my classes. I did the same thing in Dimma. In my first school year in Dimma, I topped the class in three consecutive terms, and I was given a box of soap containing thirty-five bars. I sold the box for thirty-five birrs; that was a lot of money. I bought my first pair of shoes, Adidas, and some new clothes with that money. Also, in Kakuma, I topped most of my classes. But I met tough young fellows, such as Kuir Garang (now a famous author of five books in Winnipeg, Canada), who managed to wrestle the top position from me several times.

The remarkable thing in Kakuma was that a primary school was built next to every minor group, making a total of twenty primary schools in the camp. The schools were named after major cities and historical sites in Sudan. For example, Juba Primary School, Wau Primary School, and Torit Primary School were named after major South Sudan cities. Coincidently, the school built next to Group Two (my group) was named Bhar Naam Primary School after the Naam River, where I used to fish. The same river prevented me from crossing when I first attempted to join the rebellion in 1985. It was the work of divinity to name that school after the major river in the Agaarland. The named Bhar Naam was the only thing that reminded me of home.

Shortly after we arrived in Kakuma, assessment tests were conducted to determine our school levels. I landed in grade three, the third-highest level in the entire camp. The highest was grade six. The schooling I had done in Dimma, Ethiopia, did not let me down at all: I had a good foundation. I learned that digging a pencil on paper is like digging with a hoe in the field; you always yield something. Out of nearly 17,000 pupils, there was only one grade three, one grade four, one grade five, and one grade six. The rest were grades one and two. Those who were in grade seven upward qualified to be teachers.

In the first year in Kakuma, there were no classrooms. No problem. Along the dry riverbed was a park called Lazy Man Park that had good shadowy trees. We sat under those trees and used cardboard and charcoal as pencils and books. Our caretakers and all other adults who knew how to read and write became our teachers.

We were desperate to read, but there were no books. Books were like gold and diamonds. We became desperate to the point that when you saw a piece of paper flying in the wind, you would chase that paper down just to read it. If it were blank paper, it was even better, for you would use it to take notes.

One day I visited a teacher's house. When I used the toilet (restroom) in the teacher's house, I found discarded papers and newspapers in the bathroom being used as toilet paper. As I scanned through the pile, I noticed some of the documents had perfect, readable notes—some printed and others handwritten. "Oh my God," I thought. "Why waste such good notes?"

You will not believe what I did next. I went through the pile, selected the clean and readable papers, stuffed them into my pockets, and left. I had good reads that day. And every time I visited that teacher's house, I was always tempted to visit the toilet to look for notes.

We had no electricity in the camp, so reading at night was impossible. A very few boys with wealthy parents or relatives in the camp owned lamps. I always wished I had a lamp to study every night. But another boy showed me how to make a light. All you needed was cooking oil, steel plates, and charcoal. You dipped two or three charcoal pieces in the oil and then placed them on the plate and lit it. It burned just like a candle. You continued adding oil, making sure not to smother the fire or let the charcoal burn to ashes. I stopped eating my cooking oil and used it for fuel, especially during the examination period when reading was needed.

In Zone One, there was no grade three, so I had to travel across the camp to Zone Two, about half an hour's walk each way, to go to Rajah Primary school every day.

My first teacher was Garang Thiep (currently in Manitoba, Canada). Ustaz Garang was not just a teacher; he was the deputy headmaster and eventually became the headmaster of Rajah Primary School. He taught many subjects, including math, science, and geography. Ustaz Garang was very authoritative. His no-nonsense approach to teaching was suitable for strong-headed former child soldiers like me. When you were in Garang's class, you would be quiet and attentive whether you liked it or not. I stayed away from crossing him. A good soldier always knew when he did not have enough ammunition to win the war.

We followed the Kenyan curriculum. Primary school was grade one to eight, which they called standard one to eight. And secondary school was grade nine to twelve, which was called form one to form four. After completing grade twelve, known as form four, that was the end of your education. There were no colleges or universities to attend. The UN could not afford to send students to Kenyan colleges and universities. There were no jobs available for form four graduates either because refugees could not work under Kenyan law; jobs belonged to Kenyans only. So, the only job available in the camp was teaching in primary school. But these positions were occupied by Kenyans, who had more qualifications and higher education.

The subjects taught in school included English, math, Kiswahili, science, home science, GHC (geography, history, and civic), CRE (Christian Religious Education), and art craft and music.

My favorite subject was math. I usually got high marks in math exams. I loved multiplication, addition, subtraction, and division. I had crammed my multiplication tables since I was in Pachong Primary School, which gave me an advantage over other students. My job as a logistics officer in Dimma, where I constantly counted and distributed bullets and sacks of food to task forces, companies, squads, and platoons, was an added advantage. I easily passed my classes, and I topped every class.

As I advanced to grade six, math started to get more complicated. First, we learned fractions and equations. Then it got even more complex when we learned integers. Marial Mamal (currently in Rumbek) introduced integers that did not make any sense. The teacher drew a line on the blackboard and scaled it from zero to ten to the right and zero to -10 to the left.

"When we add, we go to the right; when we subtract, we go to the left," the teacher said. "Let us say -4 is our starting point. If you add six," he moved his finger six scales to the right, "you get two. And if you subtract six," moving his fingers to the left, "you get -10. Therefore," he concluded, "minus four plus six equal two. And minus four minus six equals minus ten."

I understood the concept, but I did not know where it applied in the real world.

Each class became an adventure in learning something new; some lessons made sense, others did not. In geometry, for example, the area made a lot of sense. I farmed plots of land back home, so I knew all the shapes (square, rectangle, circle, or triangle); I just had to learn their formulas.

"Every farmer must know the size, shape of his farm, and the number of seeds needed," the teacher said. "An area for a rectangle is calculated by multiplying the length times the width. A square has four equal sides, but it's still calculated as the length times the width."

Another mathematical shape that I enjoyed learning about was the circle. "To calculate the circumference of a circle," the teacher said, "multiply the diameter of the circle with pi. Or you can also find the area for a circle by multiplying pi times radius square."

Even though the formulas did not make sense, the circle made much sense because of its cultural significance. Circular shapes symbolized unity and communalism among the Jieng people. I thoroughly explained this in my first book, The Proud People:

Traditional Agaar builders construct roundhouses, reflecting what they see in the surrounding nature, such as the earth, the sun, and the moon, which are circular or oval. Most importantly, there seems to be something inclusive about the round shape. Agaar dancers form a circle to clap, sing, and dance; spectators form another circle around the dancers to watch. During prayers and invocation, people do not only create a circle around the holy ground or sacrificial pegs but walk in a circle clockwise or counterclockwise as they chant prayers. People sit around the plate or fire to eat or warm up. In court, at meetings, and all other social gatherings, people sit in a similar round pattern. It is not, therefore, an accident that houses are also built in this manner. Circular shapes symbolize unity or communalism. Try to sit around a plate of food in a rectangle, triangle, or square; there will be people too far away from the plate. Stand in rows or lines in a social gathering, and others will be on the far side of the line. This generates advantages and disadvantages, haves and have-nots. Circular is the norm.[2]

Sports II

In addition to school, another good thing about Kakuma was the sports. My love for sports began in Dimma in 1989. After completing our guerrilla warfare training and waiting to be sent to the front line, there was nothing else to do other than play sports. The SPLA seemed to believe that sports prepared soldiers for combat by increasing fitness, channeling aggression, focusing the mind, and strengthening the ties between troops, instilling discipline and readiness to serve a common objective. So, in training centers, refugee camps, and liberated towns and cities, sports activities were encouraged by the movement's leadership.

2   Maker, W., *The Proud People*, Perth: Africa World Books, 2020, p. 175 -176

But I joined sports in Dimma for one reason: to gain fame and have the opportunity of socializing with girls. Since then, I had been passionately involved in sports such as volleyball and football (soccer). And whenever I went to a new location or country, the first thing I did was join a sports club and make new friends and contacts.

Shortly after we arrived in Kakuma, the UN distributed sports equipment like balls, nets, and jerseys. A tournament was conducted. There were four zones, and each zone had between ten and fifteen groups. Each group selected their teams (soccer and volleyball) to play against other groups. The tournament's purpose was to select the best players representing each group, zone, and camp level.

I played both football and volleyball. I did not qualify for soccer because of many good goalkeepers, including Anthony Makuach and my friend, Kuot Mathuch. But I qualified to be in Kakuma Central Volleyball Team, later named Holy Cross Parish Team.

In sport, you discover what suits you. Because I involved myself in different sporting activities, I found out what I enjoyed and what I was good at. Even though I was only 5'9 tall, short for the South Sudanese standard, I discovered that I could jump extraordinarily high and blocked even seven-foot-tall opponents. Traditionally, our dance is called *Dhëëŋ Nhial* (Sky Dance), which mainly consists of high jumps with hands curved in the air, a skill taught at an incredibly young age. I became particularly good at the game of volleyball, making me one of the stars in Kakuma. We represented the Sudanese in Kakuma, and we played against Kenyans, Rwandans, Congolese, Ethiopian, Somalis, and Burundians. We used to travel throughout Kenya, competing in sports.

Because I enjoyed the game very much, it did not take time to grasp everything about volleyball—all the rules, terms, and strategies. Subsequently, I became a Zone One coach of boys' and girls' teams while playing on the central team. Thus, I knew the game inside out.

What I liked the most about the game of volleyball was that it was not a stagnant sport. With each team of six players (three in the front row and three in the back row), the objective was to pass the ball over the net to land in the opponent's court. In doing so, the rule was each team could not touch the ball more than three times before it was passed over the net. And each player could not touch the ball twice unless one was the block touch.

Throughout the game, there were different moves, and each one served a specific purpose. These moves included serving, passing, setting, hitting, blocking, and digging. The six volleyball court positions were setter, middle blocker, outside hitter, opposite hitter, libero, and serving specialist. But the six players rotated around the court as the game was played, yet they could still play any position, provided they did it at the appropriate time.

Looking back, I could think of several wide-ranging benefits that sport brought to my life. Beyond the physical benefits of improved strength, coordination, flexibility, and overall health, sports helped me to understand healthy lifestyles at that vulnerable age. The sport was my therapy, literally.

The sports activities had kept me grounded, completely distracting me from the hardships I faced in Kakuma. Remember, I was sixteen years old when I came to Kakuma, the most challenging phase of my life, where I dealt with internal and external forces, including hormonal changes. Peer pressure was another. The absence of parents or guardians was the next, not to mention the previous combat experience, now fueled by abject poverty. These are always a recipe for depression and substance abuse among young people. But the sports activities had kept me grounded and focused on the positive side of life. I was preoccupied, and my schedules did not allow me to be vulnerable to thoughts of my abject poverty or trapped in my previous war experience.

Volleyball was therapeutic. It replaced the bad memories of the war that had accumulated in my mind, replacing them with the values of teamwork, perseverance, and commitment. As a result, my self-esteem and confidence were boosted. In addition, exercise and training repeatedly at skills with coaches reinforced a growth mindset within me. I started to believe that I could be good at something or achieve some goal when I practiced a lot. That mindset became a helpful tool throughout my entire life.

And then there was learning through failure, which is one of the long-term benefits of sports. The experience of coming to terms with defeat can build the resilience and self-awareness necessary to manage all challenges that would come my way.

While some youths were smoking, drinking, fighting, getting girls pregnant, and doing anything and everything to stop thinking about the hell that still haunted them, and others were procrastinating or feeling sorry for themselves, my conversation involved sports and our team's abilities. The entire time I was in Kakuma, I played and coached—having fun and enjoying keeping that positive momentum going.

Regular exercise promoted my mental and personal fitness. Through training, I learned my weaknesses and strengths, how to solve problems and overcome the crisis. Most importantly, the training taught me self-motivation, self-confidence, and self-management.

The leadership role I had in the group also contributed to my personal development. Being one of the head-boys, I always wanted to lead by example. As a result, boys who were younger than me looked up to me for guidance and protection. As a result, the small boys I led started to call me Uncle. In Dinka culture, any grownup is referred to as uncle or aunt by a junior if he or she is your father or mother's age-mate. The problem was that I was only sixteen years old, and those who were calling me uncle were twelve- and thirteen-year-old boys. I had grown up fast to reach that status, and the boys who craved parental guidance had no one else to turn to, no actual grown-up, saw only me.

Fallen Comrades

In Kakuma, it took a great deal of inner work and healing on the level of both our bodies and our psyches to recover our true self—the self which had been hidden and buried beneath many-core wounds caused by the traumatic experience of war.

As mentioned earlier, I was sixteen years old when we came to Kakuma in 1992. My friends and comrades were aged between ten and twenty. But we were competent beyond our generation because the lack of adequate parental support or connection had emotionally deprived us, and we had left childhood behind eagerly. In other words, we grew up quickly emotionally and became self-sufficient.

After several years in Kakuma, however, our lives started to change. For some of us, including myself, who had found sanctuary in school and sports activities, Kakuma became more enjoyable than Dimma. We traveled across Kenya, playing sports. Every time we traveled, we ate good food and drank sodas. In my job as a mini team coach, the incentives I received were jerseys and shoes. As a result, my life was good in Kakuma and way better than when I was in Dimma. Subsequently, the early traumatic experiences of my life began to fade.

Unfortunately, for some of my comrades, they saw nothing but the abject poverty we lived in. They saw Kakuma as a place of sickness, disease, violence, and everything else you could imagine. There was no adequate food or water, no education, no jobs, and no future. On top of that, they were still haunted by their past life experiences. Adolescence had just kicked in, and they had no parents or guardians to help them cope. Subsequently, the early war traumas exacerbated, shaping their identities, belief systems, and life-course trajectories.

Some of these comrades deployed self-defense mechanisms of not accepting reality because it was easy, much easier to deny than facing reality head-on. As a result, they pretended nothing was happening to them. These comrades rejected the idea that they had participated in killing when they were young, that they had not witnessed friends killed before their eyes, and that they were not living in abject poverty in Kakuma. In the end, they ended up with substance abuse problems, depression, or mental disorders.

To these comrades, anguish felt surreal. They felt like they were not in the right world. Living in Kakuma felt like they had been torn out of the world and dropped into another world where everything looked and felt completely alien. These comrades conveyed the anguish through their eyes. I saw in them the depth of character that came with suffering. They did not need to use words to describe what they were going through. I saw and felt it through their characters and action.

One of these comrades who felt the pressure of Kakuma was my friend Lhat Mabor. Lhat was nineteen years old when he came to Kakuma. Remember, Lhat was my mentor. I looked up to him because he was older and senior in the ranks. Lhat Mabor had strong leadership qualities. He was brilliant and cunning—traits that earned him five chevrons, the Red Army's maximum rank. He was our head-boy in Group Two.

Back in Ethiopia, I had learned a lot from him. Even though he was not successful in finding me a date, Lhat taught me many other things. For example, he taught me *tamir-nyigat*—an effective way of loading a gun. With the palm of your hand facing downward, you extended your index finger and curled the tip of the finger on the charging handle and, at the same time, pressed down the safety bar with your thumb. Then, with one swift move (pull and push), you unlocked and loaded the gun simultaneously. It was impressive, especially to boys who solely depended on weapons for survival.

Lhat Mabor was also adventurous and a risk-taker. In Pachalla, he exploded a grenade in the middle of the day, demonstrating to untrained boys how expert he was in the subject. When soldiers came to arrest him, Lhat said the grenade's pin was broken, and he had to throw the grenade to save himself and the people around him. He was hailed as a hero. But despite his traits, Kakuma's situation had overwhelmed Lhat, and he decided to leave Kakuma for a better place.

You needed a few things to leave Kakuma. First, you needed hope. You hoped that life was much better somewhere. But where? There were two options: you could return to Sudan to fight—kill or get killed. Or you could go to another refugee camp. Another camp was Ifo Refugee Camp in Somalia. Unfortunately, Al-Shabaab Islamic fighters formed in the area, making that camp even more dangerous than Kakuma.

The second thing you needed to leave Kakuma was the courage to take a risk. Knowledge about other camps in Kakuma was shady and full of exaggerations and rumors, like any other information in the war. But, with the keen instincts of a guerrilla fighter who had spent over ten years staying alive in the wilderness, Lhat chose to die trying, hoping for a better place ahead.

The third thing you needed to leave Kakuma was *pesa* (money). It cost a fortune to travel anywhere in Kenya. You needed money for food and transport. But the main reason you needed money was for *kitu kidogo,* a "small amount" of money you paid to every Kenyan police you encountered to avoid being imprisoned and tortured.

Lhat had all the above, except the money. He wanted to go to Ifo Camp, and he suggested that I should go with him. But I was preoccupied with school and sports activities that year. First, I was in grade eight, sitting for my Kenya Certificate for Primary Education (KCPE) exams. Second, we had a big tournament in Nakuru, one of the most prominent Kenyan cities. I could not miss taking my KCPE exams or playing in the biggest upcoming tournament. That was how both school and sports kept me grounded. So, I told Lhat I could not go with him.

Lhat said he would go alone and that he needed my help. Unfortunately, we had no single identification. The only ID we had were ration cards, which did not have names on them. So Lhat wanted me to write him a departure order.

A departure order was a traveling document used by the SPLA when we were in the bush. To travel from one place to another, you needed a departure order from your superior. The absence of this official document implied you were deserting or traveling illegally, and you would be arrested. Because I was the adjutant back then in Dimma, I issued departure orders to those who traveled. So, Lhat wanted me to write him the same departure order for his trip to Ifo Refugee Camp, located between Kenya and Somalia. Luckily, I still had a copy of a typed departure order which I had carried with me from Dimma, Ethiopia. The original document read:

To Whom It May Concern:
Please allow the bearer of this note, Comrade (full name) —— to pass through your garrison to (destination) ——. Comrade (first and last names) —— is a member of the Red Army (task force) —— (company) —— (Squad) —— (Platoon) ——. Please assist him/her in any way possible.

Your cooperation is highly appreciated.
(Signature) —— (date) ——.

There were no typing machines or computers in Kakuma, so I wrote the departure order. The forged document read:

Please allow the bearer of this note, Mr. Henry Lhat Mabor, to pass through your towns to his destination—Lodwar. Mr. Lhat Mabor is a South Sudanese refugee living in Kakuma Refugee Camp, Group Two, Zone One—Minor. Please assist Mr. Henry Lhat Mabor in any way possible.
Your cooperation is highly appreciated.

Looking back, this was a forgery and a punishable crime. But honestly, I did not know I was committing a crime. As guerrilla fighters, we were trained to believe that anything we did and got away with was acceptable. So, we called the forgery a "camouflage"—a term used in everything that was culturally unacceptable, including cheating.

After I forged the document, Lhat tested it by going to Lodwar, a bigger town located sixty kilometers away, to see if the document would work. It was a success. The ill-trained and underpaid police officers allowed Lhat to travel to Lodwar and back using the departure order, only paying a few shillings as *kitu kidogo* to support the document.

Now that the departure order had worked, Lhat Mabor was ready to go to Ifo. We now had to generate money for his trip. He needed a lot of money because he would travel across Kenya, passing through

Nairobi to Somalia. We sold some of our rations, but the money was not enough. The last resort we had was to sell our tape recorder. The problem was that Lhat Mabor, James Manyiel Mayen, Majok Kadis, and I had jointly purchased and owned the tape recorder. It cost us a fortune to buy the electronic—the most expensive and precious possession we had ever owned. Remember, it was because of a tape recorder that Akoi Atem and Arok Mabior killed themselves in Pakhok. That was how valuable electronic devices were to us. Now Lhat wanted to take our most valuable possession.

Because Lhat was my best friend and mentor, I supported him by selling the tape recorder to generate money for his trip. But I doubted whether Manyiel and Majok would allow Lhat to take the electronic device. Lhat said he knew what to do with Manyiel and Majok. By this, I knew Lhat intended to take the tape recorder without their knowledge or approval. It was a significant risk because James Manyiel Mayen (currently in Adelaide, Australia) and Majok (in the USA) were not the kinds of guys you wanted to mess with. James Manyiel Meen was already a warrior with the Agaar scarification marks on his head, running from ear to ear. He is from the Pakam section of Agaar. The Pakam are known for their no-nonsense approach, and they can be prone to violence. Manyiel possesses these traits.

Majok Majok (famously known as Kadis) was also a warrior with the Tonj scarification marks, running from his forehead to the back of his head. Back then, in Ethiopia, Majok Kadis was the second in command of the entire Red Army. When Akoi Atem committed suicide, Majok Kadis became the overall commander. He was a powerful young fellow.

Lhat Mabor, on the other hand, had no tribal marks, but he was a typical Rumbek boy who, in addition to being cunning, had mastered the art of boxing. I was the smallest and weakest in the group. And in Kakuma, where muscles ruled, I was the weak link in this group. Poor me! I have no idea how I ended up in this group of death in the first place. Now Lhat wanted to run away with the recorder, leaving me to answer to Manyiel and Majok. I was in a dilemma.

Lhat and I shared the same room; Manyiel and Majok lived in separate rooms, which meant they would want to know how Lhat got away with the tape recorder without my knowledge. They could beat the crap out of me. I was sure of that. On the other hand, Lhat was my best friend, and I did not want to betray him. I was in unimaginable limbo.

At dawn, Lhat grabbed the tape recorder and waved me goodbye. "Remember, when Manyiel and Majok ask you where I was going, tell them you don't know," Lhat warned as he disappeared into the darkness.

In the morning, Majok and Manyiel appeared. Lhat and the tape recorder were missing.

"Mayom, where is the tape recorder? Where is Lhat?" they bombarded me with questions.

"I don't know," I said, pretending to be as innocent as possible. I knew Lhat had taken the tape recorder, and he was going to Ifo. I had allowed him to take the tape recorder. I knew everything, but I denied everything. I was nothing but a master of deception.

Manyiel and Majok knew right away that Lhat would sell the tape recorder, so they raced to Kakuma town, looking for him. At that time, Kakuma only had three shops and manyatta houses. So, they turned the little town upside down. Lhat was nowhere to be found.

Knowing Manyiel's and Majok's mindsets, Lhat knew they would look for him, so he went to wait for transport a few kilometers away from Kakuma town.

However, knowing Lhat's perspective, Manyiel and Majok knew Lhat would be waiting far away from the town, so they followed the main road to Lowdar. These were the smart people I lived with. Poor me!

Miraculously, they found Lhat sitting under a bridge. Unfortunately, the driver who was supposed to take Lhat had been delayed, and he was caught red-handed. It was two against one in the arid desert, so Lhat had no option other than to surrender the tape recorder. His trip to Ifo had ended abruptly.

But Lhat Mabor was a tenacious fellow who never ran out of options. Unable to go to Ifo, he used the little money he had to return to Sudan. He intended to go and do some business to generate money for his trip to Ifo. His destination was Agoro—a market where guns and alcohol were sold and bought, which was a very lucrative and dangerous business at the same time. The Agoro market attracted a lot of young men. You bought guns from soldiers or alcohol from local people and carried the goods hundreds of miles to Agoro to sell them. Selling guns was a dangerous business because your customer could shoot you and take all the goods. Desperation had forced many young men into this risky business.

One of my comrades (name withheld), now a general in the South Sudan Army, left Kakuma for Agoro. He was in love with a girl and was generating money to marry the girl. But eventually, the girl rejected him. The comrade composed the following song:

Girl, do not talk to me with your back turned.
Look at me.
Isn't it because of you that I walk until my feet wear out?
I walk to Agoro,
While I am carrying KK on my head until I become bald.

A couple of months later, Lhat returned from Agoro, Sudan, as a wealthy man. He even bought me brand-new Adidas shoes. After that, he spent a couple of days in Kakuma before heading to Ifo. Majok and Manyiel had already forgotten about their issue with Lhat, and they ended up being friends again. Majok Kadis also went to Ifo with Lhat.

After Majok and Lhat went to Ifo, Manyiel and I became roommates. Both of us ended up in a lawsuit because of Lhat Mabor. A guy who claimed to have lent money to Lhat took Manyiel and me to court, saying we should pay him because Lhat was our friend. That was how upside-down the law was in Kakuma. Our belongings were confiscated, and Manyiel and I found ourselves in front of Sultan Malongdit—a traditional judge. Sultan Malongdit, who had no teeth, only spoke Dinka, and he found it difficult even to pronounce Kenyan cities.

"If you don't tell the truth, "Judge Malongdit warned, waving his index finger, "I will take you to prison in *Nyiduar* (Lodwar) or *Nying-gur* (Kapenguria).""

But the case was thrown out when my coach, who was also my paternal uncle, *Ustaz* Madong, showed up in court to testify on my behalf. The judge told the plaintiff, named Atem Majak, to sue Lhat, not his friends.

After one year in Ifo, Lhat returned to Kakuma. Unfortunately, shortly after he arrived in Kakuma, Lhat ran into trouble with the law. I did not know whether the same lawsuit was still pending or a different one, but the deputy camp chairman, Mr. Cirilo Majok, the ex-commissioner of Rumbek East, sent people to arrest Lhat. Because of that lawsuit, Lhat left our group and went to stay in the UN protection camp in Kakuma, where those who had insecurities, such as women running away from abusive husbands, stayed. However, other people were not allowed to visit that camp, so I could not visit Lhat. And Lhat did not come to visit me because he feared arrest.

In 1999, Lhat took a plane from Kakuma to Khartoum. I never heard from Lhat Mabor again. He vanished in Khartoum. Some people said Lhat joined the Darfur rebels, and others said he went to Ethiopia. I never heard from Lhat Mabor again.

I knew my friend was not the kind of guy to stay in one place without reappearing. And he would not wait this long without getting in touch with me. So, I suspect something terrible happened to him.

The next comrade to leave Kakuma and mysteriously disappear was Anthony Makuach. Anthony Makuach's father was from Tonj, and his mother was from Rumbek. Anthony Makuach was born and grew up in Rumbek. He lived in Rumbek Two area, where he went to school and played soccer. He became an incredibly famous underage soccer team goalkeeper in Rumbek in the early 1980s.

In 1987, Anthony Makuach joined the SPLA, where he settled in Panyudo, Ethiopia. Anthony Makuach became an incredibly famous goalkeeper in Panyudo. He was a superstar. Everywhere he went, his fans swamped him.

I first met him during the tournament in Itang in 1991, where he dominated the event. Everyone talked about Anthony Makuach. Wearing a light-blue coverall with white edging, Makuach was the best goalkeeper I had ever seen. His goalkeeping abilities were exceptionally unique. He drew a crowd everywhere he went in Itang.

I was one of the boys attracted to him. I stood behind the net in all games where Anthony Makuach was goalkeeping. I was the goalkeeper from Dimma Mini Team, so I wanted to steal some goalkeeping moves from Anthony Makuach. We had no television or internet; we copied live from others. When I saw something once, I would copy it. I watched Anthony Makuach during the entire tournament and stole his moves, how he jumped and caught the ball, and so on. I returned to Dimma as a changed boy. I used the goalkeeping style I stole from Anthony, and I made a name for myself. I became an incredibly famous goalkeeper for Dimma's underage team.

In 1992, after taking Adut with her children to Torit and returning to Kapoeta to live with my brother, I joined the Kapoeta football team. Anthony Makuach arrived in Kapoeta after being evicted from Ethiopia and joined the team. Anthony Makuach became the goalkeeper for Kapoeta Soccer Team, and I became the goalkeeper for Mini Team respectively. This was where our friendship began.

Our coach, I forgot his name, was a second lieutenant from Shilluk. He was an anti-aircraft Sam-missile launcher. Antonovs bombed daily in Kapoeta, so the coach always came to coach us with the anti-aircraft, Sam. That way, if an Antonov came, he would leave coaching for a moment and shoot the Antonov. The coach was a multitasker.

It was in Kapoeta that I got to know Anthony Makuach personally. There was a match between Mini Team and the elderly team led by the Commandeer Achuil Manoldit, Commander Deng Aguang (their goalkeeper), Ramzi Mabor, and other big-bellied commanders. Naturally, the small boys defeated the elderly team.

After the match, Anthony Makuach came and hosted me on his shoulders, congratulating me for the win. He complimented me on my goalkeeping ability. Anthony Makuach did not know that I had stolen his moves. And I did not tell him either, for there was no need. I was beaming with the excitement of being carried by the superstar.

When we came to Kakuma, Anthony Makuach left his group in Zone Two and joined us in Zone One. He was about twenty years old. We welcomed him to our group. I mean, who would not want to be Anthony Makuach's friend? We ate together, played cards together, and played sports together. We were on a volleyball team together. And on top of that, he was the goalkeeper in the Sudanese soccer team. We traveled throughout the Rift Valley Province, competing against Kenyan teams.

A couple of years later, Kakuma grew as refugees from different countries, such as Ethiopia, Zaire, Rwanda, Burundi, Somalia, and Liberia, arrived. The refugees formed a team, and Anthony Makuach became the Kakuma United Central Team's goalkeeper.

Anthony Makuach and I had a nickname for one another. We called each other *Anyuath-makou* (night grazer). Thanks to our habit of sneaking out late in the evening to go to the water point where girls collected water, the name came about. We were chasing little girls. I thought I was the only one doing that; Anthony Makuach thought the same thing too. We never told each other about our nightly camouflage until we accidentally met one night at the same water point. We were surprised to see each other there.

"So, you are *Anyuath-makou* (the night grazer)?" Makuach said. "So are you!" I replied as we both laughed. From then on, we started calling each other *Anyuath-makou*. We never told our friends how the name came about.

Anthony Makuach had a dream. He wanted to be sponsored by one of the Kenyan schools through sports. First, he planned to play in the Kitale or Kapenguria team. Then, he hoped to transition to the Kenyan national team, Gor Mahia. Eventually, from Gor Mahia, he wanted to join one of the European clubs, such as Arsenal or Liverpool. That was his vision.

I never doubted Anthony Makuach for a moment. Nothing could prevent Anthony Makuach from joining any team, even in Europe, because he was the most excellent goalkeeper. Anyone who knew Anthony would say the same.

One day, Anthony Makuach approached me, beaming with excitement. A rich Kenyan lady had sponsored him. A week later, Anthony Makuach packed his belongings and said goodbye, heading to Kitale. That was 1998. I never heard from Anthony Makuach again until three years later when I heard he had died. No one knew exactly how he had died.

Another comrade I had a lot of memories with was David Chan Wieu. From the Awan section of Gogrial, David Chan had been a friend for an exceptionally long time. We first met in Dimma, Ethiopia, in 1988. I was in Taskforce One, and he was in Taskforce Two. We used to hang out every opportunity we got. We mostly went hunting or target shooting—the only activities done in the camp. David was very entertaining, and he liked to dance to disco music.

It was until 1992 that we became roommates. David, Lhat, and I shared the same tent in Narus. This was when the international community pressured the SPLA to abandon child soldier practices, so we were discharged and sent to Narus, along with all the refugees who fled from Ethiopia after President Mengistu of Ethiopia was overthrown.

David Chan was famously known as Raymond Manyoya. Some people thought this was his real name, but it was his nickname. Shortly after arriving in Narus in 1992, the UN distributed blankets. David Chan, who did not know how to read English, asked me to read what was written on the label of his brand-new blanket. I read out the words, "Raymond Manyoya." But it was difficult for Chan to say the tongue-twisting words. As he struggled with the pronunciation to no avail, I jokingly said, "Raymond Manyoya is going to be your nickname!"

Chan hated the idea, and he started chasing me down, trying to beat me up. But before he could catch me, Lhat Mabor, who was also listening, picked up the name and started running in a different direction, yelling, "Raymond Manyoya, Raymond Manyoya!" Chan left me and ran after Lhat.

Soon, the bored boys from our groups, who wanted an excuse to run, sprung up from whichever direction, calling, "Raymond Manyoya, Raymond Manyoya!" The game went on and on. Eventually, the exhausted David Chan Wieu could not do anything. The name stuck. Chan ultimately loved the nickname, especially when he became incredibly famous for it.

I did not even know the meaning of Raymond Manyoya until I went to Nairobi for a medical checkup before going to Canada in 1999. In Nairobi, I saw a signboard that said Raymond Manyoya, the exact word written on the label of David Chan's blanket. It was a blanket factory. I laughed to myself as I remembered my friend.

I had a lot of fun times with David Chan. One time, a fortune-teller took our precious 200 Kenyan shillings in Kakuma in 1998, but he did not solve our problem.

One of my friends, Chol Kon Chol (currently living in Boston, Massachusetts), lost his brand-new pair of soccer boots. Chol Kon (famously known as Ayellow), who was on the Central football team, was issued brand-new boots. But the shoes just vanished in the middle of the day in our house—presumably stolen.

After searching everywhere to no avail, Chol Kon said he had to go to a fortune teller to identify the thief, so he went to the renowned fortune-teller Deng Unguech from the Jurchol section lived in Zone Two. Chol Kon asked me to accompany him to Deng Unguech's house. I did not believe in fortune-telling, but I had to attend to my friend, anyway. I had heard a lot about Deng Unguech and his fortune-telling abilities, and I wanted to see the men. David Chan also joined us.

The only problem was that it cost one hundred Kenyan shillings ($1) to see Deng Unguech. That was a lot of money. Chol Kon and I were broke. Luckily, Chan offered to pay the fees. However, upon seeing us, the fortune teller would have nothing to do with us. Instead, he ordered us to leave his house immediately.

"You Red Army are trouble-makers. You like to cause trouble," he said. "Get out of my house now. I don't want to solve your problem."

I did not particularly appreciate how Deng talked to us, so I told Chol and Chan we should leave this rude man's house. But Chol was adamant. He wanted to get his boots back; otherwise, he would be kicked out of the team. So Chol pled with the fortune teller, offering to pay double if the fortune teller could say who stole the boots.

When the fortune-teller heard he could receive double pay, he accepted the offer and immediately ushered us into his little house. The fortune teller's room was unique. There was fine sandy soil on the floor; it was not plastered. Under the bed were several stones of different colors, shapes, and sizes. Farther in the dark corner were other unfamiliar items. I had never been to a fortune teller's house before, but Deng Unguech's room was a little scary, to be honest.

Deng Unguech told us to sit on the bed. Then, he sat on the floor, bringing out several small stones under the bed and placing them on the leveled ground. He mumbled some words in Jurchol language as he arranged the rocks, creating some patterns, some of which looked like animal footprints.

He did not ask our names or the purpose of our visit. I was not surprised, though. After all, he was a fortune-teller who could see the unseen. So, I assumed he already knew who we were and why we had come. It was a good sign so far, meaning he knew what he was doing. We could not wait to see the thief who had stolen our boots. Next time, he would not mess with us again. Stealing from us, thinking he would get away with it? Hell no!

Deng Unguech demanded the money, and Chol handed him our precious 200 shillings ($2), which he borrowed from David Chan. The amount could feed us for a week if we ate beans and bread, which cost ten shillings a plate. If we wanted to eat like kings, a dish of bread and meat broth cost fifteen shillings. But our meals disappeared in Deng Unguech's pocket.

"Tell me your problem," Deng Unguech finally said after securing the money.

"My boots have been stolen," Chol said.

"What color?"

"Black with white stripes."

Deng Unguech rearranged the stones and drew more patterns and lines with his fingers as he mumbled some phrases in Jurchol, mixed with Arabic. The marks looked like a monkey's footprint. I did not understand the Jurchol phrases, but the Arabic terms included "*Gata el tigil u shaal mathuran,*" loosely translating, "He cut the monkey and took the intestine." I had no clue what that was supposed to mean.

But this was where I fell off with Deng Unguech. Because, according to Dinka culture, blessing, fortune-telling, invocating, or praying that did not involve the noble cow or at least the mention of cows was not holy or divine. Yes, I once ate a monkey for survival, but I was disgusted when the fortuneteller used the monkey in his fortune-telling. I mean, he might want to "cut the monkey and take the intestine" when dealing with Jurchol people because monkeys are the most important delicacies in their culture. But he was dealing with the Dinka; the best he could do was to modify his conjuring phrases to "cut the cow and take the intestine" would have appealed to me more.

After chanting the phrases and arranging the stones for several minutes, Deng Unguech asked Chol Kon to provide the names of the people present when the boots were stolen. Chol Kon gave him the names one by one, starting with Chan, myself, and several other friends and roommates. People often played cards in our house, so there were many people present.

One by one, the magician entered the names in his things, the arranged stones, and patterns, each time chanting the exact phrases: "Chan cut a monkey and took the intestine," or "Mayom cut a monkey and took the intestine."

"There they are," Deng finally said, pointing in the middle of the patterns. "I can see the color of the boots in Chan's name."

I looked closely, hoping to see the colors of the boots too, but I only saw the stones, soil, and drawings. Looking at Chan, I saw his face had turned red with anger. Chol Kon looked stunned.

Deng Unguech, in a very twisted turn of events, said David Chan was the thief who stole the boots. Chan vehemently denied any wrongdoing. But Deng Unguech kept saying, "I know you took those boots, Chan. Just admit it." As Chan kept denying it, Deng Unguech threatened to kill Chan using his powers if he did not confess to the crime. But Chan said, "Go ahead and kill me if you can because I know I did not take the boots." Deng said he could not waste Chan's life just because of shoes.

I did not believe Deng Unguech's narrative either. I tried to explain that we had been friends for over ten years, and Chan had not done anything like that before, and he was not the thief. But Deng Unguech kept saying, "My things don't lie," pointing at the patterns on the soil. Deng Unguech said Chan took the boots and gave them to "another guy who lived on the other side of the street." That guy who lives across the street sold the shoes to an Ethiopian man. Deng could not tell us the guy's name, but he described him as a very tall and skinny guy who wore ragged clothing. Deng instructed us to go and find the name of the tall and skinny guy wearing tattered clothes living on the other side of the road. The session was over.

On the way home, Chan and Chol started to argue. However, Chol did not deny or confirm Deng Unguech's conclusion. Thus, Chan implied that maybe Chol believed what Deng Unguech had said. When we reached home, Chol Kon asked my opinion on the matter, and I told him frankly that Deng Unguech was a liar and Chan did not take the boots. I told Chol we would go back to the fortune teller tomorrow, and I would prove to him that the fortune teller was a liar.

The following morning, Chol and I returned to Deng Unguech's home. Chan did not want to do anything with us or Deng Unguech. I told Chol to keep quiet and let me do the talking. When he saw us, Deng Unguech ushered us into the house. "Did you find the name of the guy?" he asked.

I told Deng that we found the name of the person who fits the description: he was tall, thin, and wearing ragged clothes. His name was Mayom Maker. I also added that Mayom Maker was a well-known thief in our group. (We did not introduce ourselves to Deng yesterday, so he did not know I was Mayom Maker).

Deng quickly arranged the stones and drew patterns as he chanted: "Mayom Maker *gata tigil u shaal mathuran* . . . Oh, yes," Deng said, "I can see the colors of the boots in Mayom Maker's name. Chan gave the boots to Mayom, and Mayom was the one who sold them to an Ethiopian man."

Chol had heard enough already. Moreover, I was with Chol the entire day when the boots were stolen, so Chol knew I was not the thief. On top of that, the description the fortune-teller gave of someone tall, thin, and in ragged clothes did not fit me.

"Give us our money back, Deng," Chol Kon said. "You are a liar. We tricked you. This is Mayom Maker. He does not fit the description, and he was with me when the boots were stolen. If you were a real fortune-teller, you would have known these facts."

Knowing he was tricked, Deng became very agitated and asked us to leave his house immediately. "I told you yesterday that you, the Red Army, are trouble-makers, and I did not want to deal with you. But you insisted. I'm not returning any money."

There was nothing we could do. Several Jurchol youths played dominoes outside, and we were in the Jurchol community. So, demanding our money by force was short of suicide. We left quietly.

Knowing that I had proven that Deng Unguech was ineffective and deceitful somehow satisfied me. But the damage had been done: we did not find the boots, we lost our precious 200 shillings, and the friendship between David Chan and Chol Kon was ruined, despite my attempts to reconcile them.

David Chan Wieu was one of the boys who were accepted to resettle to the USA. But on September 11, 2001, when the USA was attacked, and the resettlement was halted, Chan had remained in Kakuma. Subsequently, he returned to his homeland, Awan, South Sudan, where he was killed. I did not confirm where or when he was killed.

The Red Armies did remarkably well during their time in the SPLA and the refugee camp. The indoctrination and prolonged isolation had bonded us together, and we depended on each other for survival. But our problems began when we were separated. A few of our comrades, such as Lhat Mabor and Anthony Makuach, who decided to leave the pack's safety, instantly became victims in Kakuma. But our serious downfall began when we migrated to the Western world, where we scattered in different countries, states, cities, and apartments. Then, for the first time in our lives, we started to live and make decisions individually. But the absence of social skills, separation anxiety, and culture shock, in addition to the previous war exposure and trauma, made it harder for some comrades to navigate this complicated world individually.

Many of my close friends and comrades had already succumbed to illness, addiction, and other circumstances. Others hung on for lives in Canada, the USA, and Australia. These comrades were homeless, lonely, and isolated. They needed help so badly, but no one to help them. Their friends and comrades were swamped, working two jobs, taking care of their families, and studying simultaneously. They were trying to keep their lives together and have no time to babysit their fallen comrades. What was next? The fallen comrades' relatives back home could not even afford to call to say hi, let alone provide emotional support. Ultimately the unfortunate comrades started to succumb one by one.

One of the comrades was Daniel Thuch Achiek, who passed away in Kansas City, Missouri. Daniel Thuch was like my brother, and I had known him for over thirty years. And our friendship started during our days in the liberation struggle. Daniel Thuch Achiek was born in Pap Anok village, located in Lake State—South Sudan. He joined the movement in 1989, where he was trained with the Intifada Division in Dimma, Ethiopia.

I first met Daniel Thuch in Dimma in 1990, during a soccer match. Our commander in chief, Dr. Garang, had visited the camp, and we had arranged a soccer match to welcome and entertain the chairman. My task force played against Thuch's task force. I was the goalkeeper. Daniel Thuch, with a group of friends supporting their team, stood behind the net, where I was goalkeeping, and they taunted me with insults and mockery, trying to distract me. It worked. My team lost the game—a humiliating defeat in front of the chairman. And for years, Daniel Thuch laughed at me, saying, "We beat you in front of the chairman." But there was nothing I could do to him because he was a very likable young fellow everyone wanted to befriend.

The second time I met Thuch was in 1992 in Pakhok, right after my last tour of duty from Pachalla. The starvation was at its peak at the time. One day, I went hunting with friends, including Lhat Mabor. After hunting all day without success, we came across other hunters, and Daniel Thuch Achiek was among them. They had killed an animal. Unfortunately, they had already roasted and consumed the meat and were about to leave when we arrived. But Daniel Thuch gave me a piece of roasted meat that he intended to take home for later consumption. It was the first time I learned that Daniel Thuch had a generous soul; otherwise, who would give away his last meal during the starvation?

When we came to Narus in 1992, our forces were reshuffled, and Daniel Thuch and I landed in the same squad. I was the squad leader. I did not forget the piece of meat he gave me in Pakhok, which had already sealed our friendship. We shared the same tent, and our beds were side by side. I admit I treated him favorably because he was my best friend. Therefore, Daniel Thuch enjoyed the luxury of having a friend as the boss.

From Narus, we moved to Kakuma, Kenya. Again, Daniel Thuch, Lhat Mabor, James Dhuor, and I shared the same room and ate off the same plate. And for the next ten years in Kakuma, we were there for each other's darkest and brightest moments. We were inseparable.

I was three or four years older than Daniel, so I took the role of big brother, ensuring other boys did not bully him. In Kakuma, where bullying was typical, Daniel Thuch was among the least bullied fellow in the camp because you could not mess with him when I was around.

In addition to protecting him from bullies, I also introduced him to girls for the first time, and I gave him tips on how to court girls. I vividly remember the time when Daniel Thuch told me about his first crush. I was probably sixteen, and he was twelve. I took the initiative and fetched the girl he admired and locked them in our tin-roofed shack-house. Later, I asked Daniel Thuch whether something had happened between them. Nothing had happened. Like any other first-timers, they were both nervous and did not know what to do. You could only imagine my disappointment at that moment. I risked getting beaten to get the girl, and you let her get away freely? What a waste!

I know this story sounds rudimentary and childish, but these are things that bind brothers together for life. I am sure all brothers, sisters, and friends have stupid stories like this, which they keep to themselves and bond them together in life.

Later, Daniel Thuch asked me not to tell his friends and age-mates about this incident for fear they would make fun of him being incompetent with girls. Because of that incident, I teased Daniel Thuch by calling him "Young D"—meaning he was too young to handle a woman. The "D" was just the initial of his first name, Daniel. For some reason, Daniel Thuch liked the name, and he started calling himself "Young D." He even printed his nickname, "Young D," on the back of his t-shirts. That was how much he liked the nickname, and he became famous for it even in the USA.

When I started resettling in Canada, I added Daniel Thuch and James Dhuor as my dependents. But because they were not my blood brothers, they were rejected during the final interview. After the rejection, Daniel Thuch and James Dhuor were depressed. I was depressed, as well.

In my final attempt to take them along with me, I told the interviewer, a young Canadian woman, that I was not going to Canada if my friends (Daniel Thuch and James Dhuor) were rejected. The interviewer was stunned by my decision. She could not understand why I could give up this golden opportunity just because of friends. But for some reason, she was adamant about me going to Canada.

"With your attitude and resilience, you will do well in Canada," she said. "So, my advice to you is, go to Canada and work hard and support them by sending them money. Then, when they become seventeen years old, they can also resettle in Canada and join you."

I accepted the Canadian lady's advice. On December 19, 1999, I resettled in Canada, leaving Daniel Thuch in Kakuma. I left him all my clothes, shoes, and ration card. In less than a month after I arrived in Canada, I sent him $200, which was a lot of money back then, especially when converted into Kenyan shillings.

In 2003, however, the USA government decided to take 3000 of the unaccompanied minors, called the lost boys, and Daniel Thuch resettled in the USA, landing in Connecticut.

When they arrived in the USA, Daniel Thuch rented an apartment with a group of comrades, just like in Kakuma, when more than four boys could share a house. Friends who did not have jobs, money, or apartments were always welcome to live freely with Daniel Thuch Achiek.

But things were different in the USA, where individualism is the norm. Neighbors constantly called the police on them because many people were coming in and out of their apartment. Many black people living in an apartment in America are suspected of making noise and doing something illegal.

Shortly after they arrived in Connecticut, police officers came to their apartment with guns drawn. For someone who grew up dodging bullets, the first thing you did when you saw someone approaching with a gun was to run away or hide. That was what Daniel and his friends did when they looked outside and saw the police officers with guns drawn: they hid. The police sent in dogs and arrested and charged them for crimes they knew nothing about.

"I swear we did not do anything," Daniel Thuch later called and told me about this police incident. "We were in our house minding our business. But the police just came with guns drawn. Why are Americans like that?"

I could hear the helplessness in Daniel Thuch's voice. He was overwhelmed, lonely, and isolated. He did not know what to do. Daniel eventually said he wanted to move to Canada to come and live with me. But that was not possible either. Moving from the USA to Canada was not like moving from Kakuma Refugee Camp to Ifo Refugee Camp. It was not like writing a forged departure order for Lhat Mabor to travel from Kakuma to Ifo. So, I told Daniel to wait for five years to receive citizenship before moving to Canada. But the arrest made it harder for him to obtain his citizenship. He had to find a lawyer to defend him in court.

Despite all of that, Daniel Thuch was still the friendliest, most comprehensive, and humble person you meet. He always worried about others' welfare and helped them without expecting anything in return, further illustrating the purity of his generosity and friendship. No one stayed with Daniel Thuch without being impressed by his kindness. For example, in Connecticut, Thuch sheltered and fed homeless friends and comrades for years.

In 2017, Daniel Thuch called me with both bad and good news. The good news was that he had finally obtained his citizenship and passport. Fortunately, this meant we could complete our dream. Our dream was to travel to South Sudan to spend time in the Aliab where his parents lived and go to the Agaar where my parents lived.

The bad news was that Daniel was fired from his job, where he had been working for thirteen years, climbing his way up to a supervisory position. But he promised to get his act together. First, Daniel Thuch said he was moving out of Connecticut to look for opportunities elsewhere. So, in 2017, he moved from Connecticut to Kansas, Missouri, searching for better opportunities. Tragically, Daniel Thuch Achiek passed away in Kansas on June 4, 2020, after a short illness. He passed away peacefully in his sleep.

Another veteran who succumbed was James Dhuor Anok. Like Daniel Thuch, James Dhuor was also from the Aliab section of Jieng. He joined the movement in 1989, where he was trained with the Intifada Division in Dimma, Ethiopia. As mentioned earlier, I shared a house with him, Daniel Thuch, and Lhat Mabor in Kakuma.

After I was accepted to go to Canada and my dependents, James Dhuor and Daniel Thuch were rejected, James Dhuor was deeply affected by the rejection. He did not want to remain in Kakuma. Instead, he returned to Sudan to find his long-lost parents. I tried to encourage him to complete his primary school in Kakuma but to no avail. James Dhuor Anok saw no reason to stay in Kakuma when I left for Canada. He returned to Aliab, South Sudan, in 1999.

However, after a couple of months in his homeland, Aliab, James Dhuor was still emotionally unstable. He could not cope, even though he was among his people. He missed his comrades back in Kakuma. When he heard that I had not left for Canada yet, James Dhuor wanted to return to Kakuma. But there was no way he could do that; it cost a lot of money to fly from Aliab to Kenya. Moreover, there were no telephones or social media in Kakuma or South Sudan back then. The only form of communication was through the Red Cross mailing system.

So, James Dhuor wrote a letter through the Red Cross, asking me to send him money for a plane ticket back to Kakuma. I received James's letter one week before leaving for Canada. I had no money to send him. So, I replied to the letter, instructing James Dhuor to go to Rumbek to be with my mother. I promised him that when I got to Canada, I would send him money to return to Kakuma.

Upon receiving the letter with the instruction, James Dhuor Anok left his Aliab homeland and went to Rumbek, tracing my family to Wulu. My family welcomed him, and people called him Mayom's brother.

In just three months in Canada, I found a job, and I started sending money back home every month so that my brother could establish a small business. He opened a small grocery store in Wulu. As my brother, Manyang, traveled back and forth between South Sudan and Uganda to buy and sell goods, James Dhuor ran the shop. James Dhuor was a family member by now, and he became comfortable and did not even want to return to Kakuma.

But in a very twisted turn of events, James Dhuor ended up marrying the younger sister of my brother's wife. Thus, the friendship was sealed by marriage, as marriage is considered a union between families, clans, or tribes among the Jieng people.

After marriage, James Dhuor returned to Aliab with his family. But like any other veteran, James Dhuor was still haunted by that core sense of emotional isolation—the emotional maturity that haunted veterans—that lingers, even if the veteran has a superficially everyday adult life. James Dhuor went to school, worked, married, and raised children. However, all the while, it appeared he was still being haunted by that core sense of emotional isolation that dated back to the social isolation and war trauma he suffered during the liberation struggle.

Dhuor Anok started to develop post-traumatic stress disorder. No matter how hard he tried to be normal to raise his family, the flashbacks kept his body and mind preoccupied. So finally, in 2020, Dhuor went to Juba for treatment. But he vanished completely. Nobody ever found out what happened to him.

The author with his two brothers, Manyang and Makis, in Kakuma—1996.

Trying to be stylish, the author, wearing a black toque under the sweltering sun of Africa, stood in front of a beggu tree, posting for a picture—1998.

The author's friends, Lhat Mabor and Majok Kadis posting with a Somalia child in Ifo Refugee Camp. This was shortly after Lhat returned from Agoro.

The author (squatting, right) with friends, including Chol Kon (the tallest), who lost his soccer boots.

As the spectators gathered to watch, the volleyball team took a picture before a game. The author is standing with his left hand on his hip—Kakuma, Kenyan, 1995.

The author, wearing the red jersey #12, participated in a Volleyball match; Kenyan vs. Sudanese, Lodwar, Kenya—1998.

Zone One, Volleyball Team, which the author coached, posted with a trophy after winning the championship—1998. The author second (standing, right), wearing a white t-shirt.

From left to right: Augustino Mel Mabouch (assistant captain), Peter Mam Makuei (captain), William Mayom Maker, the author (coach), and Daniel Duot Ajak (assistant coach)—Zone One Volleyball Team.

211

PART FIVE

Canada

<hr/>

"I looked through the window to see my new home, and I was not disappointed with what I saw. Off in the distance, I saw the tall buildings of Halifax city. I could not believe I was coming to live in this beautiful city."

Resettlement

On December 10, 1999, I received the news when I was playing volleyball that a new set of names had been posted for flights to Canada, and my name was on the list. I did not even know the person that told me. The news of the resettlement was too good to be true. I took off running without even notifying my friends.

This was the second time I had ever raced to the UN compound. The first time I ran to the UN compound and other resettlement candidates was in the middle of November when I heard several lists had been posted. When I arrived at the compound, a crowd of men and women had gathered around the bulletin board adjacent to the main gate. I wanted to get closer so that I could look for my name, but a wall of bodies, all looking for their names, kept me away. I had to look for an opening to squeeze myself through.

A man scanned the list and turned and stomped away in anger when he saw the word "REJECTED" attached to his name. "What shall I do?" the man cried. Another man leaped for joy, stepping on my foot when he saw the word "ACCEPTED" attached to his name. "Yes," he said. "I am going to Canada."

Every resettlement seeker, even those who did not know how to read or write, understood these two English terms: "REJECTED" and "ACCEPTED."

Instead of complaining to the man who had stepped on my foot as he celebrated his acceptance, I used the opportunity to squeeze in through an opening he had created. I forced myself closer to the bulletin board with my right shoulder leading the way to look for my name. And there it was: William Mayom: "ACCEPTED." I was ecstatic.

There was one final process before going to Canada: a medical checkup. I traveled to Nairobi, along with the other twenty resettlement candidates, to get a physical checkup. The medic found my physical condition to be unquestionable. After all, I played sports, so I was extremely fit. Also, my blood was checked for the AIDS virus. The medic also checked my system for drugs. There were two types of drugs in Kakuma: marijuana and chat, the euphoric stimulant leaves chewed by Somalis. The sports, along with strong cultural values instilled in me at an incredibly young age, prevented me from drugs and alcohol. As a result, I was healthy and drug-free.

But I was not the judge. The result of the medical check was sent to Canada, and I returned to Kakuma to wait for a result from the Canadian Immigration System. The final verdict of the medical result usually had the same two options: "REJECTED" or "ACCEPTED."

Now I raced to the UN compound for the last time to see whether I was rejected or accepted. The compound usually took thirty minutes on foot, but this time it took me only ten minutes. I ran with a speed I did not know I possessed.

The sun had already set, and it was getting dark when I reached the compound. The compound was quiet, and the gate was locked. During the day, the compound gate would be swamped by hundreds or thousands of people who wanted to go inside for various reasons. There would be many police officers and security guards whipping and kicking people. Because there were many people, everyone scrambled to be in front of the line. You needed to be strong to protect your position in line. Small boys like me would be squeezed and trampled to death. Many small children and older persons were severely injured in these stampedes.

The bulletin board was outside, right by the entrance gate. The gate was locked, and I saw two security guards inside the locked gate.

I nervously went through the board, hoping not to be noticed and chased away by the security guards because no one was allowed near the compound after hours. I was sweating, my heart was pumping fast, and my hand trembled as I traced the name on the board. I did not know whether the excitement, the running, or the guards had caused the fear.

One guard got up and walked toward the gate, patrolling. But I stood my ground, displaying some bravery. As a herd boy, I was taught that running away when you were not being attacked would cause even cowardly animals, such as a hyena, to attack you. But when you stood your ground, the chances were that even a lion would not dare to attack you. So, I pretended not to have seen the approaching guard. But I was secretly watching him from the corner of my eye as I continued reading on the board. I knew that the gate was locked anyway, so by the time he unlocked the gate, I would disappear under the cover of darkness. Luckily, the guard just looked over the gate and noticed me still reading on the board, so he went back and sat down.

The bulletin board was jammed with many layers of paper. I dug through the documents from layer to layer, some of the documents dropping like leaves from a tree, but I did not care to pick them up and pin them back onto the board. Some papers were typed, and others were handwritten in different inks—red, blue, black, and green.

On the bottom, I finally noticed what looked like my name. Like an archaeologist removing a fragile million-year-old mummy, I used both of my hands to carefully remove all the pins and staples holding the paper, making sure not to tear it. I successfully removed it and looked at my name, making sure it was mine. There were fifteen people on the list. Finally, my eyes landed on my name, "William Mayom." On the top right of the paper was the posting date, December 5, 1999. On the top left, my eyes landed on one word written in the capital letter: "ACCEPTED."

"Yes," I said. I took my eyes off the list to digest what had just happened and make sure I was not dreaming. Then, I looked at it again, and my name was still there with the title "ACCEPTED."

The list of fifteen accepted resettlement candidates was divided into columns: serial number, name, departure, and destination. For example, serial number five read: William Mayom; Departure date: December 19, 1999; Destination: Halifax, Nova Scotia.

All the names on the list had been ticked except mine, meaning the other candidates had received their traveling visas. I carefully folded up the paper and held it tight in my left hand as I ran back to the camp. First, of course, I wanted to show it to my friends; otherwise, they would not believe I was going to Canada. But, most prominently, I wanted to show this paper to the security guards at the gate tomorrow to let me enter the UN compound to get my traveling visa. Without evidence that I was needed, I would never be allowed near the compound, let alone enter.

Arriving home, I found my friends huddling around burning wooden fire, enjoying the warmth on one of the coldest nights in Kakuma Refugee Camp. I could smell the fresh aroma of *ugali*, which they were eating—a thick porridge made of maize flour.

"I have been accepted for a resettlement; I'm going to Canada," I enthusiastically called to the group of friends. "I am going to Canada; look at my name on the departure list!" I repeated.

But the news was dismissed by my friends.

"Sit down and eat your *ugali* quietly," retorted Ajakdit as other friends roared in laughter. "Every time Mayom is uncertain about the fate of his *ugali* share, he always makes up pitiful stories."

But it did not take long before my friends knew I was not joking and that I was indeed going to Canada. I started the whole process as a joke. I did not even know I would be accepted for resettlement. However, in 1998, four countries (Canada, America, Australia, and New Zealand) had decided to accept refugees into their countries, so those who wanted to resettle in these countries were encouraged to submit their applications. Despite the pressure from the SPLA leaders who discouraged people from going abroad, many people applied anyway. Subsequently, on June 1, 1999, I submitted my application, along with my life story, hoping one of these countries would accept me.

A week after I submitted my application, I was called in for my first interview, conducted by a Kenyan lady. After the interview, the lady said my life story was "well written," and I had passed my first interview. She wanted my consent to send my application to Canada. She asked if I was willing to go to Canada when accepted. I said I would go to Canada, wherever that place was. Going anywhere was much better than staying in nowhere, which was the true meaning of the word Kakuma.

A month after the preliminary interview, I was called in for my second interview. This was a significant interview conducted by a Canadian lady who spoke big English words in a peculiar accent. I did not need a translator because I had learned that many people that had been rejected had used translators, which caused inconsistencies in their answers. The lady went through my life story, asking me questions, which I answered to the best of my ability.

I had no idea about that place called Canada that I would be re-settling to in a few days, where it was located, or who lived there. But I had seen Canada's red and white flag from the leaf of an unfamiliar tree on the sack of yellow corn flour and tins of butter oil distributed in the camp.

"William with food," remarked Ajakdit, "he's chosen to go to the place where yellow corn flour and butter oil are plentiful."

A buzz went out in groups one and two: "William is going to Canada!" Everyone came to congratulate me.

The following morning, I said goodbye to my friends, including Daniel Thuch and Ajakdit, and boarded a bus going to Nairobi to fly to Canada. On the bus, I met Joseph Makuach Majak, who was also going to Halifax, N.S. Joseph was older than me, so I was thrilled to find someone I knew to travel together to Canada.

From the time I saw my name on the bulletin board to the time I boarded the bus going to Nairobi, I was numb with excitement and hype to the point that I did not think about what I was doing. We arrived in Nairobi on December 16, 1999. We had only two days before our departure to Canada.

On December 19, 1999, we boarded a bus for Jomo Kenyatta International Airport. My mind was preoccupied, and I did not remember the ride to the airport. All I remember was lining up and shuffling along the line slowly. Looking outside through the glass, I saw the blue and white plane—the biggest airplane I had ever seen in my life. An entire battalion could fit inside it.

The line moved along until I arrived at the front. In my hand was a white plastic bag with the blue letters of the International Organization for Migration (IOM), which contained all my documents. I was issued this IOM bag in Nairobi and told to hold on tight to it. So that was what I did. I held on tight to the IOM bag until my hand hurt.

At the gate, a smartly dressed man was standing there checking everyone's documents. I took out all the papers in the IOM bag and handed them to the man. Without even saying a word, the man went through the file, selected the document with my picture on top, and handed me back the rest of the papers. He looked at the picture on the document, looked at my face, and then he gave the document back and waved me through.

I climbed the steep stairs to the mouth of the waiting plane, and the metal rail was hot. Some people waved goodbye to family members from the platform at the top of the stairs to the neatly assembled relatives standing down below. Others blew kisses to their loved ones down below. Finally, some people waved and shouted promises in strange languages.

I had no one to wave to because all my friends and comrades were in Kakuma. So instead, I went through a tunnel before stepping into the airplane. This was my first time to be on a plane. Excitement filled me. I was the first person of all my comrades to set foot on a plane. But I had no one to brag to.

"Welcome to KLM airline!" said a lady dressed in blue with a big smile on her face.

"Thank you," I said. I walked between the two aisles, searching for a place to sit. There were so many seats that it was hard to choose where to sit. Finally, I sat in a seat on the right section next to the aisle. The seats were filling up fast with people.

Soon, an elderly white woman came and said, "I'm sorry. But this is my seat."

I was surprised to find a white woman with Dinka manners. When a Dinka elder saw a young person seated, the elder would demand the seat, and a respectful junior expected to surrender the seat. So, I got up quietly to let the older woman sit.

She must have noticed this was my first flight, so she said, "Show me your ticket," which I did. She said, "Your seat is right there," pointing at the seat behind her. I thanked her and sat down next to the window. Joseph had also sat in someone else's seat, and the lady showed him his seat in the aisle opposite mine. The lady might have noticed from our demeanor, dress, or the IOM bags that we did not know what we were doing. I heard the clicking of seatbelts throughout the plane. Finally, a flight attendant came over to show me how to fasten my seatbelt.

Soon, a voice echoed throughout the plane. It was a man who called himself "Captain." I thought this was a military captain because I did not know that a plane driver was also called a captain. In the SPLA, a captain or any other high-ranking officer usually sat in the cap with the driver, and everyone else sat in the back of the truck. So, I assumed this captain giving instructions was somewhere in the cockpit with the driver of the plane. But unfortunately, I did not understand most of what the voice was saying.

The plane started to move slowly, making several turns before increasing in speed. I looked through the window and noticed that houses and trees were moving. Suddenly, the engines grew louder and louder. Then, I found myself pushed back into the seat. The plane had lifted its nose in a taking-off motion.

I had never seen a plane taking off before, but common sense dictated that the aircraft was doing the exact thing big birds, such as cranes, flamingoes, or eagles, do when taking off from the ground. With wings spread out, cranes start by running and then jumping as high in the air as they can. From there, they start flapping their wings extremely hard to get themselves up into the air. I did not see the plane flapping its wings, but the loud noise it was making inside the engines told me it could be using the same techniques big birds do when getting up into the air.

The plane took off. My body and my mind felt empty. I looked through the window and noticed trees and buildings getting smaller and smaller below. All the hardships (the abject poverty of Kakuma, the starvation of Pakhok, the near-death experiences in Dimma) remained behind. Finally, I was heading to Canada. I was told that Canada was one of the most peaceful places on earth.

Nevertheless, the fear of uncertainty or going to a new place was clouding my mind. The plane was already in the air but still climbing. I looked at my friend Joseph, and he seemed to be suffering from the same uncertainty.

A few minutes later, an Ethiopian woman seated two seats ahead of me cried out loud, which startled everyone on the plane, "God, where am I going, leaving my people behind?" She screamed in Amharic. A woman seated next to the Ethiopian woman started to rub the crying lady's back, comforting her.

I realized I was not well prepared for this trip. I did not have water or food. I did not even have a penny in my pocket. My plane ticket said I would land in Halifax on December 21, 1999. Two days without food or water was not a problem. I had walked in the Ajak Ageer desert four days without water, so two days without water or food would not kill me, especially since I was just sitting, not walking. I was sure of that.

My eyes grew heavy, and I fell asleep. I was profoundly sleeping when, suddenly, someone tapped at my shoulder, and I startled up. I looked, and it was the same lady who had helped me buckle my seatbelt. She was now pushing a cart full of strange food. "What would you like?" she asked.

"I'm not hungry," I said, "Thank you." But I was hungry because I had not eaten since yesterday's dinner in Nairobi. We had left the hotel early in the morning without breakfast. I spent lunchtime at the airport, but I did not have a single shilling in my pocket to buy lunch. Now, it was dinner time on the plane, and this flight attendant was pressuring me to get a plate of food, but I still had no money. You cannot order food when you have no money. It is that simple.

I remembered when my friend, David Chan, went to a Kenyan restaurant. This was a few months after we had arrived in Kakuma from Sudan. David had money, so he decided to treat himself to excellent food. But on the way, a thief pick-pocketed David's precious fifteen shillings. Unaware that his money had been stolen, David ate fifteen shillings' worth of food. And when he was about to pay, he discovered his money was gone. The Kenyans did not believe David's narrative that his money had been stolen. As far as they were concerned, David was a conman who wanted to eat and dash. So, they quarantined David in the corner. "You are not going anywhere until you pay," they told him. Luckily for David Chan, I came to the same restaurant and found him sitting in the corner. Instead of eating, I ended up using my fifteen shillings to bail him out.

So, the last thing I wanted to do on this plane was to eat the food without money so that when we landed in Halifax, the airline crew would prevent me from leaving the plane until I paid. "There is a Sudanese who devoured food without money," they would say, and it would be on the news. I did not want to make a wrong impression in my new country. Most importantly, I did not want to embarrass myself and my comrades back in Kakuma.

"Are you sure you don't want anything?" the lady said.

"No, thank you," I said.

The man next to me ordered his food. The aroma of the food made me very hungry. But I looked out through the window to distract my attention away from the food.

Down below, I saw nothing but water. Then, I remembered stories about the most significant water body in the world. The ocean was called Adek-diet because birds who attempted to cross it got tired and fell into the sea and died. According to the legend, only kites and eagles had mastered the art of crossing the ocean successfully. Each bird carried a log of an *adet* tree, a tree that grows in the swamp, light and foamy when dried. So, the kite carried the adet log, and when it grew tired, it sat on the water using the log as a floating device.

We came to Brussels, where Western mysteries took a toll on me. The first thing I noticed was how everyone seemed to be in a hurry for no apparent reason. With all these people at the airport, nobody talked with one another. "Even the metal is in a hurry, too," I thought, looking at what I later found out was an escalator running up and down.

"We have to climb these steps to go to the airplane that takes us to our final destination," said Joseph Makuach. Makuach quickly stepped on the escalator, and before I knew it, he was growing taller and taller as the escalator pulled him. So, I stepped on it, too. Big mistake! The thing whipped my feet on the ground. I grabbed the rail, but it was no use. The rail was in a hurry, running upward, too. With both the floor and the rail rushing upward, I fell back. Luckily, a man behind me held me and prevented me from falling. He pushed my back till my feet were on stable ground. I was so embarrassed I did not even thank the man.

Joseph and I followed the crowd, heading to the waiting areas. It had been over twenty-four hours since I had eaten food. When you lived in Kakuma for ten years, you began to pay attention to hunger after twenty-four hours. Flight attendants had offered water and food many times, but I had rejected them. I had no money, and nobody had told me the food was free.

My ticket said we had six hours in Brussels before taking another plane to Montreal, Canada. At the Brussels Airport, Joseph and I met an Equatorial couple, Jane Anita, and her husband (I forgot his name). Jane had an extra bottle of water, which she gave me. They were from Kakuma, but both used to work for NGOs in Kenya, and they also grew up in cities, so they knew many things, unlike Joseph and I, who grew up in the bush as a guerrilla fighter. From this couple, I learned food and beverages served on the plane were free of charge. My flight from Brussels to Montreal was perfect because I ate everything that was offered to me. Of course, the food did not taste that good, but I was once a guerilla who ate strange foods to survive.

Welcome to Canada

Finally, the captain announced over the PA that we were landing in Halifax, Nova Scotia. The crew walked down the aisle, telling the passengers to fasten their seatbelts for landing.

"This is it," I said to myself. "I have arrived in my new home." After being evicted by war and poverty from three countries, I felt like a foster child moving from home to home in the adoption chain. I was filled with mixed emotions: happiness and anxiety. I was happy that I had found a new home. And I was anxious whether the new home would be more likable or worse than the previous one.

I looked through the window to see my new home, and I was not disappointed with what I saw. Off in the distance, I saw the tall buildings of Halifax city. I could not believe I was coming to live in this beautiful city.

Soon, the plane slowed down, jerking a few times before descending gradually. Finally, it touched the ground and ran for a while before stopping. Everyone clapped, appreciating the safe landing.

All the passengers filed off the plane in a single line. I was unsure where to go or what to do, but I grabbed my IOM bag and followed the line. We passed through several tunnels and hallways before emerging in an open area. All the Canadians around me talked, laughed, and walked proudly—the confidence of people who knew what they were doing. I looked like I had just landed on a different planet.

Equipped with my Kakuma Refugee Camp reading skills, I read every sign I saw, but the meaning did not register in my mind. There were signs, arrows, alphabets, numbers, and other drawings. I saw A B C D; F-1, F-2- F3; G-1, G-2, G-3, and so forth. But these things did not tell much.

The best bet was to follow the passengers who had arrived with me. I made my way through the terminal, coming to an area with a sign that said BAGGAGE CLAIM. The passengers stopped and stood around an apparatus. I followed them. The apparatus (later discovered it was called a luggage carousel) consisted of a tunnel, solid metal frames, and an endless loop. The whole system rotated around and around and around. All the passengers who had arrived with me stood around this thing, watching as it rotated and rotated and rotated. I did not understand why grown-up human beings would stand around watching this thing that was not doing anything other than rotating. "It does not take much to amuse Canadians," I thought.

I looked around to see where Joseph was. He had sat five seats ahead of me, so he got off the plane first. I noticed he was standing on the other side of the apparatus. Joseph wore the exact look I had on my face: confusion. But he was watching the rotating machine, anyway.

As I was about to join Joseph, I heard tumbling and banging sounds in the tube connected to the apparatus's rotating loop. Everyone's eye shifted to the tunnel. Something was coming from the tunnel. Before I knew it, bags rushed out of the tube one after another and smoothly transitioned onto the rotating loop. Now I knew what this thing was: it was the apparatus used for transporting bags, a labor-saving device. A very efficient and effective device, mind you.

I joined Joseph and asked whether our bags would be on this thing. Joseph said he was not sure. We had not seen them since they were taken from us at Nairobi airport. We had taken three planes, from Nairobi to Brussels, from there to Montreal, and finally to Halifax. After all the passengers had taken their bags, we finally saw our two bags rotating on the apparatus. We grabbed our bags and marveled they had followed us to Halifax.

We wandered around, unsure of what to do or where to go. The airport was gigantic, and it thronged with people. English flew around in the air throughout the airport. I understood nothing because Canadians spoke faster than my mind could comprehend.

Joseph and I followed the crowd through a series of corridors, arriving at an area where people were standing with signs. Some arrivals ran into the open arms of their loved ones to hug, kiss, and laugh. It never crossed my mind that someone would be waiting to welcome me in this land. Throughout my long journey (from Sudan to Ethiopia, from Ethiopia back to Sudan, and from Sudan to Kenya), I had never been welcomed by anyone. And I did not expect to be received by anyone in Halifax.

Then a miracle happened. A woman approached me with a big smile on her face and held a big sign saying, "Mayom and Makuach." She wore a pair of gray jeans and a brown jacket. Her silky ponytail, which looked like a giraffe tail, was long and beautiful. "Joseph and William, right?" she asked.

"Yes!" we uniformly responded. I wondered how this woman knew us.

"Welcome to Canada!" she said.

"Thank you!" Joseph, whose English was way better than mine, replied.

The word "welcome" rang at the back of my head—the first vocabulary I had picked up in my new home and a pleasant one at that.

The woman introduced herself, but I did not catch her name. She was speaking so fast, and I could not understand most of what she was saying. She said she worked for "immigration," whatever that meant. She asked me a few questions, which I answered with "yes." I did not understand what she was talking about, but "yes" was the polite word I knew would not offend anybody. Joseph was a teacher in Kakuma, so he had enough English vocabulary to spare. But I could tell his English was no match for the Canadian woman whose English flowed from her lips like water from the Nile River. Joseph could not understand the complex sentences and phrases spoken in the peculiar Canadian accent, either. As the conversation went on, I heard a lot of yeses from Joseph too. He had run out of English.

Even though I did not understand our host, the smile on her face made everything she was saying sounded pleasant. Most importantly,

I was happy to be welcomed by someone in my new home. It was a good sign so far.

The woman was friendly and welcoming, but the weather was the opposite. As we exited the airport through doors that opened on their own, the freezing temperature attacked my skin like bee stings. It was hard to describe what my body felt; it was like thousands of needles poking my body at the same time. December was the worst season of the year for a Dinka who did not even have a name for snow to come to Halifax. That thing called snow had covered everything: the trees, the houses, the cars, you name it. I could not see the grass or soil on the ground.

When I first arrived in the arid temperature of Kakuma, Kenya, I thought God was absent-minded when he created that part of the world. Here, I thought God had utterly lost his mind when He made this part of the world. Even heavenly bodies like the sun did not know their functions. In Africa, the primary function of the sun is to provide heat. The Canadian sun provided light, no heat. Flakes rained from the sky, not water.

As I walked from the building to the parking lot, I lost sensation in my fingers and ears. My body was chilled despite the several layers of clothes I wore. The air I was breathing in did not feel right in my lungs. Now I knew why Canadians were so white: these extreme weather conditions turned them that way.

We exited through another door that opened on its own. The woman hustled us to the parking lot, where cars were parked. I had never seen so many cars in my life. When I visited Rumbek Town as a child, I thought I had seen many cars. But what I saw in Rumbek was nothing compared to this. The vehicles looked like herds of cattle in the Dinka land with different sizes, shapes, and colors.

We came to a white van. The woman opened the door and told us to get in. But then, she did a bizarre thing: she went behind the wheel, started the van, and drove. I had never heard of women driving before, let alone seen one. So, my new home turned out to be a land where impossibilities turned into possibilities.

Vroom. We zoomed along amidst the chaotic scenes of the city. Lines of cars were coming in the opposite direction while others approached and overtook us from behind. Endless lines of parked vehicles were along the road. Traffic signs and lights were blinking red, yellow, or green. There were tall buildings on both sides of the road. The scenes were both overwhelming and confusing.

After driving for what felt like an eternity through this chaos, we turned into a very tall building. On one side of the building were tall trees coated with snow. On the other side was the Atlantic Ocean. The car pulled into a parking lot and stopped next to the building.

A woman named Theresa met us in the parking lot. "Welcome to Canada," she said with a big smile. She took us inside the building. The woman who picked us up from the airport left. The house stretched for a long distance in all directions. The air felt so warm and smelled better inside the house. I had breathed recycled airplane air from Nairobi to Halifax and snow-filled air from the airport to the apartment. But this air was fresh, and my lungs welcomed it.

After walking for what felt like an exceptionally long distance through the hallway, Theresa opened a room and handed the key to Joseph. "This is your room," she said. I wanted to follow Joseph inside the room, thinking we were sharing it. But Theresa opened the next door and handed me the key. "This is your room, William," she said.

She entered the room and flickered the light on. I entered. I had never seen such a beautiful place before. Inside the room were a chair, table, and bed. That was all I recognized. Theresa opened a small door at the corner, revealing the toilet and a bathtub. Three days earlier, I had learned how to flush a toilet and turn on the water for a shower in Nairobi. Theresa also pointed at a cabinet-looking white thing. "This is your fridge," she said. "And this is your microwave." Finally, she pointed at a black box sitting on the table. I had no clue what the functions of these things were. But I kept saying "yes" anyway, even though I had no clue what she was talking about.

After Theresa left, the first thing I wanted to do was to take a shower. But when I inspected the bathtub, it had no faucet. The plumber had been very careless and forgot to install a faucet. So, I went to Joseph's room to see if I could take a shower there. Unfortunately, Joseph's shower did not have a faucet either. We did not know these were sensor-operated devices, where you just had to remove your clothes and enter the bathtub, and water would come on automatically.

The miseries of my new home were getting the better of me. I had spent eleven years in an isolated village in the Agaarland, a world that outsiders had never touched with their modernization. Then war broke out, and I joined the rebels, where I spent the next five years in the bushes, where the only sophisticated thing I knew was a Kalashnikov automatic rifle. When the UN pressured the SPLA to abandon child soldier practices, I was discharged and sent to Kakuma Refugee Camp, where I languished in abject poverty for seven years. That had amounted to twenty-three years of a wasted life. Physically, I was a young man. But mentally, I was a two-year-old boy, experiencing the Western world's miseries, such as running water, a fridge, and a microwave for the first time. While twenty-three-old Canadian young men and women were at colleges and universities learning to cure disease or fly to the moon, I was in a small apartment struggling to activate running water to no avail. What a disparity!

Without water for bathing or drinking, I collapsed on the bed. The bed was so comfortable that I found it hard to be comfortable. But I was utterly exhausted, physically and mentally. My head felt like it was filled with soil. I had not slept well since I left Nairobi.

It was dark outside. I looked at the alarm clock on the table, and it said 9:47 p.m. But when I looked at my plastic watch on my wrist, it said the time was 3:47 p.m. This was very confusing. My watch had lost its mind. I could not blame it because even the sun could not function when it reached this part of the world. My eyes felt heavy, and I slept.

At 8:30 a.m., a bell rang throughout the building. At first, I did not know where I was—the feeling one has when sleeping in a different place. But then, I looked through the window, and the snow reminded me I was in my new home.

After the bell, a voice came through speakers in the hallway: "It's breakfast time! Breakfast is ready!"

Breakfast? Who eats at 8:30 a.m.? For the past seven years in Kakuma, I had never, ever eaten breakfast. We ate once a day. If you were lucky, you ate twice a day. Lunch was at around 2:00 p.m. and dinner at 8:30 p.m. Breakfast was not in our vocabulary in Kakuma.

There was a commotion outside. I opened the door to see all these crazy people who wanted to eat that early. I saw a group of older women, some in wheelchairs, all heading in the same direction. It turned out that this was a retirement home where wealthy people who had retired lived. They ate good food, and they had people who cooked and took care of them. The buffet, located on the main floor, served breakfast, lunch, and dinner. Coming from Kakuma, where eating once a day was the norm, I had to learn to eat three times a day now.

An older woman passing by saw me standing at the door. She was probably around ninety years old and pushing her wheeled walker. She smiled as if I was one of her great-grandchildren.

"Come. Come," the elderly woman said, gesturing her hand in the mouth. "Eat. Eat. Breakfast."

I understood what she said. She wanted me to follow her to the kitchen to eat. I wished all Canadians could speak like her: speaking slowly and enunciating each word, and using sign language to emphasize the point.

Joseph exited from his room as the older woman hustled us along. We came to a vast dining room, where the smell of strange food filled the room. The line had already been established, and we just followed it. Three young ladies wearing white clothes stood behind a system where various dishes were set out on a table—an efficient way to feed many guests. There were about twenty people in the line, all Canadians, all women, no single man. Joseph and I were the only men, and we were young and black. The servers were the only young Canadian women.

But the older women indeed showed us the best side of Canada.

Everyone that saw us said "Hello," "Hi," or waved. The smiles on their face were hard to explain. They kept asking us, "Where are you from?" "Sudan," we said. "Welcome to Canada," they would say.

I watched and followed what the older woman in front of me was doing to avoid embarrassing myself. First, she grabbed a tray and placed two clean plates on the tray. Then she grabbed a spoon, a pronged spoon (I later found it was called a fork), and a knife. She also grabbed napkins. I copied everything she did; Joseph, who was behind me, also copied.

The buffet line moved faster, and I came face to face with a variety of food to choose from. I had never seen so much food to eat in my life. The food had an odd smell. Some of the food looked strange and unhealthy to eat. There were some rolls and a sign that said, "hot dog." I did not want to be judgmental, but dog meat was not getting on my plate, whether hot or cold. I ate a Columbus monkey before because no other foods were available. Here, the kitchen was full of food, so no need to eat dog meat. I avoided that section.

My eyes landed on what looked like an *asida*. *Asida* is a thick paste made from maize, millet, or sorghum flour. To Dinka, without *asida*, then it is not food but a snack. The sign said, "mashed potato," but it looked good to eat, anyway. I took three scoops. The stew next to the potato (I later came to know was gravy) looked like it would go along fine with it. Then there were chicken thighs and wings. I grabbed plenty of those.

My biggest shock occurred when I turned left to a section where various green leaves and sticks were displayed. I read the signs associated with these vegetables: carrots, lettuce, spinach, and broccoli. The traffic going to that section was packed; apparently, these raw leaves were Canadians' finest delicacies. But none of these raw leaves was going near my plate. Dinka culture dictated those uncooked green leaves belonged to ruminants, which chew the cud regurgitated from their rumens. Even in the SPLA, I had eaten disgusting food, but I had never eaten uncooked leaves. I passed everything and finally landed my eye on something edible: oranges. I grabbed slices of orange and placed them on my tray.

On the far side were soft drinks: sodas. In Kakuma, sodas were considered a rare treat. It was when we went to tournaments in Kenyan cities that we were treated with sodas. So, while the older women crept to the vegetable section, Joseph and I raced to the soda section.

We grabbed our plates and sat at a table. Soon, we were joined by the couple from the Equatoria, Jane Anita, with her husband, whom we met in Brussels. Sitting next to us was a man from Iraq named Mohamed. Mohamed did not know a single English word, not even hello. Unable to speak to anyone, Mohamed was depressed. The poor guy had been in Canada for three weeks, but he had not spoken to anyone because of the language barrier. So, when he learned we spoke Arabic, Muhammad became our best friend.

But what I disliked about Mohamed was that he called everyone "*Habibi.*" In Juba Arabic, *Habibi* is a term used when referring to a female companion. But in Iraq, best male friends called each other *Habibi*. So, it made me extremely uncomfortable when another man called me *Habibi*, so I avoid Mohamed because of that.

The food tasted and smelled unpleasant: the chicken was sweet, and the mashed potato smelled and tasted awful. Even the can of Coke tasted different. But I ate everything on my plate because I did not want to appear ungrateful.

After two weeks in Halifax, Nova Scotia, I received an unexpected, gracious call from a lost friend: Kuot Mathuch. The phone rang at around 8 p.m. I had never received a call from outside before, so I thought the caller was a receptionist, who called me three times a day to go for breakfast, lunch, and dinner. But she called at 8 p.m., and I wondered why she called. So, I picked the phone, and it was her: the receptionist.

"William," she said when I answered the phone. Then, as usual, she spoke so fast that I did not understand what she was talking about. All I heard were the hissing sounds English speakers made. Finally, the receptionist said something about "Someone wants to talk to you . . . hold on to make a connection." Then the phone was quiet. I hung up.

By now, the receptionist was used to my backwardness. I had never seen, much less used, a telephone before coming to Halifax. The first time the receptionist wanted to get hold of me, she called my room several times, but I did not answer the phone. Instead, I saw this black box with a cord on the table, which kept ringing, and a red indicator was flashing. I did not know what it was. My guerrilla instinct dictated that I did not touch strange objects flashing red. It could be a bomb.

Worried that something might have happened to me because I did not answer the calls, the receptionist came down to check on me. Then she showed me how to answer the phone. "When it rings, pick up, place this side (pointing to the holes on the handset) on your mouth and talk, and this side put on your ear to listen," she said. "When done, put it back here."

Less than a minute after I hung up, the phone rang again. I picked it up, and it was the receptionist. This time, she spoke slowly and clearly. "Your friend, Kuot, is on the line and wants to talk to you."

I almost screamed on the phone when I heard my friend's name. I could not believe Kuot was here. I had not seen or heard from him since he left me in Kakuma two years ago. I thought he had heard from someone that I had arrived, and he had come to see me.

Before the woman could even finish talking, I hung up the phone and rushed to the cafeteria on the far side of the building. There were still a couple of people in the buffet lineup. Unfortunately, Kuot was not in the line. One of the servers was surprised to see me again because I had just eaten less than half an hour ago. But as usual, she was friendly and professional.

"Welcome back, William," she said. "Just follow the lineup."

I told her I was not coming to eat again and that I was looking for my friend. She told me Joseph had eaten and went to his room. But I said it was not Joseph, but Kuot Mathuch. The server was confused as to what friend I was talking about. I tried to explain to her that the receptionist said my friend "Kuot was on the line," to no avail.

I exited and rushed to the reception in the lobby. It was through face-to-face communication with the receptionist that I understood what she meant. Kuot had called wanting to talk to me. So, he was on the line, not the buffet line, but the invisible telephone line where voices travel, and I was supposed to hold on so that she could make the connection.

After she explained to me what to do, I returned to my room. Five minutes later, the phone rang again, and I picked it up on the first ring. It was the receptionist.

"Your friend Kuot is on the line. Hold on to connect you," she said.

A few seconds later, a voice came. "Hello! Mayom?"

His voice had changed a little, but I recognized him. "Kuot?"

With this, we both screamed with laughter on the phone. We could not believe we were talking to each other again. Neither of us even knew where to start. We just talked and talked for hours. After two years, Kuot wanted to know everything that had happened after he was gone. I told him about some of ours friends, including Henry, who had left Kakuma for Sudan to join the SPLA. I also told him about the many trophies our team had won. We talked until 3:30 a.m. Kuot said it was11:30 p.m. in his local time. I could not understand why one country had several different time zones. I thought again that God, the Creator, had undoubtedly messed up here.

Finally, I asked him what part of Canada he was in and whether there was snow where he was. He said he was in British Columbia and that the weather was nice. It turned out that Kuot ran away from the snow in Medicine Heart, Alberta, to British Columbia

"You can't live there," he assured me. "You have to move to BC. I will buy you a ticket right away."

It was Christmas time, and tickets were costly. But Kuot was willing to pay, and a one-way ticket from Halifax to Vancouver cost $750. So Kuot bought the ticket and faxed all the information to the receptionist, who printed and gave me the documents.

On December 27, 1999, I boarded a plane from Halifax, Nova Scotia, to British Columbia. We finally reunited with my best friend of nearly fifteen years from Dimma, Ethiopia; Pakhok and Narus,

Sudan; Kakuma, Kenya; and now British Columbia, Canada. Kuot was living with six other guys, all Sudanese, in a two-bedroom apartment. We had to find another apartment.

On February 1, 2000, Kuot and I moved to our two-bedroom apartment. Kuot was working two jobs, and I survived on my social assistance of $540 a month. Later, we were joined by William K. Just like Kakuma, Kuot and I shared the same room, each with his separate bed in separate corners. William had another room.

Living with Kuot and William K. made my life easier. I learned faster because I was not ashamed to ask, and they were not hesitant to explain things in detail. I learned how to use running water effectively, operate a microwave or stove, and use the laundry. But that was not all; I also learned how to adjust the heater when it was cold and open the door by pressing nine when someone buzzed. But I had a lot more to learn.

The Telephone Call

After two months in Canada, I received an extraordinarily gracious call. The phone rang in the middle of the night, and I picked it up.

"Hello?" I said softly, not wanting to wake up my roommates, Kuot and William K, who were sleeping in their bedrooms. They both woke up at 4:30 a.m. to go to work, so they went to sleep early. I had no job, so I spent most of my nights watching television and answering telephone calls. All the calls which came at night were from Africa because when it is midnight in Canada, it is midday in Sudan. Family members, relatives of Kuot and William K, called every day asking for money, which they sent every month. This made me feel sad, miserable, and lonely because I had no relatives and family members to call me. I had not talked or heard from my mother for twenty-four years now. I wondered if she was still alive or dead.

"Hello!" a voice came from the other end of the line. "Is that you, Mayom?"

My stomach swooshed. I had never heard that name for over twenty years. My friends usually referred to me by my Christian or English name, William or Willy.

"Yes. This is Mayom," I said to the voice. "And who is this?"

"This is your brother, Ma—" the voice said before the line cut off.

"Hello? Hello?" I said frantically. But the line was dead. The caller probably did not have enough money to make a call. Most people who called from Africa talked only for seconds, enough time to introduce themselves, and asked you to call them back. But the caller did not even finish introducing himself before the phone cut off. My two brothers who were in the SPLA with me came to mind. Manyang, my older brother, was in Kakuma with me but returned to Sudan in 1996, and I had never heard from him since then. Makis was also in Kakuma, but he went to Zimbabwe in 1997. I had other close friends who also called me brother, and their names started with the same syllable. Remember, eighty percent of the Agaar male names started this way. So, I was frustrated as to who this mysterious caller was.

The caller identification said the caller was in Uganda. But I could not afford to make a long-distance call because I was on a tight budget. Every month, I received a social assistance cheque for $540, which I budgeted accordingly to the last penny, the same way I budgeted my meager food ration in Kakuma Refugee Camp. Kuot, William K, and I divided our bills equally. Half of the cheque, $270, went to my share of the rent, $150 went to my share of groceries, and $50 went to my telephone, cable, and hydro share, leaving me with $70 in my pocket for the entire month. In that month, I had purchased a pair of jeans and a shirt for $50, leaving me only $20 in my pocket. I had to keep the money for an emergency, such as a bus pass for transportation. To make a long-distance call with that tight budget was unwise.

However, I was dying to know who this caller was. So, without even thinking, I picked up the handset, pressed the call identification button, selected the number, and pressed the dial button. It rang three times before the line came to life on the other end.

"Hello?" the voice said. "Is that you, Mayom?"

"Yes, it is me," I said. "Who is this?"

"This is Manyang, your big brother," the voice said.

I remember standing in the middle of the living room with the phone pressed on my ear as memories flashed in my mind. My big brother, Manyang, whom I had not seen or heard from him since he left Kakuma in 1996? My heart was racing, my knees and hands were trembling. Finally, I sat back on the couch and got up again. "Manyang, is that you?" I kept asking.

"Yes, it's me," Manyang said.

I lost my words. I did not know what to say, how, or where to begin. This was my big brother. How did he find me? His picture flashed into my mind. Then my mother's image.

"How is our mother?" I managed to say, thinking the worst. "Is she well?" I did not think she had survived the war and war-related causes, such as ground assaults, aerial bombardments, landmines, hunger, disease, wild animals, as well as the fact that she had lost her lastborn child (me) who was supposed to take care of her when she retired.

"Yes, our mother is very well," Manyang said. "She could not believe it when I mentioned to her that you were alive and had gone to Canada. She keeps saying, 'You are just lying to me because you don't want to tell me my lastborn child is dead because you think I will die from a heart attack.'"

Who would blame her? I left when I was eleven years old, and now I was twenty-five years old. I did not believe that she was alive either because, for fifteen years, I had been a child soldier, a refugee orphan, and now a Canadian immigrant, but I had never heard from my mother until now.

"I'm delighted to hear your voice again, Manyang," I said. "But where are you now? And how did you find my telephone number?"

"I'm in Kampala, Uganda," Manyang said. "I heard you went to Canada from Kuot's brother, and he was the one who gave me your telephone number. But unfortunately, there are no telephones in Sudan, so I had to travel to Uganda here to call and talk to you."

I listened attentively to this mysterious guy who claimed to be my big brother. I could not recognize his voice at all. The only voice that stuck in my mind was a cracking one when we were teenagers. Was this my real brother or just another conman trying to trick me? My mind drifted back to the speech.

"Our mother is doing well, Mayom," he continued. "But she is getting weaker day by day because of her age and the lack of food. There is no food at all because we did not grow crops because of war. People are starving. Thank God that you have gone to a good place where jobs are available. We need your help."

I clenched my teeth with anger and sadness, picturing my mother in that condition. I needed to do something to help them. But I only had $20 in my pocket. The following welfare check was three weeks away. When the welfare check arrived, the best I could do was to negotiate with my roommates, Kuot and William K, to cover some of the bills to allow me to send $200 to my brother for his consumption in Kampala. And I must find a job right away to give money to my brother to take it to my mother back home.

"I just came to Canada less than two months ago, Manyang," I spoke. "I have not even found a job yet. But I will try to find one soon. So, in about two weeks, I will send you $200 for your consumption there in Uganda. Then I will look for a job, and if I find one, I will send you more money to take home to our mother."

I looked at the watch, and I could not believe what I saw. I had started the call at around 12:15 a.m., and now it was 12:45 am. I had talked for thirty minutes. With taxes, this call would cost me more than $20 in the next billing cycle. So, I had to end the call soon, or else my next welfare cheque would go straight to Telus, the telephone company.

"I will call you two weeks from now after I send the money," I said. "Bye for now."

I ended the call, but I could not sleep again. The conversation kept playing in my mind repeatedly. I could not believe my brothers and mother were alive.

When my welfare cheque arrived, Kuot and William K were very generous to cover my share of grocery, telephone, and hydro bills. However, I only paid my share of the rent of $270, and I sent the remaining $270 ($235 US) to Manyang in Kampala.

I started to look for a job the following morning, right after talking to my brother. But I did not know how to look for jobs. I did not know English, and I had no work experience because I had never worked in my entire life. The companies that William K and Kuot worked for were not hiring. Besides, I could not apply to any company because I was told I needed a resume first. I did not know what that was. The dream of helping my mother and the entire family back home seemed impossible at that moment.

The First Paying Jobs

After promising my brother I would send him money, I needed a job right away. Every company I applied to would not hire me because I did not have any work experience. So, I was advised to go to a community center, where volunteers helped new immigrants find jobs. I did.

"What kind of jobs have you done before?" the agent asked.

I was an adjutant and a logistics officer in the *Anya-nya* (guerrilla), but I did not think these jobs were relevant here. "I have never worked before," I replied.

The agent looked a bit surprised, though she tried to hide it by appearing professional. "Okay," she said. "What are you good at? Anything you enjoyed doing before?"

Again, my mind flashed back in time. In Dimma, I enjoyed shooting, and I was good at it. I was the sharpest shooter in the entire battalion. In Kakuma, I enjoyed playing volleyball. I was good at it, and I coached junior teams. But I knew these jobs were irrelevant.

"I grew up in a refugee camp, so I don't have any work experience," I finally said to the agent.

The agent wrote down notes and asked me to come back next week. But, first, they had a class where they taught new immigrants how to look for jobs and what to do during job interviews.

I left the community center unsatisfied, and I did not intend to go back because they were wasting my time. I did not have time to attend classes. I needed a paying job right away to send money to my brother in Uganda.

After asking many friends, I found a company hiring everyone, including those who did not have work experience. What I liked the most was that there was no resume needed. All that was needed was proper documentation, such as a social insurance number or work visa. Also, I was told that it was a seasonal job, done only in summer. And that the job was in Kelowna, and I had to move and stay there the entire work period. It was a tree-planting job. But I did not care what kind of job it was if I was getting paid. It was an opportunity I did not want to miss, my first paying job in Canada.

"It's a tough job," the informant said.

"Tough?" I said to myself. "Give me a break! There's nothing tougher than what I had gone through as an *Anya-nya*."

I called the company (I forgot its name), which was based in Abbotsford, BC. The hiring manager gave me a list of items needed to do my job before they hired me: a pair of steel-toed boots, a sleeping bag, gloves, rain gear, and goggles. These were essential. Then there were nonessentials: mosquito repellents, sunscreens, bathing soaps, lotions, and deodorants. I also needed to buy a Greyhound ticket to travel to Kelowna, where the job was. I had to buy all of these, but I did not have a single penny in my pocket. I had sent all the money I had to my brother in Kampala. The next welfare cheque was three weeks away. I had only four days to report to work with the required items; otherwise, I would not get the job. The chance of my first paying job seemed to be slipping away.

Kuot came to my help; he was a friend indeed. He promised to buy the required items from his pocket. I thanked him profusely. To reduce the burden, though, I went through the list of the requirements, identifying needs from wants. A sleeping bag, gloves, goggles, and boots were essential. Mosquito repellents, sunscreens, bathing soaps, lotions, and deodorants were nonessentials. I had lived in the bushes for years, so the elements did not bother me.

Kuot took me to a Canadian Tire store to buy the essentials: a sleeping bag, gloves, goggles, and boots. The damage was a total of $115, which came out of Kuot's pocket. But we were not done yet.

I needed a Greyhound bus ticket from Vancouver to the job site in Kelowna, BC. Kuot drove me to a Greyhound station located in Vancouver. A one-way ticket cost $30, which also came out of Kuot's pocket. I felt terrible for draining my friend's pocket, and I promised to repay him.

We bought the ticket for tomorrow at 2:30 p.m. Unfortunately, Kuot was working that day, so he could not drive me to the bus station. Instead, he gave me an additional $10, two dollars for a sky-train ticket and the remaining eight dollars for lunch.

The following morning, I grabbed my backpack and hit the road. Instead of wasting my two dollars on a ticket, I decided to walk to the bus station. It took us over thirty minutes to drive from New Westminster to Vancouver, so I estimated it to be about four hours on foot. Four hours? Give me a break! I walked from Sudan to Ethiopia for nearly three months. Four hours was a piece of cake. Besides, I hated the sky-train because invisible drivers drove them; I did not think it was safe. By walking, I was saving my life and my two dollars.

A friend of mine had googled the directions and wrote down the instructions for me to follow, from New Westminster to the Greyhound Bus Station in Vancouver. With my essentials in the backpack, a bottle of water in my backpack pocket, and ten dollars in my pocket, I walked from Seventh Street, New Westminster, to Third Avenue. I turned right and walked for five blocks to 12th Street. I followed 12th Street to Burnaby, where it changed to Kingsway. I walked on Kingsway for about two hours to Vancouver, where it changed to Main Street. I walked on Main Street for about thirty-five minutes and turned onto First Avenue. From there, I walked one block down and turned onto Station Street. And there it was, Pacific Central Station, 1150 Station Street, Vancouver, BC. It took me three hours and forty-five minutes, and I was not even tired.

I arrived there at around noon, two hours before my departure time. After a nearly four-hour walk, I was hungry and wanted to refuel. So, I went to McDonald's, located within the building, and ordered the only thing I knew how to order: a cheeseburger with Coke and fries: $4.50. I gave my precious $10 and received my change of $5.50.

This amount was enough for my tomorrow's lunch. Eating two or three times a day was not my thing. I was used to eating once a day in Kakuma. At work, I was told that meals were available, deducted from the paycheque, so I was not worried. Besides, I was once an *Anya-nya*, and the *Anya-nya* never went hungry in the wilderness, for there was always something to eat, being wild animals, fruits, or tubers.

At 1:45 p.m., we queued up at the bay to board the bus. It was my first time on a Canadian bus. And what surprised me the most was how peaceful and organized the passengers were in the line-up. Back in Kakuma, I would be kicking and elbowing my way in and out of the line. There were no peaceful queues in Kakuma: at distribution centers, or water stations, or entering the UN compound; you needed muscles to protect yourself or else you would not get served. But at the bus station, everyone just lined up one after another without anyone cutting the line off, with no security guards or police swatting people.

Soon, the driver opened the door, and we boarded. I took a seat right in the middle of the bus. All the seats were filled up one by one. A few seats remained vacant, but the bus picked up other passengers along the way. No one sat beside me, so I had two seats for myself.

I looked around, trying to see someone who looked like me, to no avail. English flew around me. Everyone seemed to know what they were doing and where they were going, except me. I had no idea where I was heading and how long it would take to get to my worksite.

I got up and went to the driver. "I am going to Kilona," I said.

"I am sorry," the driver said. "Where are you going?"

"Kilona," I said.

"Let me see your ticket," the driver said. "Oh, yes. Kelowna. I know where that is. Sit down; I will let you know when to get off."

It was 2:00 p.m. as the bus trundled from the depot, rocking us from side to side as we traveled these unfamiliar roads; my brain could not afford the time to daydream or rest. Some chattered; their voices rose and blended in the sweet ritual of friends.

Twenty minutes into our trip, a woman who was sitting on the opposite aisle walked up to me and said, "Would you mind if I sat next to you?"

She was sitting alone in her seat, and I wondered why she came to my seat. "No problem," I said as I scooted over, pressing myself to the window.

"Thank you," she said as she sat down. "It's going to be a long trip," she said as she put her brown handbag on her lap. "Are you going to Alberta?"

"No, I'm going to Kilona," I said.

"I'm sorry, where?"

I removed the ticket from my chest pocket and showed it to her. "Kilona."

"Oh, Kelowna," she said. "You have such a lovely accent," she said. "Where are you from?"

"Sudan," I said.

"Wonderful! How long have you been in Canada?

"Two months and a half."

"Amazing! Only two months? Your English is excellent."

I was flattered by the women's compliment. It was my first time holding a conversation with a Canadian without an interpreter, and I was proud of that. We talked on the entire trip; several times, we resorted to writing what we were attempting to communicate, passing the notes to each other. She kept asking many questions, and I answered them to the best of my ability. I told her I was going to Kelowna for work. She said she had retired a couple of years earlier and that now she just liked to travel. She was returning to Saskatoon after visiting a family member in Victoria. Her name was Carnahan Bernice.

The Canadian woman reminded me of my mother, mainly when she talked about retirement. If I had not left my mother, she would have retired by now. I would have married a wife; then my mother would live with my wife and me, only traveling to visit my other brothers and sisters. This was because I was the lastborn; lastborn children were expected to take care of their aging parents. I was glad that I was going to my first paying job, and I would send money to my mother.

My daydream was cut short when the bus stopped in Chilliwack, and the driver told us we had thirty minutes to stretch our legs and grab something to eat. So, everyone got off the bus and rushed to fast-food restaurants nearby. My new friend, Carnahan Bernice, offered to buy me something, but I said I was not hungry. I was hungry but not starving. Eating two or three times a day was an unnecessary luxury. But Carnahan gave me $20, anyway. I was hesitant to take money from a stranger, but she insisted. I figured that she wanted to show me how welcome I was in Canada. Besides, Dinka culture dictated that a gift from an elder, no matter how trivial it was, was good luck or blessing. Therefore, not taking an elderly gift was ungrateful, but it was considered bad luck. So, I took the money and thanked her for her generosity.

Now I had $25.50 in my pocket. If I did not get the job, this money would take me back to Vancouver. I was sure of that. It would not buy me a bus ticket, but I did not need it. It was a four-hour and a half drive from Vancouver to Kelowna, and I estimated that it would be at least a three or four-day walk back to Vancouver. $24.50 would buy me several bottles of water and cheeseburger meals to take me back to Vancouver. It was doable. Easily doable.

We reached Kelowna at 5:00 p.m., and the driver told me it was my destination. I thanked Carnahan for her company and her generosity. She took my telephone number and address and asked me to keep in touch. She also wrote her address and telephone number on a piece of paper and gave it to me.

I exited the bus and headed to a nearby gas station. I was advised that whenever I was unsure of the direction, I could go to any nearby gas station for some directions. I found a young cashier in the store, and she said the campsite was not too far away and showed me the direction. I thanked the cashier and headed south. It was around 7:30 p.m., and the summer sun was still shining.

One block away from the gas station was a McDonald's restaurant. My stomach started rumbling when I saw the restaurant. It had been seven hours since I had eaten the cheeseburger, fries, and Coke in Vancouver. I realized one thing about Canadian foods: they do not stay in the stomach for too long. You eat now, and two hours later, your stomach is empty. No wonder they invented what they call "desserts" after every meal and "snacks" before the next heavy meal. Back home, we ate *ugali*, a thick porridge made from maize flour or other flour, such as millet or sorghum flour, and it was sometimes mixed with cassava flour. It was cooked in boiling water until it reached a stiff or firm dough-like consistency. Then it was served with all kinds of vegetables, soups or broths. It was filling and stayed in your stomach longer, unlike these Canadian foods.

I made a mental calculation. If I spent another $4.50, I would remain with $20.50. This amount would still buy me four meals as I walked back to New Westminster if I did not get the job. So, I entered the restaurant and ordered my cheeseburger, French fries, and a Coke. Now I was becoming a real Canadian because I ate twice a day.

I arrived at the campsite at around 8:00 p.m. I met my manager, named Shukri, from East India. The manager pointed at a tent, saying I should go there and meet my supervisor, named Sebit Muorwel, who would show me where to stay.

The name Sebit Muorwel told me this supervisor must be from my tribe, Agaar, because every Agaar name carries a story or two. His name was Sebit, meaning he was born on Saturday, and his father's name was Muorwel, meaning "man of his words."

Indeed, Sebit was from the Agaar. I was also glad to find several Sudanese and Kenyans working there. Kiswahili, Arabic, and Dinka languages flew in the air. I was at home.

At 5:00 a.m., we started the job, planting trees. Sebit, my supervisor, showed me how to do the job. First, you thrust the shovel into the ground, then pressed the shovel deeper using your right foot before you tilted the shovel to create a hole. Next, you had to make sure that the hole was not too shallow or too deep. After making the hole, you grabbed a seedling with your left hand and placed it in the hole, making sure not to put the tree in the planting hole too deep that any part of the trunk flare was covered with soil. Finally, you backfilled the hole. Then, you counted five steps and planted another tree.

It was $0.15 to plant one tree, and you were paid based on how many seedlings you had grown. On my first day, I planted a total of 500 seedlings, making $75. On the second day, I planted 1000 seedlings. My mental calculation told me I had a total of $150 in my account. I was immensely proud of myself. My money was growing like the seedlings.

Most people consider the job to be tough. The seedlings were in a truck. Everyone had a pouch that looked like a mailbag. You carried 150 seedlings at a time, fifty on your right hip, fifty on your left, and fifty on the back. Then, after planting, you walked back to the truck to get more. Sometimes, a helicopter placed the seedlings on the mountain top, and we had to climb up and down to get the seedlings and plant them.

While all my coworkers complained about living in the wilderness, I enjoyed every moment of it. Living in the wilderness on the mountain top reminded me of Dimma. With the seedlings dangling like magazines and the shovel in my hand like a Kalashnikov, I was scaling the mountain at ease like a mountain goat. Sometimes, I sang revolutionary songs as I worked. This singing fueled me to work even harder. All the things that had happened to me in the past turned out to be the main foundation of my future.

By the end of the first week, I was planting an average of 2000 seedlings a day. This was $300 (200 x $0.15). Money was growing in my account faster than the trees I was growing. After one month, the planting season was over. After taxes and expenses incurred, such as food and other costs, were deducted, I was given a cheque for $4,500. I was immensely proud of myself. My sweat had resulted in a fortune.

With the cheque in my pocket, I got a ride from Kelowna to Abbotsford. I did not know that I could cash my cheque anywhere. I kept the cheque, hoping to come and cash it in New Westminster, where I did my transactions. It was when I had arrived that Kuot told me cheques were cashed anywhere in Canada.

I bought a Greyhound ticket from Abbotsford to Vancouver, using the $20 that Carnahan Bernice, the Canadian Good Samaritan, gave me. The funny thing was that the bus stopped at a station in New Westminster, closer to where I lived, but I did not know it. So, I had to go all the way to Vancouver, and then I walked for 3:40 hours from Vancouver to New Westminster with the cheque in my pocket, mind you. None of that bothered me; I was used to learning things the hard way.

After I arrived in New Westminster, the first thing I did was to write a letter to Carnahan Bernice, thanking her for her generosity. I told her that the $20 she gave me had helped me immensely and that it was much appreciated. I also said that her gift was a piece of good luck and that I got the job and earned a lot of money.

One week later, Carnahan Bernice replied. I did not understand most of what she wrote because she used big words, and her handwriting was all joined letters. But surprisingly, she put another $20 inside the envelope. So that was more good luck.

After cashing my cheque, I sent $1,500 to my brother, who was still waiting in Kampala, so that he could buy food and clothes to take back home to our mother. I had left with $3000, plus the $20 gift from Carnahan. Kuot's car had broken down, and he did not have enough money to repair it. So, I gave him $1,500 to buy a transmission for his car. Like Dinka says, "Friendship is about the hand going and the hand coming," meaning giving and receiving. It was Kuot who bought me a plane ticket from Halifax to British Columbia. And he purchased my work essentials such as a sleeping bag, steel-toed boots, goggles, and gloves. It was my turn to help him when his car broke down. We had been looking out for one another since we met in Dimma in 1989.

I used the remaining money to buy myself shoes and clothes. I paid my bills, including the money that the government used for my process of resettling in Canada.

Now, with work experience in my belt, finding my second job was extremely easy. I heard about a company named Morning Star Nursery that was hiring. I was hired on the spot when I applied. My job included planting, weeding, watering, or pruning flowers. It paid $9 per hour.

This job was far away, and there was no public transit. So, a company van picked us up. But sometimes, when the van broke down or the driver did not come to work, we stayed home, and we were not paid. I did not like to stay home and not get paid. I had stayed home and not got paid for nearly fifteen years in Kakuma and Dimma. So, I did not want to stay home and not get paid in this beautiful country, where anyone willing to work gets rewarded. So, I had to look for another job.

I applied at Autogas Propane, and I was hired as a pump attendant. We sold gas, diesel, and propane. There was also a convenience store, so I was both the cashier and pump attendant. This job was relatively easy, and I enjoyed it a lot.

Like any other job, though, I preferred and loathed other aspects of my job as a pump attendant. My coworkers were genuinely lovely and friendly. I particularly liked the owner of the company, Bob Good. He worked hard. Even though he was the owner of the company, he stayed late. It was when I was about to close that he would leave. Sometimes, he even drove me to a sky-train or bus station. I liked the job so much that I looked forward to going to work every day.

But the other loathed aspects of my job were shortages. Sometimes, customers drove away without paying. And you, the employee, had to answer to your supervisors and managers why and how the customers drove away without paying. You had a lot of explaining to do, especially if you had not written down the plate number of the customer, who had driven away without paying. Sometimes, you had to pay the shortages from your pocket that occurred during your shift. Luckily, I did not have many drive-away incidents on my shifts.

But some of my coworkers wanted to get me in trouble. So, at the end of my shift, I counted the money, put it in an envelope, sealed it, wrote my name and the total amount of money on the back of the envelope before putting it in the safe. In the morning, when the manager was balancing the book, $20, $40, or $60 was missing from the envelope. What was surprising was that the envelope was not ripped or torn.

I was called in for questioning almost every week as to why cash was missing from my shifts. I did not understand why money kept disappearing from the envelope. I knew someone wanted to get me in trouble. But there was no way I could find out who the thief was. The situation was so bad that I wanted to quit. But my manager, named Akbar, from Iran, knew it was not me. After all, who would take money from his shift knowing he would get in trouble? So, the manager told me not to quit and that he would get to the bottom of this.

One week later, the culprit was found. Secret surveillance cameras were installed inside the store. We, the employees, did not even know; only the managers knew about the cameras. That day after the end of my shift, I counted the money, put it in an envelope, sealed it, and put it in the safe. The culprit who relieved me opened the safe and used a pocketknife to loosen the flap without tearing the envelope. Then he took $60 before re-sealing the envelope. Everything was recorded live on the tape—he was caught red-handed. He tried to deny any wrongdoing, only to be shown the footage of him opening the envelope and taking the money. He was fired immediately.

After one year with Autogas, I was promoted to assistant manager. This is one of the good things about Canada. Companies like hard workers. If you work hard, you will be acknowledged and rewarded. I always devoted my full attention to the company and never had problems with my bosses. My guerrilla warfare training and indoctrination taught me to obey seniors' orders, which had become handy in the workforce. I had never been written up or fired in any company I had worked for since I moved to Canada.

While working for Autogas, I found my second job working at Chevron. I worked at Autogas from 6:00 a.m. to 2:30 p.m. From there, I went to Chevron and worked from 4:00 p.m. to midnight.

With a double paycheque, big bucks started rolling in every two weeks. I established a small business for my brother back home and paid all my debts.

It puzzled me that some Canadians, especially young people, took this country for granted. People did not want to work hard but instead blame others, and they did not appreciate what they had. In some parts of the world, young men and women do not have these opportunities. I did not understand how anyone could be homeless in this beautiful country where there were opportunities. I did not know English fluently, yet I had been hired and worked two jobs.

With my two jobs, I bought my first car, a red Acura 2002. First, I needed a driver's license. Then, I went to ICBC (International Corporation of British Columbia) to take the "Knowledge Test." I took my driver's license exam, and I failed. I got a seventy-five percent mark, and you needed eighty percent to be issued a permitted Class 7. I returned home and studied the book for two weeks. In my second attempt, I got eighty percent. I passed, and I was issued a class 7 L.

There were some restrictions. First, I had to always drive with someone with a full license in the car. In other words, I should not operate the vehicle alone. In addition, I had to display the red-letter L on my car's bumper to show other road users that I was a learner. Also, I should not drive after midnight.

Kuot taught me to drive in our neighborhood. Driving looked easy when Kuot was doing it. But when I sat behind the wheel for the first time, it was a different story. What threw me off the most was the position of the wheel. I could not balance in the middle of the road because the wheel was placed on the left, not in the center, where it was supposed to be.

Another problem was the pedal. I could not feel the pedal with my shoes on, so I jumped on the pedal, almost hitting a parked car. But everything has a solution. In my first lesson, I drove bare-footed, and this made it easier for me to feel the gas and the brake pedals.

I learned what we call "the *Anya-nya* way," meaning a guerrilla knows things in unconventional ways. With this mindset, I drove my car to work one day. I was not even comfortable yet because I had not taken many lessons from Kuot. I was overconfident of my non-existent abilities.

The first time I drove my car alone was on Saturday, and there were not that many drivers on the road. It had snowed that day, so I had to go slow and careful. But the major problem was that the windshield became foggy, and I did not know how to turn on the heater or wipers. No problem. I did it the *Anya-nya* (unconventional way), and I used rags to wipe the windshield. Every five minutes or so, when the windshield became foggy and I could not see properly, I would pull off the road and manually wipe the windshield with the rags. I did this repeatedly until I reached the worksite safely. One of my coworkers eventually showed me how to turn on the defroster, heater, and windshield wipers.

No buses were going to my work site, so I had to drive. I just had to be careful not to get caught driving with a Learner's license. I was caught once by the police, who gave me a double-violation ticket of $146, $73 for driving without a supervisor, and $73 for not displaying the L sign. The police also gave me two options: either call a friend with a full license to drive the car home or have it towed, and I would pay the towing fees. So, I called a friend to come and drive the car.

Many of my friends had similar stories. They were determined to learn to drive by any means possible. One of these friends was Peter Mangok Gum. Peter Mangok received many violation tickets because he drove without a supervisor. But he was determined to pay the ticket and drive the next day again. Back then, Canadian police were good. I do not know what they did to Peter's car. But as soon as Peter started his car, the police would show up out of nowhere and said, "Peter, where are you going? You know you are not supposed to drive without a supervisor."

Shortly after I was issued that doubled-violation ticket, I took a road test, and I failed. The examiner said I did not slow down in one of the school zones. I was also not shoulder-checking regularly. I also received demerits in parallel and reverse parking. The examiner advised me to work on these things before booking my next road test. Two weeks later, I retook the road test, and I passed. I received my Class 5 new driver's license.

Trucker

Working at Autogas Propane as an assistant manager, I made $14.50 per hour. However, I learned that truck drivers made between $20 to $28 per hour. That was that. I figured out I was wasting my time working at the gas station. I was going to be a truck driver to make more money. And nothing was going to stop me.

I went to the Insurance Corporation of British Columbia (ICBC) office to inquire about what it took to be a truck driver. A gray-haired man sitting behind the desk took my license and busied his fingers on the keyboard, checking my driving records. They were clean.

"Take this book," the gray-haired man said, handing me a guide for professional drivers. "And go to a driving school of your choice to take air brake courses. Then you come back to take a knowledge test. If you pass the test, you'll get your commercial vehicle license."

Before finding a driving school, I read the book first. I learned all kinds of trucking know-how, from heavy vehicle braking systems to identifying signs, signals, and road markings, needed before getting behind the wheel.

In 2005, I enrolled in a commercial driving school in Surrey, British Columbia. It was the beginning of my new adventure, which I first found to be invigorating and intimidating at the same time. This seemed like an improbable adventure because I had only ridden on the back of a truck twice in my entire life (from Dimma to Pakhok and from Lokichogio to Kakuma, Kenya). I had never sat in a cab before, let alone driven the truck. Additionally, I had never driven a manual transmission before. Thus, I was probably the most unlikely candidate to become a truck driver in the world. But my philosophy was, "If others can do it, I can do it too."

There were about twenty of us in the class. Our instructor was a

Canadian man who liked to flavor his sentences with many F-words, a testimony that he had been in the trucking business his entire life. But he knew the subject he was teaching. He emphasized air brakes, which was the main reason why we took the course:

Air brakes work using compressed air instead of hydraulic fluid. Air brakes can be either drum brakes or disc brakes, or a combination of both. An engine-mounted compressor pressurizes air. The air compressor then pumps the air into the air storage tanks, which store the compressed air until it is needed to stop the tractor-trailer.

Sitting in the class, I found the air brake components were far more complicated than the Kalashnikov components. They included an air compressor, reservoir, foot valve, brake chambers, airlines, brake shoes, and drums. As a truck driver, I should know exactly how much hard work it took to guarantee that every vehicle component was working at optimal capacity, which was why I had to take these courses.

After passing the course, I was issued a certificate to take to the ICBC to do the knowledge test. The certificate allowed me to take the test three times, and if I failed three times, I had to return to school to retake the courses. It cost me $600 to take the classes, so I would have to pay another $600 to retake the courses if I failed the test.

At the ICBC, I was shown a computer. There were thirty-five multiple-choice questions, and I needed to answer twenty-eight of them correctly to get eighty percent, which was the passing mark. In my first attempt, I got twenty-seven out of thirty-five, which was seventy-seven percent. I had failed. No problem. I still had two attempts.

The following week, I went back to take the test after I had studied a lot. I got thirty out of thirty-five questions, which was eighty-five percent. A big smile registered on my face, even though I was alone with the computer. I went to the counter to have my photo taken and issued my commercial driver's license.

With my learner's license, I started building firsthand experience behind the wheel. But getting a trucking experience was the most expensive thing I had ever encountered. It was $85 per hour to go to driving practice. Since I had never driven a manual transmission before, the instructor estimated that I needed at least forty hours. Eventually, the instructor made a deal with me that I could pay $3,500 and take as many hours as needed until I passed my road test and got my license. That sounded like a good deal. I paid the money.

For the first couple of days, I sat in the truck with other students watching how to shift up and down, turn, brake, double-clutch, and so on. The instructor emphasized double-clutching, the act of using the clutch pedal twice during a single shift between gears.

When it was time for me to start my actual driving lesson, I had about thirty minutes of verbal instructions before climbing into a Peterbilt truck laced with rust. I fired it up, and the engine diesel roared like a tank, reminding me of the days when I was in the battle. The quavering roar of the diesel engine drowned out the sounds of the entire world around me. With the instructor beside me shouting instructions, I drove on a low-traffic route in Surrey, BC, learning how to shift through thirteen gears of the eighteen-wheeler or the tractor-trailer.

The training consisted of many parts. First, I learned coupling and uncoupling—the connecting and disconnecting of the tractor and trailer. Then, I provided a verbal commentary of an inspection of the tractor and trailer. Next was backing up, which was the most challenging part of being a truck driver. There were two types of backups: straight-line backup and a forty-five-degree backup, where you back up at an angle. None of these were easy.

"When the trailer goes left, steer left," the instructor yelled. "When the trailer goes right, steer right."

After I practiced driving for over forty hours and the instructor felt I was ready to take the test, I booked my commercial driver's road test at my local driver's licensing office and filled out all the paperwork. The examination began. The ICBC examiner sat beside me as I showcased what I had learned. I was nervous. Extremely nervous.

Starting with coupling, I backed up the tractor, aligning it to the trailer. Then I exited for a visual inspection, ensuring that the tractor's fifth wheel was aligned to the trailer's kingpin. Both apparatuses were correctly aligned. Next, I entered the cab and backed up under the trailer until the trailer's kingpin slid under the groove in the fifth wheel. The kingpin caused the locking mechanism to engage, which kept the trailer locked to the tractor. Finally, I checked to make sure that the fifth wheel was thoroughly lubricated for a smooth turning.

The coupling and uncoupling (the connecting and disconnecting of tractor and trailer) took me around ten minutes. I had thirty-five minutes left to make my pre-inspection trip. The instructor took notes and watched the time. I had between forty-five and fifty minutes to complete the pre-trip inspection test and two hours for the driving test. I was doing good so far.

After the tractor was connected to the trailer, I started the pre-trip inspection test. First, I started inside the cab, checking the seats and seatbelt, the horns, the gauges, the pedals, etc., ensuring that every part worked and there was no damage. Then I exited and opened the hood, checking everything under the hood, including oil, antifreeze, and steering fluids, as well as all other parts and components.

Finally, I walked clockwise around the tractor-trailer, checking everything from tires to brakes to the body of the tractor-trailer. While inspecting, I touched every component and told the examiner the name of the part and what I was looking for. For example, for tires, I checked pressure, wear and tear, and tread depth. To check the tread depth, you used a toonie. You slipped a toonie in between your tread blocks. If the tread reached the bear's paws, your tires have lots of treads left. But if the tread gets only as far as the word 'DOLLARS' (or 'CANADA'), your tires are worn and need to be replaced.

"Very good," the examiner said. "You have passed your pre-trip inspection test."

I smiled, and my confidence boosted. But I still had the most crucial test. I must demonstrate all the trucking skills I had learned—everything from starting, stopping, shifting gears, turning, backing up, parking, merging on highways, and so much more. I got behind the wheel and adjusted the seat and mirrors. I put it in gear and released the parking brake. The truck eased forward, spinning a few times before finding traction. I cruised along, double-clutching to shift up. The examiner, sitting next to me, watched me closely, taking notes now and then.

Everything went well until I went up the hill. The truck was losing both speed and power, so I tried to downshift. In doing so, I missed a shift, and I could not put it in gear. I ended up stalling. I had to stop and restart the truck again. This caused me demerits. Also, when I was going down the hill, I tried to shift up, but I missed the gear again, and I was in neutral for a while before I managed to find the gear. More demerits were added.

But my major problem occurred during the backup test. To begin with, I had forgotten to honk before backing up. This mistake automatically failed me. But the examiner allowed me to carry on with the test, anyway. Knowing I had screwed up the major part, I already lost confidence, and I became extremely nervous. I knocked out several cones during the actual backup between obstacles, which I was not supposed to touch. The final verdict was that I passed the pre-trip inspection test and failed the driving test. Backing a sixty-five-foot tractor-trailer was extremely difficult. Even the examiner knew this.

"It's going to take you at least one year before you become comfortable backing up," the examiner said. "The reason I failed you was because you did not honk before backing up."

I took more backup lessons. And in my second attempt, I passed, and I was issued my class one commercial driver's license. Finally, I was ready to roll and make the big bucks.

But first, I had to decide whether I should do local, short-haul, or long-haul trucking. I chose long-haul because I knew it would be easier to drive on highways than congested local roads. Finding a trucking job was easy because many companies were hiring. But, first, I was teamed up with a guy named Alan to get some experience. Alan, a driver from Winnipeg who had been driving for forty-three years, constantly bragged about his ability to persevere through rides that other drivers did not dare attempt.

In our truck, a brand-new Volvo, we had a doubled bed bunker inside the cab, where we slept. We also had a small fridge, a TV, and a DVD player. So, while one person drove for a maximum of twelve hours, the other person slept or watched movies, relaxing until his shift returned.

Our first run lasted for twenty-one days. We took a load from Richmond, BC, to Spokane, Washington. From there, we grabbed another shipment to Florida, Miami. We made several pickups and drop-offs within the USA before finally taking a load to Toronto, Ontario. From Toronto, we took a load to Winnipeg, Manitoba. Since my co-driver was from Winnipeg, we spent three days in Winnipeg; Alan stayed in his apartment while I stayed in the truck. From Winnipeg, we took a load back to Vancouver. Again, I spent three days in my apartment while Alan remained in the truck. Then we left again.

In the first round trip, we drove for about 15,000 miles. I was paid $0.27 per mile, meaning I had a total of $4,050 before taxes and deductions in my account. The income was appreciated because I had many debts and bills to pay. I had borrowed money from the bank and sent it to South Sudan so that my brother could open a business to take care of our mother, plus the $3500 I borrowed from my bank to get my license. I also still had to pay the money the government used to resettle me to Canada. Then I had to pay my bills, car payments and insurance, credit cards, and so on.

After driving with Alan for two months, I joined one of my friends, Tong Unguech, who worked for Trans-border Logistics. Driving with Tong was better because we shared the same culture, language, and we liked the same music.

But I intended to gain experience and drive solo. There were disadvantages of team driving. It was always hard to decide when to relax, which route to take, which music to play, and how loud you wanted it played. If you were alone, you made decisions, doing as you wish. So, after driving for several months with Tong to gain experience, I started driving solo.

What I liked about truck driving was that there were no formal work shifts. Timecards and regular shifts were foreign concepts. Instead, load pickups and deliveries were made at different times. One piece of work, for example, began when I backed my tractor-trailer into the dock to be loaded and ended when I backed it into another dock to be unloaded, whether it was dawn or dust, midnight or midday. This unpredictability extended to the routes I took. Truckers did not take a single way; even if you were doing pin to pin, they changed their routes.

Another thing I liked the most about being a truck driver was being my boss. My *Anya-nya* mentality still kicked in now and then, especially when I encountered bosses who were overly arrogant in their authority. However, when away for any length of time, whether a few days, weeks, or months, as a solo driver, I made the most of my decisions because I was doing my job satisfactorily, and no one got in my face.

My first solo trips were memorable: I took a load from British Columbia to Alberta. It took me all day to reach Calgary. The warehouse opened twenty-four hours, so I backed the trailer into the dock at around midnight. I exited and watched the forklift truck emptying my trailer. When done, I pulled out of the dock, closed the door, grabbed my signed bill, and drove to a nearby truck stop to get fuel and food before dialing the dispatcher, notifying him that my trailer was empty. The dispatcher told me there was a load in Lethbridge going to Mississauga, Ontario. That was over 2,000 miles away. The only thing that makes a trucker grin is a lot of miles. But a 2000-mile trip turned my grin into a big smile. A lot of miles meant a lot of money. It was that simple.

But it was my second load from Lethbridge to Mississauga that tested my patience and resilience as a trucker. I backed into a dock at a warehouse in Lethbridge, and my truck was loaded with eggs. After I pulled out of the dock to find a scale to weigh my load, it was 48,000 pounds. The maximum weight my truck could take was 45,000. So, I was 3,000 pounds overweight. This was problematic. I could get a hefty fine at any weigh station for being overloaded.

I went back to the company to take some of the load off, but unfortunately, they were already closed for the day. It was Friday, and they were not open until Monday. The shipment was "hot," meaning the load was needed urgently. If I waited for the warehouse to open and reduce the load, I would be at least two days late. On the other hand, if I took the load, I could be ticketed on the way. I was in a dilemma.

I called the dispatcher and told him about this nightmare. I yelled at the dispatcher, literally, for assigning me to this load, knowing it was over the limit. That was another good thing about being a truck driver. When you knew you were right, you screamed your lungs out to the manager or dispatcher. There was nothing they could do. Because if they screamed back, I would quit right there and leave the truck anywhere. I would find another job right away or take a flight home. The company had to fly another driver to that location and drive the truck back home. It cost the company a lot of money. So, the managers and dispatchers avoided antagonizing their drivers. The dispatcher apologized and asked me to do the best I could to deliver the load.

I had no choice but to take the risk. I had to drive at night, hoping that most of the scales were closed. Driving on Trans-Canada Highway, it was apparent that the snowplows had not done an excellent job. Snow was about three inches deep, and it was slippery. I held my speedometer below fifty. The only advantage I had was being overloaded, which increased traction on the slippery road.

Arriving at Sudbury, all hell broke loose. I had a nearly five-mile-long downhill grade ahead of me. I was told that many drivers had lost their trucks and lives in this place. I could feel the sweat running down my arms, and my hands were shaking. The road surface was a mixture of rain, slush, and ice.

I downshifted my thirteen-speed transmission to fifth gear, slowed to twenty-four mph, and set my Jake brake to all cylinders. The Jake brake (an air compressor inhibitor that turned the engine into the primary braking system) sounded like the Howitzer as it worked to keep my heavily loaded truck-trailer under control. Looking at my tachometer, it was at 2,000 rpm, and I was at twenty-fix mph. I brushed the brake to bring the speed down to twenty-three mph. Before I knew it, I overcame the obstacle easily. That was it. My confidence peaked, and I thought I could drive in any weather condition.

For the next two years, I long hauled across the eight provinces of Canada and forty-eight states of America, driving almost through every major highway and city in Canada and the USA. The once child soldier who trekked from Sudan to Ethiopia and Ethiopia to Kenya now cruised across North America. He was getting paid big bucks while cruising, mind you.

Further Education

Less than a month after I arrived in Canada, I went to school. But after two weeks in school, my brother called and told me how much they were suffering at home because the war was at its peak; people could not grow crops or rear cattle. I did not see any reason to study when my mother and siblings were dying of starvation. So, I left school and went to work, planting trees, pumping gases, and finally driving trucks, so I could pay my bills and support my family back home.

After my family was well off and I had paid off my debts, it was time for me to go back to school. I knew how crucial education was. Even when I was a truck driver, I had registered in a self-paced program in Pearson Adult Learning Center, where I could take all my assignments and do them on the road. While waiting to be loaded or unloaded, which sometimes could take an hour or more, I used this time to do my assignments. After one month or so away, I returned to spend three days at home before taking another load. In those three days, I would take all my completed assignments to school to be marked, take all the necessary tests or exams, and grab another bundle of assignments before hitting the road. The progress was slow but effective because I persisted.

In Kakuma, I had reached grade ten (form two). I thought I knew English very well. But when I came to Canada, it was a different story. I realized that my English writing was the equivalent of a Canadian second grader, and my speaking had no equivalency. So, I knew I had to work hard to get an education in my new country.

When I first registered in school in Canada, I was twenty-two years old, and I was not allowed to join high school; the only option was to go to adult school to take the English as a Second Language program. A friend of mine, who had been in Canada for two years and knew English very well, took me to Pearson Adult Learning Center, located in New Westminster, BC. He acted as my translator.

As soon as we entered the office, a young woman approached us and inquired about our visit after greeting and introducing herself as Trudy. My friend, the translator, explained to Trudy that I wanted to enroll, and he continued answering Trudy's questions on my behalf. But eventually, Trudy told the translator to stop talking and that she wanted to hear from me, her student. She asked me a few questions, such as my home address, where I was born, and when I came to Canada. I thought I answered the questions very well. And I felt good talking to a Canadian teacher in English less than a month after I had arrived in Canada. But my dignity was hurt when my friend whispered to me that I used Dinka more than English in my reply. Of course, he had exaggerated, just to make fun of me, like he always did, every time I tried to speak in English. My enthusiasm to talk in English faded away as a result.

Discouraged by my friend's remarks, I just wanted to shut my mouth up and leave quietly. But then I realized it was not possible to shut your mouth in Trudy's presence, no matter how laconic or terse you thought you were. The woman could talk. That was a fact. Because even after the registration was completed, the questions continued flowing from the woman's lips at a speed I could not imagine.

"Willy, do you have any questions?" she said, apparently trying to squeeze every piece of English vocabulary out of me to determine my grade. "Willy, you are coming to school tomorrow morning, right?

Willy, do you know which bus to take? Willy...? Willy...? Willy...?"

I did my best to answer her questions. I told her I would ride my bicycle to school. I also wanted to know a safe place to park my bike every time I came to school. But because I did not know how to pronounce the letters "P" and "F" differently, the words "park" and "fuck" sounded similar. The F-word was easy to pronoun because my friends, who always listened to Black Entertainment Television and rap music, used it a lot. So, at the end, when Trudy said, "Do you have any questions?" I set my tongue wagging. "Where can I fuck my bicycle?"

My friend tried to conceal laughing but to no avail. Trudy repeatedly told him to stop laughing before she asked me to repeat what I just said. Finally, I repeated the exact words, "Where can I fuck my bicycle?"

Trudy just looked as if she was thinking, "I have a lot of work to do this semester!" She finally said, "Oh, you want to know where to park your bicycle?" trying to correct me. "Let's go outside to show you the bike rack."

"Do you know what you've just said to that lady?" my friend said, still laughing when we were on our way home. "You told her you wanted to make love to your bicycle!"

I was so embarrassed. But to make things even worse, my friend proceeded home and told this story to the rest of our friends.

"You have no idea why Willy wants to go to school so badly!" he said mockingly. "He wants some privacy with his bike to f★★k it. That's what he told the teacher!"

The group of guys who had just emerged fresh from their usual place—a nearby pub—roared in laughter. And they continued to mock me for months. Whenever I came from school, they would say all sorts of nasty things.

"How's your day in school with the bicycle?" they would say. "Pleasurable, I suppose. Hahaha!"

Nevertheless, their mocking compelled me to go to school every day because I wanted to know English to avoid the mocking and embarrassment.

The following day after I talked with Trudy, I sat for an entrance examination that tested my English and math levels. I did well in math and took three consecutive exams to find my level. I did not do well in English. I was put in level H, called Purple, because we used an English book with that color. I did not know what grade that was. Perhaps grade four or five.

I registered in four classes: English, math, social studies, and history. English was divided into three: grammar, reading, and comprehension. I took history and social studies mainly because I wanted to know the history of Canada to pass my citizenship test.

I worked hard in class at Pearson Adult Learning Center; I did all my assignments and came to class early even though I was working a full-time job. My first teachers, included Trudy, L, and Alan, were incredibly supportive. Their office remained open during school hours so that any student who needed help could walk in. What amazed me was that every teacher was willing to sit down with me one-on-one in any subject, even if it was not the subject they taught. All the teachers were warm, accessible, and caring.

The teachers were inspirational. When I was struggling with English, especially essay writing, to the point that I wanted to quit, I received unwavering support from all the teachers, who encouraged and motivated me to keep trying harder. When I skipped essay classes, thinking I would get away with it, my first English teacher (I forgot her name, maybe Patricia?) made sure I did not get away with anything. Every time I missed a class or two, she would save all the assignments for me. As soon as she saw me, she would hand me bundles of handouts that I "must" complete and give them back to her for marking. She always said she wanted the assignments "next Monday," which meant I had to do them on the weekend because I worked Monday to Friday. I missed too many weekend parties because of her. On top of that, she kept telling me that I could not go to the next class, let alone college, without mastering essay writing.

Another time, I was writing a five-paragraph essay, but I ran out of words after writing only two paragraphs. Frustrated, I went to Trudy and told her I was stuck and did not want to complete the essay anymore. Trudy just looked at me and said, "We are all stuck, but we still have to do our best to complete our essays." Then she opened her computer and showed me the assignment she was working on when she was teaching and studying at the same time. Again, I was left with nothing other than to console myself that I was not as dumb as I thought I was after all because even my teacher—a reservoir of all English vocabulary—struggled with her essay too.

Small gestures like that motivated me to pay attention in class and listen to teachers' advice. For example, Paul had advised me to keep my writing clear and straightforward. He said this because I had bought myself a dictionary and crammed big words to impress the teachers. But the problem was that I did not know to put these words into meaningful sentences, which caused me bad grades in essays. So, Paul told me to stay away from big words or vocabulary that I did not know how to construct into a sentence; instead, I should use simple words.

Another teacher called L had given me excellent advice. He mentioned in the class that he read every night before going to bed and that anyone who wanted to improve their English should do the same thing. "All intelligent people read every night before going to bed," he said. Since then, reading and writing before going to bed became one of my habits.

I did a lot of reading. One day a friend showed me the New Westminster Public Library. It was my first time in a library, a house of books, and I could not believe the number of books in this house. At first, I thought this was a supermarket where books were sold. Then I was told the books were free. You just had to register and receive a library card, and I could have all the books I wanted.

All the books I ever wanted! My mind flashed back to Kakuma, where I ran after papers flying in the wind to catch and read them, or when I collected notes and newspapers in my teacher's restroom. Now I could read as much as I wanted. I grabbed five books that day, and the library became a frequent haunt for me.

But at first, adjusting to the Canadian classroom and school environ-ment in the Pearson Adult Learning Center was challenging. I had never seen such displays of affection in a school before. There was a Canadian couple (a boy and a girl) who sat directly behind me. They kissed and smooched, not only in front of other students but also the teachers. What struck me as odd was that the teachers allowed them to do so. In Africa, you could never hold a girl's hand in school, let alone kiss her.

These were high school dropouts in their early twenties, and they badmouthed everyone, including the teachers. The boy liked to call everyone "stupid." The girl liked to say, "fuck off." I was shocked the first time I heard that word from her mouth. In Dinka culture, girls would never say such a word in public.

The couple was very disruptive. They constantly talked, even during the tests or lectures. When a teacher told them to be quiet, they would not listen. And since they sat directly behind me, they dis-tracted me a lot because I could not pay attention to what the teacher said. One day I was angry, and I turned around and shushed them.

"What the hell are you saying?" the guy said. "Don't you even know how to talk? Why are you so stupid?"

"Be quiet," I said, thinking he did not understand the hand gesture I made to silence them.

"Fuck off!" the girl said.

Since that incident, they started disliking me. The couple called me stupid because I did not know how to speak English. This insult did not even irritate me because they called everyone stupid, includ-ing the teachers. And whenever I asked a question in the class, they laughed at my funny accent and incorrect English.

One time, I became angry with them when they called me stupid, and I said, "If you are that smart, why are you in the same class as me?" Of course, this question got on their nerves, and they hated me even more. But I did not care.

They were getting in my last nerve, almost waking up the *Any-nya* version buried inside me. Fortunately for them, they had mocked me in the class but avoided me outside.

But it was in the midterm that they found out I was not as stupid as they thought I was. When English results were given, they were thrilled with their marks. I overheard them bragging—the guy had gotten sixty-five percent and the girl sixty-eight percent. I had not received my result yet, and I was expecting the worst because if they got those grades and English was their first language, my paper would be awful. But I was astonished when I saw my result. The teacher handed the paper to me and whispered, "Very good!" I looked, and I could not believe it. Knowing they would be peeking over my shoulders to see what I got, I placed my paper visibly on the counter, facing up. They looked and saw a seventy-five percent mark. The looks on their faces said it all: they were wondering how the hell I got a better mark than them when I could not even speak the language that well. But they were even more surprised when math (my favorite subject) exam papers arrived. I scored ninety-three percent. They never called me stupid again.

But they did not stop talking in class during the lectures. One day, they made a teacher incredibly angry. It was in the Communication 11 class. I forgot the name of the teacher. I hated that teacher because of the remark he made in the class. Because of this young couple's disruptive behavior, the teacher generalized the entire class instead of talking to the culprits who were disrupting the class.

"You are all adults, and you should behave like ones," the teacher remarked. "Remember, there is a reason why you are still in primary level when you should be in colleges or university. You are all here because of your bad choices. Remember that."

This statement hurt me so badly, as it was not fair. The teacher did not know what opportunities we had had or not had because most of the students in our class were immigrants. And we had not had the opportunities to finish our studies in our respective countries due to war and other causes. So, the reason we had not studied was not our fault. Even if we were all dropouts, this remark would still have hurt us because there is something about pointing out the obvious that makes the words hurt more. Perhaps the teacher in question thought he could criticize us into better students, but the way he dragged out those words, enunciating each syllable with venom, told me otherwise.

I had a few friends at school. One of my first Canadian friends was a girl named Ashley. She was gorgeous. She approached me one day and introduced herself. In Dinka culture, a girl never approached a man. No matter how interested a girl was in a man, she always hid her feelings until the man approached her first. Approaching a man implied that the girl approached every man she met. So, Ashley's behavior was a turnoff.

Then I remembered a story told in Kakuma. When many young men were applying to go abroad, the elders made up bogus stories intended to discourage young men from going abroad. One of the stories told was that Canadian and American women liked to date refugees. Then they mistreated you. And when you broke up with her, she saw into it that you were either arrested or killed. Some girls would willingly sleep with you. Afterward, she would call the police saying you raped her. Others would trap you and become pregnant. Then she would dump you and demand child support for seventeen years. The government would then take every piece of ID you had, making sure you did not go anywhere.

Some of the stories were true. Shortly after we arrived, some of my friends ended up getting their wages garnished because they had failed to pay child support. A friend of mine who was in the USA was sentenced to ten years in prison for rape. His was a complete cultural misunderstanding. The friend in question had invited an American girl he was dating to his house. The girl came alone. This was when things went wrong. You see, in Dinka culture, when you invite a girl into your house and she comes by herself, this signals that she wants to sleep with you. A girl who does not want to sleep with you would come along with a friend or two to see the man she was dating. So, when my friend invited an American girl into his house, and the girl came alone, he thought the girl wanted sex with him. So, he began his advance on the girl. The girl said no, but she did not resist when the guy removed her clothes. But again, a Dinka girl often says no at first, but she eventually gives in when a man persists. So, the guy continued with his advance. When they were done, the girl went straight to the police station and reported the rape. My friend ended up in prison for ten years.

It was because of this cultural misunderstanding that I avoided Ashley. I did not want to be another victim. Besides, I had learned my lessons the hard way in Ethiopia when my friend Lhat Mabor and I started running after girls.

Luckily, there were many Sudanese women in New Westminster, Burnaby, and Surrey. I thought dating someone from my country would not cause any trouble because we knew our culture. But I was wrong. I learned another lesson the hard way.

I first dated a woman from the Kakwa tribe. It did not take long before I found another girl who caught my interest. She was from my tribe, Dinka. I did not see anything wrong with seeing two women because, in Dinka culture, a man could see as many women as possible. Polygamy was (and still is) the norm among the Dinka.

During a Christmas gathering, the entire Sudanese community in British Columbia had gathered for a Christmas party. Sitting at a table with the Dinka woman, the Equatoria woman felt ignored. So, the first thing the Equatoria woman did was go to the parking lot and broke every piece of glass in my car. Then she came inside to confront the other woman and me. A fight broke out between the two women inside the hall. They were separated, but they snuck outside to continue their fight, and they ended up hurting each other. Police were called, and the party ended prematurely. The Dinka woman had a shattered knee, and the Equatoria woman's eyebrow was bitten. I did not get away freely either: I ended up paying thousands of dollars to get my car fixed. Remember, this happened in front of the entire South Sudanese community, and other Africans were invited to the party. My dignity was gravely wounded, too, because of the embarrassment.

Nevertheless, I learned another lesson the hard way: I rejected the Canadian woman, Ashley, thinking I had avoided trouble, but I ended up in even more trouble.

Despite all the parties I was going to, I did not stop working jobs and studying. After completing my ESL program at Pearson Adult Learning Center, I went to Douglas College. They asked for my transcript, and they were interested in two subjects: math and English. I had an A in math and C+ in English. So, the college wanted me to take an English "assessment test." I did not know the meaning of assessment, but I was willing to take that test, anyway. I had studied hard at Pearson Adult Learning Center, and I was not afraid to take any test. The test was one week from now, I was told.

I returned to wait for one week. What I hated about English was that I could not study for a test. You have general formulas in integers, calculus, and areas that you needed to know in Math. But English does not have formulas.

One week later, I went to Douglas College, and I was shown a classroom where the test was taking place. Upon entering, I found a woman sitting at the desk by the door who asked for my name. "William Mayom," I said.

"Welcome, William," she said with a big smile. "Sit anywhere there and log in."

I looked where she had pointed, and I saw a row of computers and chairs. My nightmare had begun. I had never sat close to a computer before, let alone operate it. I sat on the chair anyway and stared at the black monitor.

There were about fifteen students. Every student seemed to know what they were doing, and each sat down and touched the computer here and there, and their computers came to life. Everyone's computer was turned on except mine.

After all the candidates had arrived, the instructor introduced herself as Micah and wrote some numbers on the board. These were the keys to log into the computers to access the test. Again, all the students busied their fingers logging in except me. I did not even bother to touch my computer because I did not know where to begin. After Micah had finished talking and the test had begun, I raised my hand.

"Yes, William," she said as she walked over.

I was not surprised that she remembered my name. It was not like I could just blend in, as I was the only black person in the room.

"I don't know how to operate the computer," I said.

All the other students looked at me. I did not know what they were thinking. It was like jumping into the river with other swimmers when you did not know how to swim. "Why the hell did you jump in when you knew you could not swim?"

"Okay!" Micah said, eyes dotting from side to side, probably thinking fast for a solution. "I will be right back," she finally said and left the class. A minute later, the teacher returned with a printed version of the test and placed the papers in front of me. "There are two sections," she said. "In this section, you read each passage and choose a correct answer from these multiple-choice questions. And in the second section, you choose one topic from these three topics and write a three-paragraph essay. Make sure your handwriting is clear so that I can read it."

By the time I completed one section, the other students were already done and leaving the room. Micah told me to take my time because I had started the test late. I completed the first section and wrote an essay. I do not remember the topic I talked about.

The following day, I returned to see my result. I had passed the assessment test, and I was accepted to Douglas College. But Micah wanted me to take two courses of "Developmental Studies" (whatever that meant) before I registered in actual college courses. The developmental courses turned out to be English courses, which I easily passed with the "Mastery Grades."

Also, Micah advised me to go to a computer lab every day to learn to use computers. Luckily, some volunteer tutors helped struggling students like me in the library. As a result, I learned basic computer skills, such as logging in and out, opening an email account, and typing. I also developed some skills with Microsoft Word, Excel, and PowerPoint presentations.

I then started college courses. But my first semester was a failure. I took four courses in one semester: English 1130, computer, business essentials, and economics. Taking these classes was more difficult than I thought. In Kakuma, I took up to eight classes, but I had the whole year to complete them. But four courses in three months and a half took a toll on me. I failed computer and economics that semester. It was the first time I had failed courses, and I was very embarrassed. But I knew I had to adjust to the Canadian classroom and the constant bombardment of English to pass my courses. I failed a few classes, and I retook them and worked harder to pass them.

Professor Rosilyn Coulson taught economics. She knew her subject very well, and she was always ready to explain no matter how many times one asked questions. But I was having a hard time in this course because formal economic concepts were difficult for me to understand.

What I dreaded were the graphs. I had a hard time interpreting the graph. And then there was this term called "curve" that appeared on almost every page of the entire book. You could not talk about economics without graphs. And you could not talk about graphs without curves. There were many kinds of curves: the supply curve, which "slopes up and to the left," and the demand curve, which "slopes down and to the right." Then, you add equilibrium, elasticity, other lines, and more curves. But that was not all. Prices and quantities were also added to the graph. Now I visualized this complicated nonsense (the whole graph), and the result I got was a spinning head.

I failed the economic course terribly, only getting thirty-eight percent, the lowest grade I had received in my entire life. But this horrible mark did not discourage me. I retook the class with the same professor. During my second attempt, I received a sixty-eight percent mark. The professor wrote "SOLID!" in capital letters and an exclamation on top of the paper. I did not ask what Professor Rosilyn Coulson meant by that statement, but I assumed she was impressed by my determination. I passed the economics course on my second attempt.

I noticed I was doing well in writing. Any assignment that had to do with writing was my favorite. In addition, I received feedback from many professors who said I wrote clearly. This positive feedback motivated me to take more English classes.

But one of my highlights was in the fourth year when I took a creative writing course as one of my electives, taught by Professor Richard Maddocks. I won a publication award in that class, and my piece was published in an anthology book, Pearls 35.

In 2017, I graduated with a bachelor's in business administration with a focus on finance. After graduating, I worked for the government of Canada as a financial reviewer. In 2020, I wrote and published my first book, *The Proud People.* The naked goatherder who turned into a child soldier was now a degree holder and author of three books and working for the government of Canada. What a journey!

PART SIX

South Sudan

◇◇◇◆◆◆◆◆◆◆◆◆◇◇◇

"[Many] things had happened while I was away. Firstly, culture and all other things had changed in my absence. In my hometown, Rumbek, neighborhoods, economic systems, and recreational pursuits had considerably changed. People had changed with the culture, and I could not identify the familiar symbols, customs, and attitudes I once remembered. Subsequently, I felt like an alien among my people."

Family Reunion

I sent money back home every two months or so. There were no banks in South Sudan, so my brother had to travel to Uganda to receive the money. There were no telephones in South Sudan either, so we only talked when he came to Uganda. Even though I sent money and messages home every month to my mother, she could not believe I was still alive.

"Your mother does not believe that you are still alive," my brother kept saying every time he came to Uganda to talk to me on the telephone. "She thinks you are dead, and I'm just keeping the bad news away from her. She keeps saying, 'If my son is still alive, why doesn't he come?'"

At that time, I did not have my Canadian citizenship yet, so I could not visit. My first plan was to ask my brother to bring my mother to Uganda to talk to her on the phone to assure her that it was me and I was alive. But again, I realized she could not even recognize my voice; the voice she knew was her eleven-year-old boy, and I was now a twenty-nine-year-old grown man—it had been seventeen long years since her eleven-year-old last born had left. The only way she could believe I was alive was when she saw and held me in her arms.

Then things changed for me in 2005, five years after I arrived in Canada. First, I became a Canadian citizen. Then, after I received my passport, it was time for me to visit home to see my mother. War was still going on in the country, and my mother lived in a small village called Wulu, several kilometers away from Rumbek, the capital city of Lakes State. My brother would meet me in Kampala, and then we would go to South Sudan together. Canadian friends said it was not a good idea to visit and that it was dangerous. But I did not care. I had to go and see my mother.

I boarded a plane from Vancouver to London, from London to Nairobi, and finally to Kampala. It was the same route that I took five years ago when I was migrating to Canada. Back then, I had nothing but an IOM white bag, which alerted others that I was just a refugee who had no home and did not know where he was traveling. Now I was a Canadian citizen, and I was returning to my homeland to see my mother. What a feeling that was!

Throughout the flight, I kept wondering how my mother would react when she saw me. It had been seventeen years since she saw me, and I was a child then. Now she would see a grown man. Would she recognize me? Would my arrival overwhelm her? The good thing was that I had already told my brother to inform her that I was coming; this would reduce the shock.

We spent four days in Kampala buying goods for my brother's shop and all the clothes I would distribute to my relatives. After we purchased all the goods, we rented a truck. My brother and I sat in the cab. Traveling through Equatoria, there was no town that I passed without meeting a comrade I knew. Most of the fighters who liberated that region were my comrades from Dimma. They were surprised when I told them I had come from Canada. Someone said he heard I was killed in action in Tula. Yes, I was on that mission, but another Mayom from the Black Army was killed in Tula, not me. It was a great reunion with comrades, but I could not wait to reunite with my mother.

The roads were terrible. The truck could only travel less than thirty kilometers per hour because there were potholes and broken bridges that the truck had to negotiate. The truck broke down several times on the way.

Finally, we pulled into Lakes State—my childhood home, of which I had no memories. We came to a small town called Wulu. The truck stopped in front of a small store. While the goods were being unloaded into the store, my brother and I walked for about five minutes before coming to three grass-thatched roofs encircled by a bamboo fence. I recognized my mother sitting on a *bambar* stool, smoking a pipe. She saw me and got up. "Makol, is that you?" she called me by my childhood name. Makol means I was born at midday.

"It's me, Mother!" I spoke.

"Wuwuu," she cried.

We hugged, and seventeen years of emotion spilled out of me. But I suppressed the emotions. Men are not supposed to show emotion or shed tears in public. My mother, on the other hand, did not cry because crying was considered a bad omen. You only cry when someone has died. There were many other ways of showing happiness, one of them is singing or dancing. That was what my mother did; she let me go, allowing others to greet me, as she abandoned herself in a chant, calling her ancestors and divinities who had been looking out for me throughout these years and finally bringing me back to her safe and sound.

The crowd gathered as neighbors and relatives swamped the homestead. Small boys swamped me, not to see me, but the video camera I held to record this momentous reunion.

Three older men came forward. They were my paternal uncles, and I recognized one of them, Uncle Majir Tuil. He was carrying a sacred device called *yuƐl*, made from a giraffe tail intricately attached to an ebony stick, used to symbolize his holiness. He was and still is believed to be endowed with special curative powers.

I got up to greet them, but they ignored me.

"Let them cleanse you first," my mother yelled out to me.

I knew what that meant; I had to go under the blessing ritual of whirling a sacrificial rooster over my head.

Uncle Majiir barked out orders to, "Bring water and a rooster." Water was poured into a bowl and handed to him. The elders walked around the perimeter, pouring water in every entrance and exit. He was reciting invocations as he was doing this: *"Acë piath të cien bƐn ke puɔl guöp. Nïn ku pääc,"* Uncle Majir said. "It is good that he has come healthy and alive. He will always sleep and wake up healthy and alive."

After completing the circle and invocation, he came and poured the blessed water on my feet and over my head. Then he dipped the sacred device, *yuɛl*, in the water and flicked it into the crowd, blessing them with the blessed water. While standing in a circle of onlookers, Uncle Majir greeted me. And the crowd started to hug me one by one.

Again, the rooster was brought and handed to Uncle Majir. The crowd moved back, forming a circle with me in the middle. Uncle seized a rooster by the leg and told me to stand still as he circled the rooster over my head three times. Then he pinned the rooster's legs down with his foot, held its head, and cut off the rooster's head. The headless rooster flapped its wings on the ground until it was quiet. Uncle Majir kept barking orders to the dying rooster.

"There it is," he said. "Now turn your legs to the east and your head to the west. Stop right there. There it is. Straighten your legs. There it is."

I watched as the rooster made its final kick before it died, legs pointing east and head pointing west. This signaled that the rooster had accepted it would die and take a message to the spiritual world. The spiritual world consists of *Nhialic* God and His associate messengers such as jak divinities and ancestors or the living dead. So, this small sacrifice was given as a gift to appease *Maayuäl*, communion with Him, and thank Him for protecting and bringing me back home alive.

After the rooster was dead, Uncle Majir took the knife and pointed it up three times, each time letting me touch the blooded blade with my tongue. The intention was to taste the fresh blood with my tongue to complete the cleansing ritual. But the Canadian inside me was uncomfortable tasting the blood. So, I looked for the dry part of the knife to put my tongue on slightly. The tasting of blood bestows a great blessing to the taster and drives away any evil spirits.

After that, a war song dedicated to *Mading-Ding* Divinity was sung. It was the same song that I sang in the desert when I almost died of thirst. The song is exceedingly long, and the following is an abstract:

Kë ci wën Wundiör maan,
Ka ye thimic ë nyier.
Maadïŋdïŋ aba kuöm piny në duaar.
Acë möön cëmën ë luat de.
Madiŋdïŋ aba kuom piny në duaar.

The thing that the Son of Wundior hates,
He sprinkles it with the drizzles.
Mading-Ding (the Dark-Grey Divinity) will cover me with clouds.
It is as dark as the cloud.
Mading-ding will cover me with the bloom.

The chants and dances continued for several days as distant relatives continued to come. Several animals were slaughtered, and people feasted. Whenever other relatives arrived, the celebration started all over again.

In addition to this momentous occasion of the family reunion, a more significant monumental event occurred while I was home. It was in 2005 that the peace agreement was signed between the SPLA and Sudan government. Southerners were given five years before voting to break away and form a new country or remain one country. And indeed, six years later (2011), Southerners overwhelmingly voted to become an independent country, creating what is now known as the Republic of South Sudan. So, I left my mother to join the war, and seventeen years later, I reunited with my mother while the peace was signed. It was indeed the act of divinity.

The celebration of the peace agreement shortened my visit. One month flew by in Wulu. Before I knew it, I had only one week left before I caught a plane back to Canada. When I declared my departure, my mother could not understand why it had taken me so long to come and see her, and then I planned to leave so abruptly. She had lived in that isolated world, and she assumed everywhere was nearby. I was worried about missing my flight because my mother kept saying,

"You will go next week or next month." There were no calendars and schedules. One day had twelve hours of sunshine and twelve hours of darkness. Suppose I could not travel today, no problem, as tomorrow was another day. If I missed a car going to Uganda, several other cars would come tomorrow. If I missed a plane, that was not the end of the world; I would catch another plane tomorrow.

I finally convinced my mother that I was returning to Canada to finish school. She understood that part because she had taken me to school before. I promised to come back and spend a lot of time with her after I completed my studies. I took a car from Rumbek to Kampala, then a flight back to Canada.

Reverse Culture Shock

My second visit to my homeland was in 2017. By now, I had been away from home for a total of thirty years. During this time, I had always defined myself as a Dinka culturally. If I was not doing a good job distinguishing myself, individuals from my host country kept asking me, "Where are you from?" Additionally, terms such as "refugee," "immigrant," or "naturalized citizen" reminded me that I came from somewhere. So, I always knew my origin and culture: Dinka.

With this mindset, I had been adjusting culturally for the entire time I was away from my homeland. When going abroad, I always anticipated facing significant differences in customs, values, and social mores. This phenomenon is known as culture shock.

Strangely, when I returned home after thirty years away, I encountered the same culture shock as that which I had experienced when I first arrived in Canada. This phenomenon is known as "reverse culture shock." I was not expecting this reverse culture shock when I returned home. Instead, I expected to pick up from where I had left off. But I was wrong.

Two things had happened while I was away. Firstly, culture and all other things had changed in my absence. In my hometown, Rumbek, neighborhoods, economic systems, and recreational pursuits had considerably changed. People had changed with the culture, and I could not identify the familiar symbols, customs, and attitudes I once remembered. Subsequently, I felt like an alien among my people. So, I had to readjust to my culture. But readjusting to my culture appeared more difficult, time-consuming, and frustrating than adjusting abroad because the latter is expected.

Secondly, I had changed, too. I was astonished by how significantly I had changed while I was in Canada. And because I had enjoyed a remarkable transformation in diaspora, I returned to find my old homeland, a new homeland, which looked massively different. Friends, family members, and relatives felt like strangers. The Agaar culture that was once so familiar had become alien, and home seemed indefinable and vague.

The change was not only in my eyes but also in the eyes of my friends, family members, and relatives, who kept reminding me that I was not quite Agaar anymore. I had developed a new approach and attitude towards problem-solving, thinking, and managing everyday life. And everything I did or the attitude I portrayed in Rumbek was pointed out as being foreign.

The trouble began when I brought one of the Western concepts—dieting—into the Dinka society in South Sudan. After spending nearly two decades in Canada eating junk food and exercising less, I was fat. And my best thought-out plan was that I would burn off all the fat in Rumbek by sweating under that sweltering African sun and dieting.

But dieting simply does not exist in the Dinka culture. The Dinka do not even have a word for it. According to the Dinka philosophy, you eat food (any type of food) and fast when there is no food. Based on these relevant facts, your body will make its own decision, whether to get fat or thin. But this idea of telling your body what to eat, when to eat it, or how much to eat was unusual. My mother, as well as my brother's wife, thought this dieting was absurd.

Despite the disapproval from the entire family, my recently acquired Canadian culture told me to continue dieting, anyway. The diet food that I chose was asida with *mullah kombo. Asida* is a solid porridge made of maize or sorghum flour, served with *mullah-kombo,* a broth of green leaves or okra, cooked with dried fish or meat, and thickened with peanut butter; all seasoned with traditional herbs and condiments. It is organic food without fat. It was my favorite child-hood food as well, so I was both dieting and satisfying my craving at the same time.

I instructed my brother's wife to cook the *asida* and *mullah-kom-bo* dishes for me every day. My brother's wife's name was Christine, but she preferred being called Man-Sebit, meaning "Sebit's mother" as Sebit was her first-born son. This is a respectful way of calling or identifying a person by their children, often the firstborn child among the Dinka. So, Man-Sebit cooked the *asida* and *mullah-kombo* every day. And after eating it for a month, I lost lots of weight. My big belly disappeared, and so did the lumpy rings on my neck. I got back in shape, and I felt great. I could walk and even run a distance with-out breathing heavily. I was ecstatic, and I could not wait to return to Canada and impress my Canadian friends with my new look.

But my mother and Man-sebit loathed the fact that I lost weight. They thought I was becoming malnourished. My brother's wife took the matter seriously and personally. She could be accused of under-feeding me, her brother-in-law, by the community. So, she took the cooking to the next level, and she was a good cook. Every day, she cooked a variety of dishes—bread, *kisira*, macaroni, or rice served with beef, lamb, chicken stew, soup, or broth and she placed them at my disposal, encouraging me to eat them. But I wanted none of that and only ate the *asida* and *mullah-kombo*. Man-Sebit was outraged as a result.

One day, my mother and Man-Sebit had enough of my picky eat-ing habits and confronted me. We were sitting on a veranda, and I was sitting on a plastic chair. Smoking a pipe, my mother was sitting on a blanket spread out on a cement floor. My brother's wife (Man-Sebit) was sitting next to my mother. Both women faced me head-on. I felt trapped. I could tell they had planned this earlier.

"You refuse to eat nutritious food," Man-Sebit protested, "until you become thin to the point of horror. Have you seen yourself? Was that why you came here, to starve in our hands?"

While my brother's wife was making her heartfelt speech, my mother was quiet the entire time. But I knew she was not on my side in this matter. Soon, my mother took the pipe out of her mouth and put it down. She was ready to fire at me, I could tell.

"Why do you come with this bad habit, my son?" my mother finally spoke. "Why are you afraid of food? You have been eating only one type of food for a month, and you do not even eat that much. You will surely starve to death. First, you came looking fat and healthy, but now you look terrible. I do not know what happened to you. Can you just eat like a normal Agaar?"

To my family and friends in the Agaarland, being thin is terrible and associated with hunger or sickness. And being fat is a good thing because it is related to general health or wealth. In contrast to my relatives and friends in North America, being thin means wellness, and being fat implies un-wellness. Do you see the cultural misunderstandings I am trying to explain here? Two cultures see one thing differently. How confusing! And we, the expatriates, are caught up in these cultural escapades. We are accused of bringing our bloody cultures and rejecting the integration into our host countries. And in our countries of origin, we are accused of bringing foreign culture and abandoning our own culture. We, the immigrants, are on the receiving end of these misinterpretations.

But my mother thought the world was beautiful and that it was me who was behaving strangely. Language had changed, and I found it hard to express myself the way I wanted in my mother tongue, alarming my mother. People kept correcting me, pointing out that I was speaking weirdly or in a strange accent, which distanced my mother and me. As far as my mother was concerned, I was not the way she remembered me, and these new aspects were disconcerting. For example, Mother specifically asked me when she had enough of my cultural shortcomings, "My son, why do you talk and act like a *jur* (stranger)?"

I could not blame her. I left her when I was around eleven years old, and I came back when I was around forty. This meant I had only spent twenty-five percent of my entire life with her and seventy-five percent away from her. I had learned several other strange languages, apart from the language she taught me—the Dinka. But again, I did not even speak Dinka consistently without getting carried away and throwing in English, Arabic, or even Kiswahili vocabulary. I admit that the only things that had not changed were my skin tone, hair, and other physical characteristics. But my accent, language, and behavior had changed drastically over the years. So, my mother was right: I was a stranger to her.

Apart from the language, my actions were also questionable. My strange behavior was visible when I decided to leave our family's home because it was "overcrowded"; instead, I rented a nearby lodge where I spent a couple of days with friends. My main reasons were to have privacy with friends and, at the same time, to reduce the burden mounted on my brother's wife, who was constantly cooking day and night. But what I thought was a polite thing to do turned out to be rude. Leaving the family home and spending nights in the lodge was despicable on many levels.

Firstly, it is disgraceful to leave a family's home for any reason, let alone when you have not quarreled with anybody. Secondly, my move showed that I did not care about them or miss them. Finally, the implication was that the least I could do was spend the entire visitation period with them instead of sleeping in a hotel as if I did not have a home.

Things even went from bad to worse when my mother learned that I ate at restaurants. She lost her mind. Why eat at restaurants when there is plenty of food at home? What a waste! She could not understand my "strange behavior," and I could not give her any satisfactory explanation. Eventually, she concluded that I had "truly become an *asuma*." *Asuma* means a city-dweller who lacks decent manners.

Another incident happened when I gave my mother some money. Since she was short-sighted due to her age, she asked me to count the money. But the way the illiterate populace counts money differs. They do not count the bills five, ten, fifty, or one hundred South Sudanese pounds. No. They identify the bills based on color and shape, and then they name them in their unique way, which a stranger like me could not understand.

Unable to count the money for my mother, I summoned in one of my nieces to count it. But I tell you, I felt pathetic, having failed in communication with my mother. My mother, on the other hand, seemed entirely puzzled by the fact that I couldn't count the money, and she just looked at me as if she were thinking, "I thought I taught you the language! But how the hell did you become so illiterate suddenly?"

After my niece successfully counted the money, my mother turned to me and asked, "You don't even know how to count the money?"

My mother could not understand how I came with such a large amount of money that I distributed to the family, relatives, and friends, yet I did not know how to count it. I just laughed and told her that "we count the money differently." But I did not think my answer made any sense to her. After all, what did I know? I was just an *asuma* and a *jur*—the typical foreigner who lacked decent manners.

Apart from my direct family, my friends thought my behaviors were bizarre, too. Because I wanted to exercise and lose weight, I walked on foot every day. And I loved it. After driving cars for decades in North America, I just wanted to walk in my motherland. The walking made me feel physically and emotionally connected to the land I had been away from for thirty years. Walking brought back to life all my childhood memories. I felt joy walking on the soil, for the lack of a better word.

But every time I walked on the road, a friend or even a total stranger would pull up in his car or motorbike beside me and offer a ride. I would tell them, "I'm okay, thank you. I just want to walk." But they would look at me as if I had lost my mind. I must be insane. Otherwise, how could a normal human being refuse a luxurious car ride and choose to walk on a dusty road under the sweltering sun? I

knew there was nothing I could do or say to justify my strange behavior. So, I walked, and the insanity stuck.

After nearly two decades in Canada, I had adopted Canadian values and priorities. But, for example, the time-conscious quality of
Western society had aroused considerable antagonism, and I found
myself judging and condemning my old culture, which seemed like it
had considerably changed and yet remained the same.

My friends could not understand why I was in a hurry all the time
for no apparent reason. When I was invited to an event, I was always
the first one to arrive and the first one to leave. I kept getting asked,
"Where are you running to?" I kept saying, "I'm invited somewhere"
or "I'm going to take a nap," just to find an excuse to leave. The truth
is, I was always bored sitting in one place for up to eight hours, doing
absolutely nothing but chatting and playing cards.

Out of nowhere, I was nicknamed *"Kawaja-athuot"* (the black-
white man). There is no doubt about that. I am a *kawaja-asuot*. After
spending nearly two decades in North America, I am used to rushing
or hustling. I rush to work on time, rush home on time, and rush to
pay the bills on time.

But in South Sudan, there is no rush. Rushing is a foreign concept.
They have patience, and you must learn it when you are there. *"Acin
mishkila"* (no problem) is the soothing phrase they often used to kill
all the worries and hurries in you. *Acin mishkila* is a broken Arabic
word that was partially Dinka. Late for work? *Acin mishkila*. You will
go eventually. Cannot make it to an event on time? *Acin mishkila*. The
event does not always start on time.

One time, for example, a friend invited me for dinner at his home.
"You must come to see my home," he said. That is a typical way of
inviting people. They do not just say come for dinner or lunch. No.
That is inappropriate. The appropriate way is to say, "come to see my
home," or "to see my wife," or "to see my children." When I asked the
friend what time I should come to his place, I swear to God, the guy
pointed at the sky, gesturing toward the sun, even though he had a
brand-new watch on his wrist: "Come when the sun is here," he said.

The act caught me off guard. I thought this was the kind of thing people used before the invention of the watches. But I was wrong. I looked around, trying to see if the other five guys, who were also around, were as surprised as I was. But no. Everyone looked normal, and they understood the indicated time.

I got the point: this Western mentality was messing up my reasoning capacity. Not everyone had a watch. Besides, why deal with the complex nonsense of watches: the hour hand, minute hand, and second hand when you can point toward the sun so everyone could see? The natural way is more accessible and less complicated.

I did not want anybody to think I was too dumb to tell the time by the position of the sun, so I noted the position of his hand, which was perpendicular, made a mental calculation, and assumed the event would start at around noon.

The following day, I was at his house at noon. Surprisingly, no one was there but him. When I asked him where everybody was, "*Acin mishkila,*" he said very calmly. "They will come." They did not come until around 5:00 p.m., and the event began at 6:30 p.m. I had to learn to be patient—*acin mishkila.*

Datelines and schedules are always flexible, even on a national level. For example, I went to a travel agency (name withheld) in Juba. There was a huge queue when I arrived. People were pushing and shoving in the line; the strongest wanted to get in first. Baffled, I queued up behind the last person in the line, not because I had no muscles to force my way in, but because I felt it was shameful, unethical, and animalistic to trample the weakest and force my way in.

Soon, a man arrived, flanked by two armed bodyguards. He was probably a high-ranking officer or minister. His bodyguards moved people out of the way for the man to enter the office. He was traveling somewhere and wanted to purchase a ticket, just like everybody else. But because he had the power and authority, he could not wait in line. An agent emerged to welcome the arriving dignitary. "Come in, honorable," he said. The man went inside with his bodyguards.

I was still the last one in line, but the line was not moving at all. The African sun was pushing on top of my head. I was sweating profusely. After a few minutes, a man emerged from the office and walked right up to me. "Honorable, come inside," he said. I looked back, thinking he was talking to someone behind me. But no, he was talking to me. The way you dress determines your status in South Sudan. I wore a clean suit, which made me looked like I was a minister or something. I had never been called honorable before. This title felt a little weird. I almost told the man, "Hey, man, I just came from Canada, and there's nothing honorable about me." But hell no! I kept my mouth shut. Opportunity comes once in a lifetime. The privileges of honorability were too precious for me to ignore at that moment. I was getting in and buying my ticket first. So, what the heck! Without hesitation, I accepted the honorability and followed the man inside, where I was seated next to the general with his bodyguards.

Soon, I was called to the ticket counter. "I need a ticket," I said. "When is the next flight to Rumbek?"

"*Mikin bukura,*" the agent said in Arabi-Juba. "Maybe tomorrow."

This answer, full of uncertainty, worried me. But I bought the ticket anyway and went back to Shalom Hotel.

First thing in the morning, a friend of mine picked me up in his car and took me to the airport. The main airport terminal was under construction, so there were makeshift structures made of tents and plastic sheets. I checked in my bags, and I was shown the waiting area inside a worn-out tent. The tent was hot and overcrowded. There was no oxygen. Even though it was morning, the sweat trickled down my back, free-flowing like condensation on a windowpane. All seats were occupied, and many people were standing. I stood there sweating like hell. A Caucasian was standing a few feet away. He was in bad shape, much worse than I was. The pained look on his face told me he was not having a good time in South Sudan. His fragile skin was not made for this weather condition. When I first landed in Halifax, I felt the same thing; I realized my thick skin was not meant for the extreme Canadian weather conditions.

After standing for a couple of minutes, a young officer in uniform stood up and offered his seat to me. "*Fozol,* honorable," he said. "Welcome, honorable." By now, I was enjoying the name. I grabbed the seat. Who would not? I mean, I had to be insane to turn down the term "honorable" with all the courtesies and respect that came with it.

After about six hours at the airport, an agent came to make an announcement.

"Sorry, people," he said in Juba Arabic, 'the flight to Rumbek has been canceled because the pilot is sick."

Everyone left quietly, except me. All other passengers were used to these unnecessary postponements.

"When is the next flight?" I asked the agent.

"*Mikin bukura,*" he replied. "Maybe tomorrow."

I retrieved my luggage quietly and headed back to the hotel. The following morning, I headed back to the airport. Again, there was no flight to Rumbek because it was the weekend. I grabbed my bags and went back to the hotel quietly. On Monday, I went back to the airport. Again, there was no plane going to Rumbek. I did not even bother to ask again; I already knew the answer: *mikin bukura.*

It took me almost two weeks before I finally found a flight to Rumbek. I checked in my bags before we were hustled toward a small, Russian-made plane. From afar, the aircraft looked nice and new. But when I got closer, I could see it was a piece of junk. In some countries, that plane would be in the junkyard. Seriously, the plane was rusty, and some screws and nuts were either loose or missing. I doubted if the plane would even get off the ground. But I had no choice but to take it.

Soon, two Russian men—a pilot and an engineer—arrived. The engineer took a ladder and climbed on top of the left wing of the plane. He tied a rope onto the propeller hook. I did not know what he was doing. Then, the pilot jumped into the cockpit and started the plane. Two propellers (right and front) worked, but the left one did not. Then, I realized what the engineer was doing; he was starting the left propeller manually. With one swift move, the man yanked the rope, making sure it was off the hook of the propeller. Then, miraculously, the propeller came to life. It was the first time I had seen a plane started manually.

We boarded the plane. Some people started mumbling prayers. Others were writing on Facebook, "Pray for me; I'm traveling by plane from Juba to Rumbek." Your prayers seem insufficient or insignificant in that situation, so you must mobilize the entire world to pray for your safety. There were no trusted, experienced South Sudanese pilots that passengers should rely on them. Foreign pilots operated most planes. But many of these pilots were green pilots who were not permitted to fly in their respective countries because they had no experience, so they had to go and practice in South Sudan. South Sudan's aviation system did not exist, so all sorts of planes were dumped into the country. Because of this, passengers put their faith in God, not the airline or government. The two Russians, too, mumbled something, possibly calling on their Russian gods.

What made things even worse was the plane was overloaded; some passengers were seated on the floor in the aisle. The plane started to move slowly and increased its speed gradually. It was shaking, rattling, and vibrating violently. It had a pathetic climb rate, sluggish top speed, poor build quality, and the inability to perform sharp turns in the air. I spent fifty-five agonizing minutes from Juba to Rumbek. Miraculously, though, we made it to Rumbek safely. Thank God!

These cultural inadequacies stirred up different emotions inside me. I was utterly caught up between two different cultures (South Sudanese and Canadian). And for the first time in my life, I realized I had two different mentalities: the recently acquired North American mentality and the old African mentality. Therefore, I understood the reactions I had received from my friends, family members, and relatives in Rumbek. I was an Agaar, trying to figure out how to fit in back in after thirty years of being away.

It became clear my efforts to bridge the cultural gaps would not always be successful, so I had to adjust and readjust my behavior appropriately. Throughout my journey, I had learned many lessons through these experiences and reflections.

I was determined to relearn the culture at any cost. I knew it would be easier to learn from children. The children did not care about my cultural incompetency. Whenever I said or did something wrong, they thought it was funny. So, I befriended the children. Luckily, there were more than ten nieces and nephews in our family's home, all living under one roof. I befriended them, intending to learn from them. But they did not know my intention.

My five-year-old niece, named Easter, was a very vibrant young girl and became my instant informant. Easter was very talkative and very articulate. I appeased her with money. She spoke with a lisp: I need *"guyuc ka nguan,"* she would say, demanding "four moneys." Four was her magic number. It did not matter what kind of denominations; if there were four pieces, she was happy. Instead of identifying the bill based on the digits (one hundred, fifty, or twenty-five) like the way the literate people do or based on color and shape like the way illiterates do, Easter counted the bills physically, one, two, three, and four, irrespective of their figures, colors, or shapes. She made things simply straightforward.

Every day, I would go grocery shopping with my nieces and nephews. A nearby shop was about a fifteen-minute walk away. Surprisingly, the shop owner was an Arab, a Darfurian, who seemed to have found peace and prosperity amidst the Dinka societies after fleeing violence in Darfur, western Sudan. I tried to talk to him to find out more about how he ended up there and whether he was happy or not living in Rumbek. I also wanted to know whether he was in culture shock. But we could not communicate effectively because of the language barrier: he spoke no English, and I understood nothing in his classic Arabic. So, *Acin mishkila*, I had to be patient and observe how he interacted with his regular customers—my nieces, nephews, and the entire neighborhood.

My nephews and nieces (about nine of them) were mainly under the age of ten. One morning when I took them to the shop, I stood there watching an episode unfold that I had been waiting for. My learning process had just begun. The children enthusiastically ordered their goods. The shop owner was more than willing to provide both goods and services.

My nephew, Malei, who was barely a teenager, oversaw the business negotiations. He knew what was needed and what was not. The children did not think I was their student. To them, I was just a treasurer. No, I was more than that: I was a banker. I was the bank. I instinctively knew I would eventually dip my hand into my pocket to complete the transactions. That is the beauty of being an uncle.

Oh! Did I tell you my nieces and nephew do not call me by my name? Please! It is disrespectful for a child to call a grownup by their name. So, forget about Willy, William, Mayom, and all of that. Instead, they called me "*Walen*," which means uncle. And they said it in different ways: the lisped five-year-old Easter made it nice and neat: "*Wayen*." And a two-year-old little guy, Manuer, made it short and brief: "*Lën*." It did not matter how they said it: what mattered the most was that I was the uncle, and I had to act like one. I had to pay the bills and give everyone some pocket money to maintain my status. Later, when my nieces and nephews grow up, I would be obliged to "catch a shaft (**wai dɔm**)," meaning I would contribute a lump sum of cows as a bride price when each nephew got married. Similarly, I would get my share of cows received as a bride-price when each of my nieces got married.

Now, the business had already reached its peak. "We want six *kotobi*," Malei said. I had no clue what *kotobi* was. I would soon find out. Before I knew it, the shop owner brought six scoops of sugar at our disposal. The *kotobi* was a unit measuring sugar. I did not know what language it was. I needed to learn fast, and I had just picked up my first new word.

The children ordered simultaneously. But the shop owner did not miss a beat. The goods kept rolling in: sugar, salt, tea, cookies, juices, and much more.

Easter pitched in, too. She demanded her goods: "*Ayawa yuban ka nguan,*" she said with the lisp. I heard and understood that. She needed "four chewing gums." The store owner handed them to her.

Even the two-year-old little Manuer was in a business mood. But he was too short to see the goods on the counter. So, he tiptoed, trying to have a clear shot of what he wanted, but to no avail. Finally, he raised his arms. "*Jot,*" he screamed, demanding I "lift" him. I hoisted him onto my shoulder. He knew what he needed.

"Big-Boom," he said, pointing at candies that looked more like lollipops. The shop owner put three candies in his hand. I gathered Big-Boom was the name of the candy.

I thought about the creative marketer who came up with the name Big Boom to target these young demographics affected by war. The name Big-Boom would not be appropriate for North American children, but to children born in a war-torn country, like little Manuer, whose favorite toy was a wooden AK–47, it was the coolest name ever. That is an adaptation mechanism—*acin mishkila.* I would adapt too.

The shopping ended with me—the Uncle—getting the children extra cakes and biscuits as snacks to eat on the way home. Surprisingly, the children took the snacks and stuffed them into their pockets. "Eat them," I told the children. But Easter quickly answered matter-of-factly, "People don't eat on the street!" Oops! I forgot, again! Patience. Why eat on the street, like birds, when you could go home, sit down, and eat like a normal human being? *Acin mishkila.* I got the point, Easter!

Even the two-year-old Manuer had a perfect reason for not eating on the street. While we were on our way home, I unwrapped the Big-Boom candy and gave it to him. But Manuer grabbed the candy quickly and hid it behind his back. I did not know what he was doing. At first, I thought he was just playing with me. But his facial expression told me he was serious about something. "Eat it," I told him. He pointed at the sky, saying, "*Gop!*" I looked up but saw nothing other than the clear blue sky and the blistering sun. I still was not sure what he meant until my teacher, Easter, stepped in to help. "He said the kites would snatch off (*gɔp*) the candy if you eat outside," she said. Lesson learned. You cannot eat in an open area because the birds will attack you.

I remembered my encounter with the kites when I was about six or seven years old. My mother gave me a very juicy bone that I intended to chew on all day. I do not remember what I was doing exactly. But all I remembered was a big "swoosh!" and the bone was gone, leaving me with nothing but a scratched hand and an empty stomach.

But in Canada, there are no kites to snatch food out of people's hands, so people usually eat on the street. But that is not the main reason. People eat on the road because there is no time to settle down and eat. Time is money. The money is never enough, and neither is time. At work, for instance, they give you a fifteen-minute break or a thirty-minute lunch. By the time you run across the street to McDonald's or Burger King, five minutes is already gone, leaving you with only ten minutes. You stand in line, place your order, and pick it up; another five minutes is gone. With the remaining five minutes, you grab your burger and munch it on your way back to work. You do not want to be late, or else you will face supervisors or managers—sadists who enjoy making others miserable. Everybody counts minutes and seconds in the West. Nobody wants to be late. It is one of the norms—that is why they have schedules and deadlines. You must finish a project in a specific hour or day or month or year; doing any project before or after the deadline is unacceptable. But in South Sudan, schedules and deadlines are flexible. If you cannot finish the project today, *acïn mishkila*, it is not the end of the world. Common sense tells you that endless hours, days, months, and years are ahead.

Day by day, I used my common sense to learn through observation and adaptation. After all, the Dinka culture is mainly based on common sense, so it was not hard for me to readapt and successfully blend into society. What made the reintegration easier was that most of the cultural values were instilled in me during my childhood. I only had trouble with minor cultural norms, which had evolved in my absence, but I muddled through simply fine as the time progressed.

After I had been in Rumbek for two weeks without the internet, I started to panic. I realized how the internet had become a massive part of my life. I could not function without my gadgets, and the devices (laptop/iPod/cell phone) could not work without the internet. I needed the internet for communication, education, and entertainment. Most importantly, I needed to do online banking to pay my bills (rent, loans, credit cards, hydro, etc.) in Canada. Without the internet, I could not pay the bills, and all my services would be discontinued. I was in a frenzy of rage as a result. I wanted the bloody internet badly.

I was relieved when a friend told me the closest internet service nearby was at Rumbek Airport. It was far away from where I lived, Akuach, but the distance was not the problem. The problem was how to get there. Boda-boda motorbikes were the most common transport service used but operated mainly by unlicensed immatures who erratically weaved in and out of the traffic. It was completely unsafe! Most cars lacked air-conditioning, so sitting in a car in fifty degrees to get there would be like sitting in the oven. The inconvenience! The only safest and most convenient mode of transport I trusted was my feet. I walked places.

In the morning, I grabbed my gadgets and trekked to the airport. It took me an hour and a half to reach the place. Indeed, internet service was available. What a feeling! My hard work and dedication were rewarded.

Surprisingly, the building where the internet appeared big, clean, and more advanced than other buildings in the area. It was the only building that had running water. Then, I noticed a bizarre thing. The signboard at the gate contained three letters which I was not expecting to find in that part of the world: U.S.A. The building belonged to the United States of America.

Inside, I met one of the employees, who happened to be a relative from my mother's side. He explained that the building was built by USAID (United States Agency for International Development) to provide service to Rumbek people. Fair enough.

At around 2:00 pm., I left the site. I wanted to stay there all day, but I was hungry. Starving. There were no restaurants nearby. It was not Canada where fast-food restaurants (KFC, Burger King, or McDonald's) had popped up everywhere; this was South Sudan. In Vancouver, restaurants look for you; in Rumbek, you look for the restaurants. The closest restaurant was about thirty minutes away.

I raced down a bumpy road in a cloud of spiraling dust under the sweltering sun, going to the city center where good restaurants were. On the road, I met three youths—one man and two girls. The man, who was about six feet tall, with six scars on his forehead and yellowish-dyed hair, seemed to be in his late twenties. His demeanor and physical characteristics fit an *adheng*, a gentleman. They were also heading to the market. Their physical appearances told me they were typical Agaar youths (*aparapuool*) from cattle camps who had never been exposed to the world-gone-mad conditions, such as education and modernization. But the acceleration of technology seemed to be driving the rate of change among these young people. The young man had an electronic device in his hand.

"Brother, help me with this," he said, handing me an object which looked like a mini radio.

I reluctantly took the object and realized it was an oversized cell-phone commonly used by the warriors. The traditional warriors named the cellphone *Dom-ba-laac*, meaning "hold it so that I can pee." The phone is so big that it cannot fit in your pocket and so beautiful that you cannot put it down, for it will get stolen or damaged, so you must hand it to a friend to hold when urinating. This was the impli-cation of *dom ba laac*.

"How can I help you with it?" I asked.

"Find my friend, Marial Mabor, inside here," he said. "I want to talk to him."

He was illiterate, so he wanted me to go into his contacts, find his friend's name and telephone number, and dial so that they could talk. I was not sure if I could be able to operate the device. But I had lived long enough in the West, and Westerners never admitted to not knowing anything without trying and failing miserably. With that in mind, I examined the device, trying to figure out where the turn on/off button was to no avail! The device was incredibly worn out. The turn on/off button was not there, letters and digits were not visible on the keyboard, and its cover and other broken parts were taped and glued back in. I want to be politically correct here, but I cannot find a better term to describe the device other than to say it was a piece of junk.

Unable to operate the device, I told the *aparak*, "Sorry, I don't know how to work this." The *aparak* looked disappointed and confused. In his view, I was a city-dweller *(tueny)*, and I had to know how city things worked. If I went to cattle camp and asked him, he would be an expert in any subject. So, he expected a city-dweller to be fully competent with modernization. The opposite of *tueny* is *athuma, adhaba,* or *saluk.* To the youth, I fit the latter definitions.

I changed the subject by turning my attention to the girls who were quiet the entire time. They were probably sixteen or seventeen years old. Their demeanors were friendly, outspoken, and respectful—qualities acceptable for Dinka girls. One of them appeared talkative, and the other one was quiet and reserved. I approached them in a typical Dinka mutual flirtation style: "Girls," I said, "I want to know your names."

The girls looked at each other's faces and smirked. "We don't tell our names to strangers on the street," the talkative one said.

I was expecting such an answer because Dinka girls never easily surrendered their names. They played hard to get because appearing easy could send a signal that they were promiscuous. Patience, persistence, and perseverance were highly anticipated in the courtship process. I knew that.

"Are you from the Rek?" the quiet one asked.

Her question caught me off guard. I was not expecting to be called *Muony-Rek* in Rumbek. I had spent thirty years abroad being alienated, and I finally returned home only to be viewed as an outsider: Dinka Rek.

"No, I'm from the Agaar," I replied. "Why do you think I'm Rek?"

"Because you speak with a Rek accent," she said before they both roared in laughter.

They were probably right. In my entire life in SPLA and refugee camps, most of my friends were from Rek. So, I might have picked up the accent when I tried to fit in, though I was oblivious to it.

Nevertheless, being called Rek in Rumbek, especially by girls, meant a different thing. Rek people were known for their circumcision, a practice abhorred in Rumbek. The girls were indirectly and jokingly accusing me of having a mutilated or deformed private part. They were cunningly hilarious girls. Very smart too.

But I categorically denied having any association whatsoever with Rek. Nevertheless, they kept me entertained until I reached my destination. Then, even though the young girls were joking, I was called Rek in my community, which made me feel alienated.

In conclusion, it was a long journey across four different worlds. First, I was born in an isolated village, a world that outsiders had not touched. Second, I transitioned into a world-gone-mad of guerrilla, where constant brushes with near-death experiences were the norm. Third, when the international community pressured the movement to abandon child soldier practices, I was discharged and sent to the refugee camps, a world with its own rules and regulation. Fourth, I finally transitioned to the Western world, where I had to adapt to the modern world's miseries, such as running water or microwaves. Throughout this long journey, I had changed through living in different cultural contexts. And when I returned home, I ended being a stranger in my culture and among my people. The whole experience was the bargain of a lifetime. I had trekked across different worlds.

www.ingramcontent.com/pod-product-compliance
Lightning Source LLC
Chambersburg PA
CBHW021851020426
42334CB00013B/282